THE DOCTORS WHO'S WHO

CRAIG CABELL

JOHN BLAKE

Published by John Blake Publishing Ltd,
3 Bramber Court, 2 Bramber Road,
London W14 9PB, England

www.johnblakepublishing.co.uk

www.facebook.com/Johnblakepub   facebook

Twitter @johnblakepub   twitter

First published in hardback in 2010
This edition 2011

ISBN: 978 1 84358 500 8

British Library Cataloguing-in-Publication Data:

A catalogue record for this book is available from the British Library.

Design by www.envydesign.co.uk

Printed and bound by Group (UK) Ltd, Croydon, CR0 4YY

1 3 5 7 9 10 8 6 4 2

Papers used by John Blake Publishing are natural, recyclable products made from
wood grown in sustainable forests. The manufacturing processes conform to the
environmental regulations of the country of origin.

This book is dedicated to Samantha, Nathan and Fern –
keep watching and build your own special dreams.

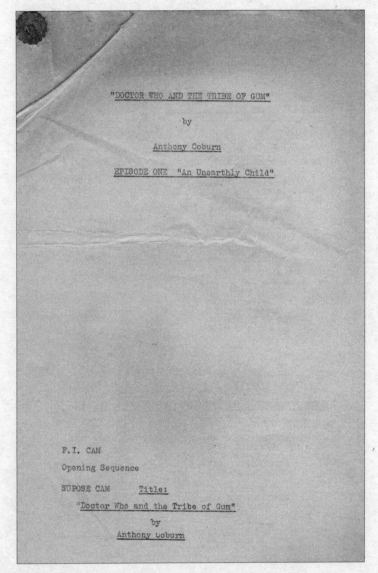

"DOCTOR WHO AND THE TRIBE OF GUM"

by

Anthony Coburn

EPISODE ONE   "An Unearthly Child"

F.I. CAM

Opening Sequence

SUPOSE CAM   Title:

   "Doctor Who and the Tribe of Gum"

                by
         Anthony Coburn

Anthony Coburn's first draft of the very first script, 'An Unearthly Child'.

'We are such stuff
As dreams are made on; and
Our little life
Is rounded with a sleep…'

- *The Tempest*
William Shakespeare

ACKNOWLEDGEMENTS

WHEN I WAS writing my biography of crime writer Ian Rankin, I was often reminded of my idea for a *Doctor Who* biography, as he mentioned the Doctor in his autobiographical writings and the *Rebus* series several times. The serendipity that has led me from that book to this one is something, I'm sure, that will bring a wry smile to Rankin's face, so thank you for that!

I would also like to thank the following people who have helped me in a more direct way with this book: Deborah Charlton, Louise Jameson, Christopher Lee, Ray Harryhausen, Brian Aldrich, and those I have spoken to and/or been in correspondence with over the past 30 years: Patrick Troughton, Jon Pertwee, Tom Baker, Peter Davison, Colin Baker, Sylvester McCoy, John Nathan-Turner, Lalla Ward, Dick Mills and Tony Burroughs (not necessarily in regard to this book). Indeed, to write anything about the Doctor Whos, your knowledge and contact has to go way back, and I would specially like to thank those who are not alive to see this book into print but were so kind to me in the past – as a much younger man – most notably again, Patrick Troughton, Jon Pertwee and John Nathan-Turner.

I would also like to thank *Greenwich Time*, the manager of Pleasures of Past Times (Cecil Court), John O'Sullivan, John

Collins, John Blake, John Wordsworth, Simon Gosden at Fantastic Literature, and Moira Williamson.

Also thanks to Samantha, Nathan and Fern, for the constant requests to watch a certain Time Lord and Anita for being so good about it, especially when I had to as well! Also many thanks to my father for searching through his extensive collection of old movies for some obscure gems (yes, Will Hay was great fun!).

Also thanks to Howard Gibbs, Andy Beglin, Latha Arun, Teresa Earl, Alka Patel, Kim Packham for the DVDs, they really helped. And finally many thanks to Sydney Newman, Verity Lambert, Anthony Coburn, Donald Wilson and Tony Williamson for making and preserving a legend.

Sincerely, many thanks to all.

Craig Cabell
London, June 2010

CONTENTS

PART TWO – FILM, TV AND THEATRE HIGHLIGHTS

INTRODUCTION

'Behind every man now alive stand thirty ghosts, for that is the ratio by which the dead outnumber the living. Since the dawn of time, roughly a hundred billion human beings have walked the planet Earth.'

2001, A Space Odyssey
Arthur C Clarke

THE BIGGEST SHOW on television is BBC TV's *Doctor Who*. The title role is that of an alien with two hearts who travels around the universe in a battered police telephone box saving the universe with a string of eclectic companions.

Playing the lead in *Doctor Who* is a life-changing experience for any actor, because, once you have taken the controls of the Tardis, you are immortalised in TV history.

No other role in television is as iconic, demanding or as anticipated by its legion of fans as *Doctor Who*. It is an enigma and one that will endure and adapt, as it has done since its humble beginnings on 23 November 1963, the day after the assassination of President John F Kennedy.

The lead actor may change, but the lead character never does, and that is the successful formula of *Doctor Who*. Of course, one could argue that the Tardis (in the guise of a police telephone box) and the signature tune are the other two indelible ingredients of the show's success and were fundamental to its successful comeback in the new millennium.

The actors who have played the central role have, for the most part, had distinguished and diverse careers, but they will *always* be known as Doctor Who, one of an elite group of people who were privileged enough to be invited to take on this most demanding role.

Doctor Who is the longest-running SF television series in the world, and it seems that with every passing decade its popularity grows. Never before has there been a single book that focuses its whole attention on the actors who have played the Doctor and their otherwise largely unappreciated careers.

Throughout this book, I will discuss many of the milestone movies in the Doctors' careers, some forgotten gems, others both famous and iconic: films such as *Brighton Rock*, *Hell Divers*, *This Sporting Life*, *Jason and the Argonauts*, *The Curse of Frankenstein*, *The Omen*, *Carry On Screaming*, *Nicholas and Alexandra* and *Withnail and I*, and TV series as famous as *Worzel Gummidge*, *All Creatures Great and Small*, *The Brothers*, *The Second Coming* and *Our Friends in the North*. Then there are the great theatrical productions from the RSC's *Hamlet* and *Love's Labour's Lost*, through to *The Pied Piper* and even the stage play of *Doctor Who* itself. And let us not forget all the great actors and actresses who the Doctors have played alongside during their careers, names such as Laurence Olivier, Cedric Hardwicke, Maggie Smith, Robert Newton, Jeremy Brett, Patrick Stewart, Sean Connery, David Niven, Stanley Baker, Will Hay, Richard Harris, Richard E Grant, John Gielgud, Derek Jacobi, Billie Whitelaw, Christopher Lee, Lee Remick, Margaret Rutherford, Joan

Hickson, Gregory Peck, Rex Harrison, Peter Sellers, Peter Ustinov – the list goes on and on.

There is much to celebrate in the careers of the actors who have played Doctor Who, and this book gives us the opportunity to discover – or rediscover – that work.

So is playing the Doctor a blessing? The ultimate actor's dream? No, it hasn't quite worked out that way for all of them. Paul McGann was given only one feature-length bite at the cherry, while Christopher Eccleston gave up after one solitary season. In contrast, there is Tom Baker, one of the most popular Doctors, who tackled the role for seven years – he even married one of his companions for a short period – and then came back to the role through the audio series. And what of David Tennant and his final words as the Doctor, 'I don't want to go'?

Doctor Who has been both saint and sinner to the people who have played him, and this book analyses the magnitude of the part and how it has worked its magic, or its curse, on all the Doctors.

This book is exactly what it claims to be: the real-life story of many men who have played one famous character. And that character is brilliant. One of the greatest in television history, most definitely one of the most successful and iconic to a legion of fans.

I would like to stress early on that – unlike many other books – this one is not about the history of *Doctor Who*. Although the opening chapter concerns the birth of the show, it only does so to explain where the main character came from and his unique personality. You won't find chapters concerning the iconic monsters, such as the Cybermen, Daleks and

Weeping Angels, or blow-by-blow story analysis and episode breakdowns. Each chapter is a mini biography about each actor who has played the Doctor, where the part fitted into his career, what effect the character – and the show – had on him and, most importantly, what else he did as an actor. Part Two of the book focuses on individual career credits for each actor in order of appearance. It also includes an essay about the programme itself, analysing the show's great moments, in an effort to explain why the show has been so successful and why the leading actors will always be part of the *Doctor Who* legacy with the rest of their careers dragging behind them.

This book doesn't try to be a definitive biography – many of the Doctors, such as Jon Pertwee and Tom Baker have done that already – this book is a clear look at where *Doctor Who* sits within the great scheme of each actor's career, something I personally don't think they can do themselves and, indeed, so far haven't.

I've found this book an incredible one to write and research. Over the years I have spoken to and been in correspondence with six out of eight of the original Doctors and some of their companions, and all these people have met me with overwhelming warmth and enthusiasm. The first interview I ever did – at school no less – was with the then producer of *Doctor Who*, John Nathan-Turner (and indeed a photograph from that session is included in the photo section of this book), so the insights for this book literally span 30 years of my life and it has been a most interesting ride.

Doctor Who has attracted so much love and respect both inside (the cast and crew) and outside (the fans and the media) that it has become an extended family to many people. But the one thing I find strange is that nobody has overtly identified –

although noticed – the thread that runs through the show, through all the Doctors; indeed, many of the Doctors naturally make the comparison themselves, and one actually played the character on stage just before becoming the Doctor... see if you can work out who it is.

Doctor Who is a fairy tale itself, and like many, it holds its own energy and level of reality.

Not convinced? Then consider this: when my son once asked me – as children inevitably do when contemplating the existence of the Tooth Fairy and Father Christmas – if the Doctor really existed, I told him, 'If somebody categorically told me that there wasn't a Time Lord spinning around the universe in a battered old police box constantly saving the day, my life would be so much sadder.' And I meant it too!

'Don't adventures ever have an end? I suppose not. Someone else always has to carry on the story.'

The Fellowship of the Ring

J R R Tolkien

Craig Cabell
Woking, September 2009

PART ONE
THE LIFE AND TIMES OF DOCTOR WHO

CHAPTER ONE
DOCTOR WHO

'He wondered, then, if the others who had remained on Earth experienced the void this way.'

Do Androids Dream of Electric Sheep?

Philip K. Dick

WHO IS RESPONSIBLE for creating *Doctor Who*?

It's not an easy question to answer. A TV show has many people who play a major role in creating it, from its initial idea through to its first transmission, but Sydney Newman must be recognised as the catalyst, the person who laid down the fundamental building blocks for *Doctor Who* and, most importantly, the main character.

Sydney Cecil Newman was born in Toronto, Canada, in 1917. He was educated at Ogden Public School and the Central Technical School, Toronto, where he studied painting, stagecraft, industrial and interior design. His skills were put to work as an artist, designing posters for cinemas and theatres in Toronto, but he soon branched out.

In 1938, Newman decided to go to Hollywood, where he was offered a job by the Walt Disney Company, who were impressed by the young man's skills as a graphic designer. Unfortunately, he couldn't obtain a work permit and had to return to Toronto where, in 1941, he secured employment with the National Film Board of Canada as an assistant film editor.

Later, Newman returned to America to study their film techniques. He would incorporate what he learned into the ever-growing Canadian broadcasting industry. In the 1950s, he moved across to Britain and became Head of Drama at ABC (former Thames Television), where he created SF shows like *Pathfinders in Space* and such cult TV series as *The Avengers*.

One of Newman's strengths was his ability to gather the right team of individuals together to make a quality TV series. This was quintessential to his success and, ostensibly, the individual show's success too.

In 1962, Newman moved from ABC to the BBC. Again Head of Drama, he was given the task of trying to fill the gap between *Grandstand* and *Juke Box Jury* on a Saturday afternoon. For the time slot, the show had to be for children. Traditionally, the spot had been filled with a classic serial, such as *Oliver Twist* or *Kidnapped*, but it was time for something else. Something different.

Donald Wilson was appointed Head of Serial and Series, and began to forge the initial ideas of what would become *Doctor Who* with Newman; but what would the show be about?

A report concerning the development of the show, written in July 1962, stated that 'bug-eyed monsters' were out but time travel was in. The idea continued to be developed and, in March 1963, a second report proposed a 52-week serial featuring 'scientific troubleshooters', with a time machine. The characters would include a handsome young man, an attractive young woman and a 'mature man' somewhere between 30 and 40 years of age, with some kind of twist to him.

Sydney Newman wasn't totally happy with the report. He

didn't like the 'scientific troubleshooters' bit. He wanted the show to be different and, for a SF show, educational. He also wanted to include 'a kid' who would get into trouble, perhaps somebody the young audience could identify with.

Newman developed the idea further himself, writing a three-page document about 'Dr Who' (who is this man? Nobody knows – 'Dr Who?'). 'Dr Who' was 'a frail old man lost in space and time…' but apart from that nothing else was known about him. From here, the show really started to take shape.

The script unit was now brought in. C E Webber (aka 'Bunny Webber' to his friends) was the first to try to make sense of this unusual show. It is unclear if Webber wrote a script or an extended treatment based upon Newman's idea of the regular characters being shrunk to the size of a pinhead and exploring a school laboratory. What is clear is that the script/treatment was rejected and David Whitaker was brought in as story editor and Australian writer Anthony Coburn as scriptwriter. Coburn would eventually write the first useable script. But first Newman and Wilson decided to find a producer. It was Newman who suggested a young lady from his former employer, ABC Television, Verity Lambert. They interviewed her and almost immediately she was offered the job. She accepted.

Verity Lambert and the director of the first *Doctor Who* story, Waris Hussein, did the casting. Lambert cast a friend of hers, Jacqueline Hills as Barbara Wright, while William Russell was cast as Chesterton. The casting of Susan came about by accident, when Hussein glanced at a girl, Carole Ann Ford, while passing a set one day, and was struck by the way she presented herself on and off camera. Hussein instantly asked Lambert down to the set, who agreed with the director that Ford was exactly what they were looking for and soon offered her the part, which she duly accepted.

Ford remembers the chance meeting: 'I was doing one of *The Wednesday Plays*, when Waris Hussein, the original director of *Doctor Who*, spotted me. He was up in the control box and I was on the set – screaming. I think they chose me because they wanted a good screamer. I certainly did an awful lot of it!'

Casting the Doctor was slightly more difficult. Both Lambert and Hussein had their own ideas, which included Cyril Cusack and Leslie French, but the actors weren't interested. William Hartnell became the next choice. Hartnell was an actor worried about being typecast. He had played an army sergeant in the movie *The Way Ahead* and the TV series *The Army Game*. He also appeared as one again in the very first *Carry On* movie, *Carry On Sergeant*. It seemed that, if there was a soldier or hard-man role, he would be cast, but the role of the Doctor presented a new challenge. He was offered the part despite Lambert and Hussein's concerns that a mature actor such as Hartnell wouldn't want to take on a single role for 52 weeks. But their fears were short-lived, as Hartnell accepted the part and delighted in telling all his friends that he was to star in a children's television series.

The main ingredients of what was to become the longest-running SF TV series ever had now been gathered together. Newman, Wilson, Lambert, Whitaker and Hussein were the main people who devised the show and then brought it to the screen.

It was essentially Newman who shaped the lead character of the Doctor on paper during the early reports, but David Whitaker was not a sleeping partner in this process. In fact, his original idea of introducing the Doctor at the end of a road in a swirling fog (titled 'Nothing at the End of the Lane'), while not used on screen, was later used in book form, at the beginning of the first novel spawned from the show *Doctor Who and the Daleks* (Muller, 1964). Slightly different from the TV show, Whitaker wrote the first *Doctor Who* novelisation introducing the characters the way he had originally visualised them for screen, and then he amalgamated the show's second broadcast story, about the Daleks, as the main story (which of course the first broadcast story wasn't). So the writer had strong ideas that he could see through to their natural conclusion, albeit in a slightly different medium, and combined with Terry Nation's Daleks – creatures that were not developed until the late summer of 1963 – he could create a one-off novel.

Newman certainly liked tried-and-trusted people around him. Verity Lambert was a known entity, as were David Whitaker and Anthony Coburn.

Coburn wrote the first episode, the first draft of which was completed by the end of April 1963. It was 43 pages long and entitled 'Doctor Who and the Tribe of Gum', subtitled 'Episode One "An Unearthly Child"'.

The first draft of this script has only recently surfaced and is one of the most important documents in our understanding of how the show was developed. At the time of the first draft script, the characters were still far from formed. Although the script was essentially what later became the first ever episode, it had some very different dialogue to that which we see on screen. Firstly, the script did not mention the 'Tardis'. The Doctor's ship is indeed a police telephone box but no reference is made to its name, unlike in the first transmitted episode. Additionally, in order to pilot 'the ship', as it was referred to, the Doctor had to sit down at the control panel and strap himself in, so some traditional 'rocket' ideas hadn't been ruled out by the time of the first draft script.

What is also interesting is that Barbara Wright's character is called Miss Canning and the reason she wants to talk to fellow schoolteacher Ian Chesterton about the bright but strange 'Suzanne Foreman' is that she is new at the school and wants to confide in another teacher and not bother the headteacher. In the copy of the first draft script used in research for this book, the first time Miss Canning's character is mentioned in the script her name is crossed out in pencil and the name Barbara Wright is inserted.

It was after this first draft that Miss Canning was developed into Barbara Wright, and 'Suzanne' became 'Susan'. Also Newman wasn't one hundred per cent happy with the script in other areas. There was an expensive element to it to begin with: when the two schoolteachers jump into 'the ship', it is still a police box, it was only when the door was shut that it transported them into the main control room. It was decided that this piece should be kept simple, losing a very eerie moment in which Suzanne's favourite music is being played in the empty police box but the schoolteachers can't see where it is coming from.

Another important part of the first draft script is where the Doctor refers to himself as 'Doctor Who'. He says that in Earth language his name is translated to 'Doctor Who'. This is important in regard to the six-page breakdown of the developed show, which was sent out to people by Whitaker when being offered to write or act in the show. It clearly stated on that document that the companions refer to the Doctor as 'Doctor Who', which is what happens in the first ever TV episode. Also Miss Canning is suddenly Barbara Wright in the six-page breakdown. This is very important because it is clear that Carole Ann Ford didn't read the first draft script (where she is 'Suzanne' not 'Susan'). That was only sent to writers before casting, and as an aide-memoire of how to write for the show. The version Ford got was the final version of the script with the names changed and plotlines and main character developed (in line with the six-page synopsis). This is a great shame, because, if she had read the first draft script, she could have found out what her relationship to the Doctor actually was (one of the show's great mysteries).

The nuances of the first draft script of 'An Unearthly Child' have only recently been appreciated. Susan, or 'Suzanne', explained that her parents are dead and her world is gone and that all she has left is her grandfather and the ship. Little insight perhaps until the Doctor refuses to let the schoolteachers leave the ship. Suzanne tries to help them understand but they are worried about her welfare and argue with the Doctor, who they believe is deranged.

It is here that a very sinister piece starts, which was changed dramatically in the final draft of the script. To begin with, Suzanne states, 'I'm trying to save you both', implying that the Doctor wants to kill them. She goes on to say that '... if you both behave like... like primitives. If you insult him... He won't listen to me.' So Suzanne was scared of the Doctor and, more importantly, he considered human beings below him and, if they provoked him, he would destroy them both. In fact, that's what he says: 'We must destroy them [Suzanne]'.

This was far too scary for children, moving the Doctor character away from a potential hero and into a potential murderer, or kidnapper at least. In the final script, it is an accident that sends the two schoolteachers and the Doctor and Susan on their journey through time and space. And the rest of the dialogue was lost also, which is unfortunate, as this is where Suzanne's history is explained, who she was, where she came from, her relationship with the Doctor and the reason for them being on Earth in 1963, i.e. all the things we – and Carole Ann Ford – wished to know and have been a mystery for the past 50 years.

Suddenly, the Doctor calls Suzanne 'Findooclare'. He explains that, if he let the schoolteachers go now that they had seen the ship, they would tell people about it, and, although many people wouldn't believe them, the enemy would. It is here that parallels with David Tennant's story 'The Family of Blood' start coming into the equation. It becomes clear that Susan is being hunted. The Doctor says, 'Everywhere [the enemy] he listens. He searches for you, Findooclare... for you. His victory is not complete until he destroys you.'

It is clear that Susan is an important figure, again as the Doctor explains: 'Findooclare would rule! Findooclare would be Queen in a world greater than any your minds could dream of. But her people are enslaved by the Paladin hordes.'

Ian Chesterton thinks that they (the Doctor and Suzanne) are both mad – and says as much – whereupon the Doctor states, 'You would insult a Lord of the House of Doclare', meaning him. Then *Doctor Who*'s greatest secret is explained away in one sentence from Suzanne: '[Findooclare] It's a name he has for me. I was a baby when the Paladins attacked our world and he saved me. We got away in this machine... It was the first our people made.'

If one were to put this into context of the present *Doctor Who* mythology, it would suggest that 'the ship' was indeed a Tardis, which would make both the Doctor and Susan [Suzanne] Time Lords, maybe at the time of the Time Wars. What it concludes, answering one of the great unexplained questions of the show, is that the Doctor and Suzanne are *not* related and that she is simply just another companion, albeit an important one, and indeed one that feels so incredibly thankful and affectionate towards him, because he managed to save her while the rest of her race – the Doctor's own race – perished. So the Doctor's first ever companion is a fellow Time Lord? Yes, and an important one. If we follow the first draft of the script, Suzanne is the one who is hiding and, following 'Human Nature/The Family of Blood' idea, it is Susan who has taken human form to hide from the enemy, the enemy that need a Time Lord and the Tardis. So what important Time Lord was Suzanne and why did the Doctor eventually let her slip away into obscurity (in a later story 'The Dalek Invasion of Earth')?

The simple answer is that she may well have been the Queen – not the President – of Gallifrey, and eventually the Doctor allowed her to stay human and find love (see again 'The Dalek Invasion of Earth') and protect her evermore, or leave her safe until it was her time to reclaim her throne.

Newman needed the whole section about the home planet and death threats cut out. He didn't want to set the Doctor up as a bad guy and didn't want his past – and that of Suzanne's – explained away, he wanted it left unknown, and it has remained that way for 50 years.

Someone Newman sent a six-page story/character breakdown to, along with a copy of the first draft script of 'An Unearthly Child', was Tony Williamson. Tony had written for *The Avengers* among other things, but decided not to take part in the series because of other work commitments. He preserved the script until his death, ten years after which his widow sold it to a private collector, whereupon it was used in research for this book.

Once the script was rewritten (with the character names changed), the six-page brief of the show, with final character names and descriptions, was sent out with the *final* draft of the script 'An Unearthly Child'. And there the great mystery began: the aliens' history had been taken out; we learn that they are exiles from their own planet but nothing else. Who is he, Doctor Who? And what relationship does Susan really have with the Doctor?

And there was the liquid gold that captured children's imaginations. The intrigue and legend began. Of course, Newman was absolutely right to make changes and create a mystery that complemented the title of the show; however, it is fitting that only now, around the 50th anniversary of the show, we truly find out what the relationship between the Doctor and Susan really was.

The Daleks are a major part of the continued success of *Doctor Who*. After the introductory pilot, the first story's viewing figures were poor – between two and three million people – which was a disaster by BBC standards. And, although 4.4 million people allegedly sat down to watch the first ever episode, the caveman story 'The Tribe of Gum' lost some of those viewers as the story went on. Verity Lambert confessed that the drop was the result of a poor choice of opening story. In interview, she stated that she would never have commissioned a caveman story, but the decision was not hers at the time.

However, after the first story was over, the second brought in the Doctor's most fearsome enemies and suddenly viewing figures soared to between eight and ten million viewers. Children in playgrounds the length and breadth of Britain were shouting the word 'Exterminate' and Dalekmania gripped the nation for the first time.

Newman was outraged. The show had very quickly fallen into the 'bug-eyed monster' category that he was so keen to avoid. Lambert denied the accusation, saying that the Daleks were humans who lived inside protected casings in the future.

Newman wasn't happy, but, as the show progressed, he admitted that the Daleks were what made such an enormous success of the programme.

The Daleks were the brain child of ex-comedy scriptwriter Terry Nation, an influential Welshman (not unlike Russell T Davies, who is primarily associated with the blockbuster return of the show in the new millennium), who was lucky to write for the show in the first place. When Whitaker approached Nation through his agent, the writer was in Nottingham writing a stage show for comedian Tony Hancock. Hancock apparently joked, 'How dare the BBC approach a writer of your calibre to write for children's television!'

That should have been the end of it, but that night Nation and Hancock had a huge row and the writer found himself on a train back to London the following day with no job. Remembering the offer made through his agent, he called her and asked if she had turned the job down yet. She said that she hadn't had a chance to do so. So he changed his mind. He wrote a treatment for Whitaker, who loved it, and history was made.

Although Nation came up with the idea of the Daleks and wrote clear instructions as to what they would broadly look like, it was Raymond Cusack who would design the first Dalek. His idea however, was too expensive to make, so he sat down with two other designers, Jack Kine and Bernard Wilkie, and together they designed the armoured pepper-pot much loved by *Doctor Who* audiences for the next 50 years.

Surely though, William Hartnell had something to do with the success of *Doctor Who* in the early days? He was, after all, the first actor to play the part, and his interpretation must have been most important, providing the blueprint that his successors would follow?

The Doctor was born way back in those original reports,

where Sydney Newman ensured that the character would prove to be different from anything else ever created. The Doctor would be a 'crotchety old man' and the audience would only know that he and Susan were exiles from their own planet.

Along with Verity Lambert, Newman had another major success on his hands. In fact, when David Tennant made his final farewell as the Doctor on 1 January 2010, the Doctor is seen attending a book signing of a female descendant of a lady the Doctor nearly married when he was made human (like Susan?). When one glances at the book jacket of the lady's book, it is clear her name is 'Verity Newman'.

Doctor Who was a joint effort from many different talented people, not just the programme makers, and one cannot underestimate the influence of the great William Hartnell.

Hartnell was the first ever star of the show, the man who would convince the viewing public to suspend disbelief for a while and travel through the universe with him in his time machine. That gentle mocking smile, that knowing twinkle in the eye were all Hartnell's, and many of the first fans of the show will maintain, to this day, that Hartnell was the very best Doctor Who. Indeed, he was the most mysterious. But how did *Doctor Who* change Hartnell's life, both personally and professionally?

An interesting question, and one that requires a detailed answer...

'But what sort of man is he? You must judge for yourself.'

Time Enough for Love

Robert A Heinlein

CHAPTER TWO
WILLIAM HARTNELL

'I think that if I live to be ninety, a little of the magic of *Doctor Who* will still cling to me!'

William Hartnell from *The Making of Doctor Who*

Malcolm Hulke and Terrance Dicks

WILLIAM HENRY HARTNELL was born on 8 January 1908 at 24 Regent Square, South Pancras, London. His mother, Lucy Hartnell, was a commercial clerk. To his dying day, William Hartnell never knew who his father was or where he originated from. His mother had come from Taunton, and Hartnell maintained a love of the West Country throughout his life. This may explain why he lied about his birthplace on *Desert Island Discs* in 1965, claiming that he came from Seaton in Devon, which of course he hadn't.

Hartnell's formative years were in a tough, working-class environment. His illegitimacy would have caused him some embarrassment and he would get into scrapes as a young working-class boy. If we are to believe a journal he left behind after his death (written in the early 1920s and mentioned in his own granddaughter's biography of him), he was fostered by a family called Harris while his mother took employment as a nanny in Belgium. In Hartnell's biography *Who's There* (Virgin, 1996), written by his granddaughter Jessica Carney, it relates that he would again live with his mother in Holborn sometime later, but he continued to be a wild-card into his teens, when he had to choose a profession.

At the age of 16 (1925), Hartnell took to the boards, but not as an actor. He joined Sir Frank Benson's Shakespearean Company as an assistant stage manager, property manager, assistant lighting director and general dogsbody. It was a two-year apprenticeship in theatre and classical acting skills, with the occasional opportunity of taking a walk-on part. It was all tough work at the end of the day, as Hartnell explained: 'It was good training. Not only in Shakespeare, but in keeping fit. Sir Frank Benson believed in keeping actors in good health and we were organised into hockey teams and cricket sides.' Benson was in his late sixties by then, so little chance of him exerting himself too much!

By the age of 18, Hartnell was touring the country as an actor, the bug to perform finally taking him over. He no longer wanted to hide backstage, but wanted to progress his love of comedy. For six years, he would tour in comedy and song and dance shows, understudying such respected actors as Bud Flanagan (from the infamous Crazy Gang). From this, he progressed to understudying in London's West End, but would take the main role when the play left London and toured the provincial cities. So Hartnell built his skills slowly and became quite well known in the acting world as a player of farce. This progressed to short comedy films in the 1930s, such as one of Hartnell's favourite roles (albeit only a 50-minute feature) as a man, Edward Whimperley, who eats an explosive, in *I'm an Explosive* (1933).

Comedy was a love of Hartnell's as he confessed, 'my real

guiding light was Charlie Chaplin. He influenced me more than any other factor in taking up acting as a career.' A lot of actors adopt an initial love of comedy before settling down to another genre, for example, horror icon (and one time Doctor Who) Peter Cushing had an early role opposite Stan Laurel and Oliver Hardy in their movie *A Chump at Oxford*, in 1940.

Hartnell played in over 20 films before the outbreak of the Second World War, not all of them comedy, but many quite short character roles with his parts quite minor.

Hartnell's career was stopped by the war. He was drafted into the Tank Corps but very quickly had a nervous breakdown and was invalided out after 15 months. 'The strain was too much,' he said. 'I spent 12 weeks in an army hospital and came out with a terrible stutter. The colonel said, "Better get back to the theatre. You're no bloody good here!"

'I had to start all over again. I was still only a spit and cough in the profession and now I had a stutter which scared the life out of me.'

Hartnell worked hard to overcome his illness, which he did with gusto. In 1942, he had an uncredited role as a German soldier in the Will Hay classic *The Goose Steps Out*. Although his part in this film was very minor, Hartnell was working with a major comedy star of his day, which gave him much exposure. In fact, Hartnell's cold image in the film set against Hay's chaos is noteworthy and was a taste of what was to come. As Hartnell's roles got larger, they also grew colder.

His first real praiseworthy appearance was in a movie called *Sabotage at Sea* (1942), where he played a villain under heavy make-up and moustache. Through this role, Hartnell learned that you didn't need much make-up to be a sinister character. A normal-looking man with much facial expression could be just as cruel; so Hartnell developed and grew with each significant role he played.

In 1943, Hartnell was approached by film producer Sir Carol Reed to play an army sergeant (Ned Fletcher) in the film *The Way Ahead*, alongside David Niven and a young John Laurie (later Fraser in *Dad's Army*). Hartnell's role was very gritty. The film centres on a group of conscripts and how they deal with military life. It opens in 1939 with Chelsea pensioners stating that if war was declared Britain would be in trouble because 'young men can't fight'. As the film was made in 1943, one could label *The Way Ahead* a propaganda movie, with just enough flag-flying to show young conscripted men that they were doing the right thing by going to war. Eric Ambler and Peter Ustinov's script is better than that though, with a down-and-dirty edge. Hartnell's gung-ho sergeant counterbalanced by David Niven's over-privileged officer commanding enhances the film further. *The Way Ahead* is a film that explains much about its time and is one of the highlights of Hartnell's career.

Hartnell's character is a stern no-nonsense regular soldier – not a conscript – who has to whip the new conscripts into shape, anticipating many of his film roles to come (including *Carry On Sergeant*). Hartnell really made an impression in the film, with his hard piercing stare and cast-iron personality.

His first scene is in itself a show of strength: heckled by a man at a railway station he holds back but looks dangerous. Unfortunately for the man, he becomes one of the sergeant's conscripts, but Hartnell's character never mentions it or shows any extra animosity towards him, which shows an impressive depth of character.

The film is very true to life in its interpretation of how the different walks of life came together in the barrack room and how they were brought together as a credible unit by their screaming sergeant, something Hartnell does an awful lot of.

The Way Ahead showcases Hartnell in his prime: a robust young actor with a resonant voice and much stage presence. He works perfectly alongside David Niven, especially when Niven questions his discipline with the men; but perhaps that discipline is as feisty as that bestowed upon him no more than 18 months previously in his own war. This strongly suggests that Hartnell was a better actor than a soldier.

The Way Ahead was a big success and Hartnell became a popular actor, albeit now typecast. But perhaps he can blame himself for that. With regard to *The Way Ahead*, he visited a real-life army sergeant, thus overcoming his wartime angst and showcasing his desire to always research his roles thoroughly.

Hartnell's typecasting became more prominent in the theatre with *Seagulls over Sorrento* (1950), which starred John Gregson, Nigel Stock, Bernard Lee and Ronald Shiner. Hartnell was Petty Officer Herbert in this nautical farce. The play tells the story of a group of volunteers in a disused wartime naval fortress, where secret peacetime radar experiments are going on. Although a comedy, Hartnell was the straight man, the no-nonsense military officer, and people began to know what to expect from him when he came on stage or screen. *Theatre World* said of the production, '... although the play has many serious moments (for all the men have their own reasons for volunteering), it is undoubtedly for its rich comedy that it has achieved such outstanding success'.

Hartnell longed to do more comedy roles, but the typecasting had taken over completely. In 1951, he took a role as a recruitment sergeant in *The Magic Box*, a movie made to celebrate The Festival of Britain and showcased many great

British character actors. The film was a biopic of the life of dreamer and pioneering inventor William Friese-Greene, including talent such as Joyce Grenfell, Margaret Rutherford, Joan Hickson, Thora Hird, Sid James, Richard Attenborough and even Laurence Olivier in a cameo role as a policeman.

One little-known fact about *The Magic Box* is that one of London's most notorious gangsters, Ronnie Kray, made a blink-and-you-miss-it appearance as an extra. Along with a group of East End kids, Kray was selected as an extra, and is clearly seen for the shortest second. Albeit in his teens at the time, it was something the fame-seeking killer would dine out on throughout his life.

Hartnell did return to comedy, albeit as an army sergeant again, in the TV comedy series *The Army Game* (1957–58, 1960–61) and the first *Carry On* film, *Carry On Sergeant* (1958), in itself a pastiche of *The Army Game* (and with parallels with *The Way Ahead*). Hartnell was really giving himself the niche role of over-serious officer that had a bunch of dead-enders to sort out; and the laughs would be generated by the dead-enders not by him.

In fairness, perhaps it was his unforgettable role as super-cool gangster Dallow against Richard Attenborough's Pinkie in *Brighton Rock* (1947) that really typecast him, less than five years after playing Sergeant Fletcher in *The Way Ahead*. A powerful role in a popular film does tend to do this, and throughout the 50s Hartnell resigned himself to playing the hard man.

Dallow was a dangerous man and although Hartnell wasn't the biggest man, his stern face, slightly gruff voice and probing eyes made a menacing presence on screen alongside Attenborough's psychotic character, Pinkie.

One does get the impression that Hartnell's character is the boss in *Brighton Rock*; his sharp suits and cool exterior set against the cavalier antics of Pinkie, certainly suggests a role of authority, made complete by Hartnell's acting skills.

Brighton Rock is a strange film, based on Graham Greene's iconic novel of post-war gang warfare in Brighton, and centres on the fact that a wife can't give evidence against her husband.

The tough roles continued. In 1957, Hartnell appeared as Cartley, the bespectacled, hard-nosed manager of Hawlett Trucking, in *Hell Drivers*, another great British movie and one that highlighted excellent young talent, such as future James Bond Sean Connery, Stanley Baker, Gordon Jackson, David McCallum, Herbert Lom, Sid James and Patrick McGoohan in one of his finest roles.

The film opens with Stanley Baker's character – Tom – approaching Cartley for a job. Cartley is quick to lay down the law, which Tom, with no other option open to him as an ex-con, accepts without question.

The Hell Drivers are the fastest road-haulage carriers around, and the faster they go the more money they make. There is much fighting and competition between the drivers, causing high tensions, but nobody of importance cares. These men are outcasts, low-lifes with nothing to lose; they are ostracised by the local people and even by their families but, for some of them, there is a crumb of pride – there is friendship. When Tom learns of a shady deal between Cartley and his reckless foreman (McGoohan), the movie quickens in pace towards a fatal accident, which leaves Tom crying out for revenge against the money men who have exploited him and his friends.

Hell Drivers is a passionate film, with quality input from McGoohan and McCallum – with their seldom-heard Scottish accents – but Connery, Baker, James and Lom are all excellent too, as are the female leads, Peggy Cummins, Jill Ireland and Marjorie Rhodes.

Although Hartnell only appears at the beginning and the end of the movie, his hard-man presence as the company boss is felt throughout the film, making *Hell Drivers* a milestone in his career, as well as a classic, gritty and tough British movie.

Hartnell did have a couple of comedy roles amidst the hard stuff. In 1959, he played alongside Peter Sellers in *The Mouse That Roared*, and he worked with Sellers again in the Boulting Brothers comedy *Heavens Above*, albeit as Major Fowler.

In 1963, Hartnell broke the mould and gave one of his very best performances, playing talent scout 'Dad' Johnson in *This Sporting Life*.

The movie starred Richard Harris and Rachel Roberts, both of whom were nominated for Oscars (Roberts eventually picking up a BAFTA).

The screenplay was written by David Storey, based on his own novel, and, from the moment the eerie Jerry Goldsmith-type opening music starts (composed by Roberto Gerhard), it is clear that this film is very different.

Roberts's character is a bitter woman who is indifferent to miner Frank Machin and his hard ways. Machin is a talented rugby player who the kind, gentle and modest 'Dad' takes under his wing to get into big-time rugby. He succeeds and, once he accomplishes this, he quietly moves on.

This Sporting Life had some great cameo roles in it, such as Arthur Lowe and Leonard Rossiter (Slomer and Phillips, respectively), which enhances the enjoyment by lightening the storyline somewhat.

It was *This Sporting Life* that brought the possibility of Hartnell becoming Doctor Who to the show's producer. Verity Lambert went to see the movie (released January 1963) and was struck by Hartnell's depth of acting ability. Hartnell's gentleness and life experience is a perfect counterbalance against Richard Harris's unthinking bullishness, and one that impressed Lambert very much.

Lambert approached Hartnell's agent to see if he would be interested in taking on the role of Doctor Who. She must have had much charm in order to persuade the agent into asking Hartnell. It wasn't his type of work after all. He had started out doing Shakespeare and adult comedy, then became the tough-guy actor. But perhaps this was Lambert's carrot on a stick: to offer something completely different to the actor, something as wonderful as the role of 'Dad' Johnson. The agent made the call and said, 'I wouldn't normally have suggested it to you, Bill, to work in children's television, but it sounds the sort of character part you have been longing to play.' The agent went on to explain that the part was 'of an eccentric old grandfather-cum-professor type who travels in space and time'.

Hartnell wasn't too sure about the part, but did agree to meet Verity Lambert and find out more. He said of the meeting: 'The moment this brilliant young producer, Miss Verity Lambert, started telling me about *Doctor Who* I was hooked.'

Perhaps it wasn't as clear-cut as that. Hartnell did go away and consider the offer and perhaps it was the diversity – the break from the typecasting – that persuaded him to take it on, as Lambert recalled, '[he] was interested but wary' when first offered the role. However, he soon made a decision and called her to accept the part.

Hartnell would find the work gruelling. He was in his mid-fifties and working 48 weeks a year, learning a variety of scripts and performing an action role, which 'was very hard work', as he admitted. Despite this, he 'loved every minute of it'.

The show became a smash hit, and Hartnell loved the idea of working for a young audience, as he said, 'To me kids are the greatest audience – and the greatest critics – in the world... You know, I couldn't go out into the high street without a bunch of kids following me. I felt like the Pied Piper.'

This was a fact echoed by his wife Heather, who used to pick him up from the railway station after a day's filming. She would say that he would get off the train and walk down the road with a stream of children behind him – not unlike the Pied Piper.

Hartnell played Doctor Who for three years and became quite wealthy because of it, earning the equivalent of about £4,000 per episode in present-day money, which was a good regular salary at the time.

Hartnell said he quit *Doctor Who* because he didn't see eye-to-eye with the BBC over the use of 'evil' in the show. He wrote in a letter to a fan, Ian McLachlan, in 1968 that, 'It was noted and spelled out to me as a children's programme, and I wanted it to stay as such; but I'm afraid, the BBC had other ideas. So did I, so I left.'

In her preface to Jessica Carney's biography of William Hartnell, Verity Lambert said that *Doctor Who* 'emanated from the Drama Department and not, as was the norm, the Children's Department'. This may be the reason why the show started to develop more 'adult' themes and ideas. As the old production staff moved on (including Lambert), more drama-based staff would take over in order to beef up the darker side of the show. This became more prevalent during Patrick Troughton's time as the Doctor – so clearly the show was naturally progressing through the department it had originally come from (Drama not the Children's Department). This genesis could explain why the show attracts a broad fan-base from people of all ages, not just children, nowadays.

Many critics think that Hartnell left for other reasons, i.e. he was pushed out because he cost too much money (other regular actors were getting a quarter of what he was earning per episode), but the original six-page treatment of the show clearly stated as a first paragraph that *Doctor Who* was 'an exciting adventure – Science Fiction Drama serial for Children's Saturday viewing'. This vindicated Hartnell's reasons for leaving.

Hartnell loved the adoration of young fans, but when the show started to get more sophisticated – more grown up and darker – his love and attachment towards the show started to diminish. This is reinforced by the fact that in 1964 he came up with an idea of a series called *The Son of Doctor Who*, in which a wicked son would wreak havoc across the universe and the Doctor would have to step in to sort things out. The BBC was not keen on the idea but sometime afterwards Hartnell said, 'I still think it would have worked and been exciting for children.'

One could argue that Hartnell's *The Son of Doctor Who* idea anticipated the new series' story 'The Doctor's Daughter', in which the audience is given the distinct idea that a spin-off series is highly likely and, above all, has the potential to be successful. In 'The Doctor's Daughter', it was the real-life daughter of Doctor Who Peter Davison, Georgia Moffett, who would take on the part.

Hartnell preserved the dignity of his 'grandfather' character during his reign as Doctor Who. In truth, his ailing health dictated that he couldn't have stayed on much longer in the role, even if he wanted to. A shame really, as four years later the show would be shown in colour. However, a story like 'Spearhead from Space' (the first Jon Pertwee – and colour – story), in which walking shop-window dummies killed innocent civilians and consequently attracted the wrath of real-life parents, would have been the final heartbreak for Hartnell.

When one appreciates how poor and unhappy Hartnell's formative years were, one can understand why he was a little over-sentimental towards children as the Doctor, not unlike the sensitivities Charles Dickens would show his young characters in his novels (he had a bad time himself as a child, while working in a blacking factory, and his heart and soul was always with the younger generation).

William Hartnell left *Doctor Who* at exactly the right time, unaware of the legacy he would create by doing so. The show was still popular, for he had quit while he was ahead. The BBC wanted it to continue, so another actor had to take over; the idea of regeneration took shape and gave the show its own excuse for reinvention. It is widely accepted that Kit Pedler and Gerry Davis came up with the idea of regeneration; indeed, they were writers of the very last William Hartnell *Doctor Who* story, 'The Tenth Planet', the first story ever to star the Cybermen.

Heather Hartnell said that her husband was happy that Patrick Troughton took over the role. Hartnell was familiar with 'Pat's' work, having worked on a film with him before *Doctor Who* (*Escape* starring Rex Harrison in 1947), so he believed the future of the show was in good hands.

Hartnell would make one further appearance as the Doctor in the show, for the tenth anniversary story 'The Three Doctors', playing alongside his successors Patrick Troughton and Jon Pertwee. He was a very unwell man at that time and had to read his short cameo roles from dummy boards, but he did it and enjoyed the experience too, spending some time with Troughton and Pertwee for publicity photographs, although he looked terribly frail by that time.

Within two years of the photo call, Hartnell would be dead from arteriosclerosis. He died on 23 April 1975, aged 67. Until her death in 1984, Heather Hartnell wrote to fans all over the world and attended several *Doctor Who* events; such was the impact and legacy of the first ever Doctor Who.

Today William Hartnell's place in TV history is secured. He was the man who made *Doctor Who* popular – magical – with children all over the world.

Perhaps one of the best epitaphs Hartnell could have had, albeit inadvertently, was within a two-page feature in the 1965 *Doctor Who* annual. Entitled 'Who is Dr Who?', the article speaks fondly of Hartnell's time traveller: 'He is mostly very gentle and kind-hearted and he has the utmost respect for life of any kind... and his heart is big enough to respect every one of the countless forms life has taken in all the ages and all the worlds.'

Hartnell believed wholeheartedly in *Doctor Who*, so much so, in fact, he lived the part more than any other he ever played, as he told Jack Bell of the *Daily Mirror* on 23 April 1966: '*Doctor Who* has given me a certain neurosis – and it is not easy for my wife to cope with. I get a little agitated, and it makes me a little irritable with people. In fact, *Doctor Who* seems to be taking over.'

Was this the reason why he left the show, the character taking him over? No, but the irritability was the first sign of his growing illness, arteriosclerosis, something not totally appreciated when he was in the role. He found it difficult to remember his lines. He lost his temper with cast members very quickly, especially new ones. All the original cast and crew had left to pursue other projects, and, coupled with his failing health, he began to feel at odds with the show he so deeply loved.

Why did he love it so much? Let us consider that in many of his post-war roles he had played an army officer and, what with such a traumatic exit from the war himself (and his love being comedy not tough-guy roles), a general dissatisfaction is clearly evident regarding the course of his career.

Another reason for his love of *Doctor Who* is encapsulated in a quote from the *Doctor Who Tenth Anniversary Radio Times Special*, where he recalls his lasting memory of the show. He had been asked to open a fete, so he dressed in his *Doctor Who* clothes and turned up in an old car owned by a friend. 'I'll never forget the moment we arrived. The children just converged on the car cheering and shouting, their faces all lit up. I knew then just how much *Doctor Who* really meant to them.'

Further evidence of the reality of the show for children comes from Hartnell's last *Doctor Who* companion, Anneke Wills, who said: '… my own children got wound-up in it. One day, while I was away rehearsing, they saw an episode in which I got carried off by monsters. They were very worried about whether I was going to come home that night. They didn't realise that the episode they had been watching had in fact been recorded the week before, and they half-believed their poor mum had been gobbled up by the wicked monsters!'

So Hartnell had made a credible character and starred in a show that had a strong young audience, but what about afterwards? Was there life after *Doctor Who*? If he was a TV icon, was Hartnell allowed to move on after the show? Also, if it was his most fulfilling role, was he happy to be a jobbing actor again?

No, would be the general answer to all these questions.

Hartnell was already booked to appear in pantomime that first Christmas after leaving the role. Handbills for *Puss in Boots* highlighted the fact that 'Television's original Dr Who' would be a major star (when in actual fact he was Buskin the Cobbler looking like Doctor Who!). If that wasn't enough, other promotional lines for the pantomime read, 'Meet the monsters from Outer Space... Super Win-a-Dalek Competition'. Clearly, Hartnell wouldn't be allowed to forget his greatest role very quickly.

Although the pantomime played to large audiences, it had its fair share of criticism, which stemmed largely from technical problems. Acoustics were a nightmare, with the orchestra being too loud and actors, including Hartnell, too quiet when reciting their lines.

Regardless, Hartnell continued to act and, in February 1967, he recorded an episode of *No Hiding Place* entitled 'The Game'. Suddenly Hartnell was back in a military role, this time an ex-Indian army sergeant turned rent collector. One reviewer was quick to spot the former Doctor Who, saying that he wished one of the cast would turn into a Dalek and observed, 'He [Hartnell] is Doctor Who' (James Hastie, *Scottish Daily Express*). Critics were harsh, and Hartnell wasn't truly allowed to move on; actors who have played the Doctor ever since might possibly be wary of typecasting simply because of the way Hartnell was treated.

But still Hartnell tried to carry on, taking on a guest spot in the popular *Softly, Softly*, in January 1968. It was here that he seemed to emerge from a low point. Due to the lack of work, harsh criticism and health problems – the main cause of his declining acting abilities – he had been drinking an awful lot; but he suddenly perked up.

On 25 April 1968, Hartnell discussed doing a Robert Bolt play at the Bristol Old Vic. It was called *Brother & Sister* and would co-star Sonia Dresdel; but it appeared that he had problems grasping the nuances of the part. The play ran for four weeks but didn't go on tour thereafter, the reason unclear. Just a couple more TV spots came his way after that, finishing with his return – in colour – in the anniversary *Doctor Who* story, 'The Three Doctors'.

It seemed that *Doctor Who* overshadowed his career after he ceased to play the role, but it was Hartnell's escalating health problems that were the main cause of this, not a lack of acting skills. His consequent depressions led to more drinking bouts and, after brave efforts to restore his health and start acting seriously again, he fell short of expectation. Perhaps in hindsight he should have retired after *Doctor Who*, but he loved his work and didn't want to give in to illness, and aren't so many people like that?

In retrospect, Hartnell had done enough to secure his memory in the hearts of the nation. He was Doctor Who? not the Doctor! When he played the part, nobody knew who the character was and where he came from; he was exciting and intriguing. Indeed, it has never been explained in the show if Susan Foreman was his grand-daughter or not, as Carole Ann-Ford explained, 'It was never really explained how she [Susan] came to be with him, but it was sort of accepted that they'd escaped together from another planet'. Was she a fellow alien, or an Earth child – perhaps an orphan? Although Anthony Coburn's original script of 'An Unearthly Child' has now been found, it takes nothing away from the intrigue that surrounded the show in its formative years.

During the Hartnell years, there was a real air of wonder and eccentricity about the character and the show itself. Even the music was strange, and its eeriness, coupled with the grainy black and white of the show, helped achieve greater thrills for the expectant audience.

One last thought and, perhaps, final compliment to William

Hartnell: when Richard Hurndall took on the role of the first Doctor in 'The Five Doctors' to celebrate the show's 20th anniversary, his character was given much respect from his successors. It was even the Hartnell character who solved the cryptic question set by the great Rassilon himself at the end of the story, which earned nothing less than an admiring shake of the head from the third Doctor. He was '*the original*' as Hurndall declared, and a great respect for the first Doctor Who has endured ever since.

It is clear that William Hartnell left the programme with a heavy heart when he knew he couldn't cut the mustard of a gruelling production schedule any more. He bowed out of show business slowly – painfully – over an approximate three-year period after that, with his only memorable performance being his return to the show seven years later for his very last TV acting appearance.

He was the Doctor of mystery, an eccentric old man and the original interstellar Pied Piper – something his successor Patrick Troughton would build upon...

'All the little boys and girls,
With rosy cheeks and flaxen curls,
And sparkling eyes and teeth like pearls,
Tripping and skipping, ran merrily after,
The wonderful music with shouting and laughter.'

The Pied Piper of Hamelin

Robert Browning

CHAPTER THREE
PATRICK TROUGHTON

'Dr Who faces the awe-inspiring *reality* of Space and Time and with wonderful human courage… He is human curiosity personified. He must see for himself; he must go *there*; he must *learn* all there is to know.

Are we not all a little possessed of the spirit of Dr Who?'

The Equations of Dr Who

The Doctor Who Annual, 1965

PATRICK GEORGE TROUGHTON was born in Mill Hill, London, on 25 March 1920 and educated at Bexhill-on-Sea Preparatory School and Mill Hill Public School. At the age of 16, he went to the Embassy School of Acting at Swiss Cottage, London, which was run by Eileen Thorndyke, sister of Dame Sybil Thorndyke. He earned a scholarship there and progressed to the Leighton Rollins Studio for Actors at the John Drew Memorial Theatre in Long Island, USA. He was in America when the Second World War broke out. He returned to England on a Belgian ship, but it hit an enemy mine and sank just off Portland Bill, in sight of England. Troughton escaped by lifeboat and always considered himself lucky to have done so.

He joined the Tonbridge Repertory Company on his return to

England in 1939 and acted there for a year. In June 1940, he joined the Royal Navy (RN) not deterred by his close escape from an ocean-going death the previous year. His first duty was protecting the coast from enemy submarines in an RN destroyer. He was then transferred to motor torpedo boats based at Great Yarmouth, where he was given his own command after the Allied invasion of Normandy. He left the RN in March 1945, but always retained a fondness for the sea.

Troughton then returned to acting and joined the Amersham Repertory Company. From there he was asked to join the famous Bristol Old Vic Company, and he appeared in *Hamlet* (1947–48) and *King Lear* (1948). He then spent two years with the Pilgrim Players performing T S Eliot's plays at the Mercury Theatre, Nottingham.

In the early 1980s Troughton said of his career, 'I like to play all kinds of people in all kinds of plays. I've got a special liking for fantasy and rip-roaring adventures with plenty of action, such as *Robin Hood* and *Kidnapped*.'

Troughton always considered himself a character actor and he cut his teeth on roles in classic Boy's Own-type adventures. He was the character actor personified, which was why he was always very reluctant to give interviews, as he explained in a rare radio interview towards the end of his career, 'It's wrong [for a character actor] to promote their own character too much… the audience get to know you too much, which makes your job harder.'

Troughton's career was long and distinguished. His first movie role was in *Escape* (in which William Hartnell also appeared) in 1948 and, in 1950, he was in Disney's *Treasure Island* alongside Robert Newton's infamous Long John Silver, a larger-than-life character actor who had been in the RN with future Doctor Who Jon Pertwee.

Troughton's first TV appearance was in 1948. 'It was the early days of TV,' he remembered later. 'About 300,000 TV viewers in London only… I was never relaxed in live TV.'

He may not have been, but he played many live roles for about 15 years before pre-recording came in. Unfortunately, many of Troughton's early TV performances, along with those by William Hartnell and, to a certain degree, Jon Pertwee, no longer exist, which makes analysis of the actor's work difficult. But many older people remember Troughton as *Robin Hood*. The six-part show was written by Max Kester and was recorded live at the Gaumont-British Studios in Lime Grove, London, between 17 March and 21 April 1953. Nowadays, Troughton's grandson Sam appears in the latest BBC interpretation of *Robin Hood* alongside Jonas Armstrong and Keith Allen.

Some of Troughton's other early roles included Guy Fawkes in *Gunpowder Guy* (alongside future *Doctor Who* producer Barry Letts) in 1950 and *The Scarlet Pimpernel* in 1956. These parts were very minor compared to his film work, which in 1955 included the part of James Tyrell in Laurence Olivier's iconic *Richard III*. Although his wasn't a major part in the film, it was memorable: being summoned by King Richard and told to murder the Princes in the Tower in a very tight two-shot, before providing a very strong voice-over during the murder scene itself. Troughton was clearly up to the job, with so much experience behind him in such a short space of time. In fact, he truly adds an additional sinister edge to the film by doing the king's dirty work against his own free will. This wasn't the first time Troughton had played alongside Olivier, having appeared in *Hamlet* (1948), which followed his own TV version the previous year.

In 1962–63, Troughton played Daniel Quilp in the BBC's epic interpretation of Dickens' *The Old Curiosity Shop*, something he mentioned as a career highlight in 1983. 'I did a lot of Dickens… the dwarf Quilp in *The Old Curiosity Shop* was a big success and a part I look back on with great love and excitement.'

Diversity was the watchword of Troughton's career and next he played the blind man Phineas in the film classic *Jason and the Argonauts*.

The movie opens with King Pelias, an evil dictator, receiving a prophecy from a Soothsayer regarding a golden fleece. He learns that a baby that will grow into a man will thwart him: Jason, a man with one sandal.

When grown, Jason saves a man – King Pelias – from drowning, and when Jason loses a sandal, during the incident, Pelias knows that the prophecy is drawing closer to a conclusion. Indeed, Jason doesn't help himself. He tells the king that he is on a quest to regain his throne and kill the evil Pelias. Knowing that he could never kill Jason in one-to-one combat, Pelias tells Jason that he isn't ready to confront the king and tells him to gather good men and a ship and prove himself first by capturing the golden fleece.

Jason and the Argonauts is a well-thought-out script with cutting-edge special effects for its day. When Jason eventually arrives at Phineas' abode and witnesses Harpies (winged demons) stealing his food and tormenting the blind man, the film takes on a mystical edge. Before Jason obtains the advice he seeks from Phineas, he sets up a trap to capture the Harpies, which his crew perform by catching them in a huge net thrown down from the top of a ruined temple. The temple used in the scene is a real ancient temple in Italy, and the actors were given special permission to climb on it.

To create any stop-motion animation requires some level of improvisation from the actor. There are no model creatures or actors in suits roaming around during shooting, so the actor is left to visualise what is going on and act solo, with the creatures being inserted afterwards. Ray Harryhausen explained the process with regard to Troughton's scene: 'For the Harpies sequence I designed several "contacts" with humans. The first where the blind Phineas is fighting off the demons and we see his stick and belt yanked from him by the creatures... Both objects were attached to off-screen wires and on my signal a member of the crew pulled them away from Patrick Troughton. Later in the animation studio I would animate the models... as though they were snatching the objects.'

Jason and the Argonauts took two years and three million dollars to make, but the end result is a magnificent piece of cinema with a great cameo role from Troughton.

Several years later, in 1966, Troughton was making a film in Ireland called *The Viking Queen* when he was asked if he would like to become the second Doctor Who. At first he didn't want to do it, feeling that it wasn't the right type of part for him. 'I was astonished that they asked me,' he said later. He had watched the show with his children and really enjoyed Hartnell's Doctor, but was unsure if it could continue when Hartnell left. 'I thought it would last about six weeks after Billy Hartnell had finished,' he said in 1983. 'The whole concept of the Doctor going on... was quite a new idea, and one was jumping in at the deep end.'

The BBC were persistent and finally convinced Troughton who felt he should black up for the part, simply because as soon as he left the role he knew that everybody would know him as the Doctor and therefore he would be typecast.

It was Sydney Newman who brought Troughton back down to earth and shaped his interpretation of the Doctor, with a throw-away comment: 'Do what you like with him. Play him like Charlie Chaplin if you want to.' (*Doctor Who – A*

Celebration, Two Decades Through Time and Space, Peter Haining, W H Allen, 1983). This appealed to Troughton, so that's what eventually happened, but only after other ideas such as 'playing him like a Windjammer captain' (very tough and hardy) had been thrashed out (*Blue Peter* interview, 1983).

It's difficult to say if the Chaplin idea was finally Troughton's or Newman's. It appears that Troughton went off the idea and Newman asked, 'Whatever happened to the cosmic hobo?' A compromise was eventually achieved, with Troughton playing the part very clownishly to begin with, but mellowing as time went on.

He reminisced on TV magazine show *Nationwide* (1983): 'First they put a wig on me and I looked like Harpo Marx, then they dressed my hair like a Beatle,' so the zany Chaplin image was toned down from very early on.

Troughton needn't have worried about being accepted as the Doctor. He was fondly regarded from the off, as highlighted in the Doctor Who Annual (1967): 'Our new Dr Who is more "with it"; he is more "switched on", more in tune with the 20th Century. There are, of course, still traces of his old personality and, characteristically, he still wears the same clothes, which are a trifle baggy on his new figure.' So the cosmic hobo was thoroughly accepted.

The cast accepted him as well, as *Doctor Who* companion Anneke Wills (companion Polly) remembers, 'We played our little joke on Patrick the first day he started. Michael Craze [companion Ben Jackson] and I ordered some special T-shirts and we greeted our new Doctor with the words: "Come back Bill Hartnell" blazoned across our chests. It was a ghastly joke, I suppose, but dear Patrick took it very well.'

Troughton remembered his three years as the Doctor with fondness: 'Of all my… years as an actor, I think these were the happiest three years. I particularly enjoyed acting with Frazer Hines, who played Jamie [Troughton's main companion in the series]. We never once had a cross word all the time we worked together.'

Frazer Hines confirms this: 'For three years Pat… and I had an absolute ball together. I think there's always room for fun when you're working – except, maybe, if it's Chekhov or Shakespeare – and I've always been a practical joker.'

Troughton got on well with all the regular cast and production crew, as he recounts, 'Innes Lloyd [who took over from Verity Lambert], the producer when I started, and Peter Bryant were [also] great to work for. I had a lot of fun.' (From *The Making of Doctor Who*, Malcolm Hulke and Terrance Dicks, Pan Books, 1972.)

Troughton enjoyed the fantasy of the show. He thought it was great that the Doctor could change his appearance, as he explained at the time of 'The Three Doctors', 'We are all different aspects of the same character. Of course it's bound to be a bit of a mystery to us, but in the Doctor's space-time machine the so-called past just doesn't exist.'

Like Hartnell before him, Troughton said that it was difficult to stop being the Doctor when the cameras were off, but, unlike Hartnell, Troughton's Doctor was not a crotchety old man, but a cosmic hobo, as he explained, 'When you're playing a part for a long time you certainly take on some of the mental attitudes of the fellow you're playing. Luckily the Doctor was a very jolly fellow and I just bubbled along.'

He would also say that having young children at the time – three under ten years old – allowed him to keep in touch with the part of the Doctor, as children loved the character so much. So again, like William Hartnell, there was that Pied Piper aspect to Troughton's Doctor and not just in the pipe –

recorder – he played, but in regard to the children who followed him. He mentioned the younger viewers in 1983: 'It [Dr Who] also gave me great pleasure coming into contact with children, for if I had not been an actor I would quite like to have been a teacher. Children keep one young.' In fact, Troughton followed up by stating that the continuing success of the show was due to new children being born.

Troughton regretted leaving the show 'very much... but you can't do something forever as a character actor'. Three years was a long time for Troughton to be involved in one particular project, as he confessed, 'If I stayed with it too long, I would get stuck.'

After *Doctor Who*, like before, he took on many memorable roles and, to him, *Doctor Who* was just one in a long line. In 1983, while shooting 'The Five Doctors' on location in Wales, producer John Nathan-Turner and former Doctor Who Jon Pertwee spent some time convincing Troughton to attend the special 20th anniversary convention at Longleat, as Nathan-Turner remembered, 'Jon Pertwee and I persuaded him to do it... And then he did cartwheels to get out of it... And [eventually] he said, "I'm not going to get out of this, am I?" and I said, "No!"'

It is important to note that Troughton and Pertwee were very fond of each other, as Pertwee was very keen to point out, 'We are tremendously fond of each other, but we made out we didn't get along at conventions because Pat's Doctor and mine didn't get on in "The Three Doctors". So it was all an act!' And a fine one too, causing all sorts of fun banter.

As soon as Pertwee had taken over the Tardis reins in 1970, Troughton was already working hard on another major project, *The Six Wives of Henry VIII*, playing the role of Norfolk. This re-established him in serious character roles, although he would continue to enjoy other genre roles in horror and fantasy, such as Father Brennan, the tortured priest in *The Omen* (1976). This was a tremendous role for Troughton, allowing him to adopt an Irish accent and pester Gregory Peck to murder his adopted son, who just happened to be the spawn of the Devil.

The Omen remains one of the greatest horror movies to this day, but, in fact, it is a typical thriller with such quality thriller actors as Gregory Peck, Lee Remick, David Warner and Billie Whitelaw.

Billie Whitelaw was terrifying in the movie and proved that the most evil person was the one who looked normal. But Troughton didn't look that normal in the movie. He had to play a desperate priest, a man with terminal cancer who papered the walls of his home with pages of the Bible and was desperate to tell Peck and Remick the truth about their son Damien. His thick Irish accent, his deathly pale features, his inner frustration and desperation to be heard – his inner turmoil – make Troughton's role a truly memorable one in the film, and his death scene is one of the most iconic in horror-movie history. Couple that with a haunting score by the legendary Jerry Goldsmith, and you have cinema history that is impossible to remake with any credit. Troughton had worked with Billie Whitelaw before in an episode of *Espionage* (1963), called 'He Rises on Sunday and We on Monday'.

After *The Omen*, Troughton took a part in *Sinbad and the Eye of the Tiger* (1977), one of Ray Harryhausen's last stop-motion movies. Troughton played the part of the wise man Melanthius. He had, of course, played the part of the blind man, Phineas, in Harryhausen's classic *Jason and the Argonauts* (1963) before *Doctor Who*, so he was not offered such parts because of his connection with the show. Indeed, he played alongside Christopher Lee in two Hammer Horror classics *The Curse of Frankenstein* (1957) and *Scars of*

Dracula (1970) (playing the small roles of Kurt and Klove respectively); so the role of the Doctor had no ill effect on his career at all. Troughton could still take on small, interesting roles like any other jobbing character actor.

Returning to *Sinbad and the Eye of the Tiger*: despite being a Harryhausen movie, the film was quite poor. It was the fourth Sinbad movie and it was clear that ideas were no longer plentiful. The over-dubbing in the film was annoying to begin with, and Harryhausen's bony demons were a poor copy of his killer skeletons from *Jason and the Argonauts* over 15 years previously.

Jane Seymour is the obligatory gorgeous love interest, just as Caroline Munro was in the previous Sinbad film, *The Golden Voyage of Sinbad*, which starred Tom Baker (see Chapter Five). That said, the wicked Zenobia (Margaret Whiting), is an unconvincing counterpart to Tom Baker's wizard in the previous film, who physically ages due to her deals with demons and the prince of darkness.

Although *Sinbad and the Eye of the Tiger* gave the appearance of being more expensive in budget than its predecessors, it was an unimaginative story that walked down tried and proven pathways with little additional imagination. So what of Patrick Troughton's performance?

Troughton had taken part in the iconic *Jason and the Argonauts*, albeit in a smaller way, and so was an inspired piece of casting for this latter movie, because there were some pretty poor choices of actor for other parts.

As Melanthius the wise man, Troughton lives in a dead city on a desert island with his daughter. He starts off cantankerous and vain, but manages to muster a sense of wonder and amazement that brings a whole new dimension to the movie, albeit a third of the way through it.

While most of the cast try to dazzle the audience with their stunning good looks, Troughton settles down behind his big bushy grey beard with an ever-building sense of humour (which must have been as contagious off camera as on). One can probably see a little of the Doctor in his character, especially when an experiment he is conducting goes wrong and explodes (to his immense joy).

Sinbad and the Eye of the Tiger is Sunday-afternoon family fodder to this day; it's just a little lazy in its creativity in comparison to other movies in the Sinbad series, and especially the Harryhausen canon.

Troughton's love of popping in and out of familiar roles is clearly shown in his strong ties to two particular novels of Robert Louis Stevenson, *Kidnapped* and *Treasure Island*. Despite being in the classic Disney movie in 1950, Troughton returned to *Treasure Island* in 1977, where he played a very convincing Israel Hands in the TV series. His portrayal of the infamous swashbuckler Alan Breck in 1952 and 1956 in TV versions of *Kidnapped* were mentioned as career highlights by Troughton shortly before his death in the 1980s. There were some stories Troughton revisited throughout his career, *Robin Hood* being another one and, of course, *Doctor Who*, which he returned to three times.

Troughton enjoyed dabbling. He even dabbled in the soaps, taking a role in the longest-running one of the lot, *Coronation Street*, playing the part of George Barton in 1974. So his character actor status was fully appreciated by all sorts of casting directors, not just those associated with action and fantasy. Troughton was an accomplished character actor and *Doctor Who* did not tarnish that in any way.

Despite severe heart attacks (in 1978 and 1984), Troughton continued to work hard, taking on cameo roles in *All Creatures*

Great and Small (opposite future Doctor Who Peter Davison in an episode entitled 'Hair of the Dog'), *Minder* and *The Two Ronnies 1984 Christmas Special*. He took a more permanent role in TV sitcom *The Two of Us* with Nicholas Lyndhurst in 1986 (on a rowing machine in one particular scene!). He was also the first person ever to be murdered in *Inspector Morse* (George Jackson in the very first story 'The Dead of Jericho') in 1987. Troughton's last performance was in the TV comedy *Supergran* also in 1987.

Patrick Troughton died on 28 March 1987, in Atlanta, USA. He was attending the Magnum Opus Con II in Columbus, Georgia. While taking part in the panel Q&A, he complained of feeling unwell and retired to his room. He suffered a fatal heart attack the following morning after ordering his breakfast and was found lying on the floor. He was pronounced dead on arrival at the hospital. He was 67.

When people discuss Troughton's great roles, the part of the Doctor is always there, but his Quilp and Breck, even so long ago, are also considered classic performances, as is his portrayal of Cole Hawlings in the BBC six-part fantasy for children *The Box of Delights*. If we look at this role against that of Father Brennan in *The Omen* and then his roles in *Coronation Street* and *Doctor Who*, Troughton's diversity and skill as a character actor is quickly showcased and appreciated.

Patrick Troughton was the quintessential British character actor, never staying in one place – or one role – for too long. Perhaps *Doctor Who* fans were initially upset by this, especially the way he would talk about his other roles with equal or more love, but they soon came to understand why Troughton was sometimes shy of public appearances and interviews. He didn't want to give too much of himself away or for them to get to know his true character. That said, he did return to *Doctor*

Who several times, in 1973 for 'The Three Doctors', in 1983 for 'The Five Doctors' and yet again – because he enjoyed the comeback so much! – in 1985, for 'The Two Doctors'. This last appearance – an excellent story featuring his faithful companion Jamie [Frazer Hines] alongside then incumbents Colin Baker and Nicola Bryant – showcased Troughton's love for and humour in the role (through one 'dinner party' scene at least, where he is momentarily transformed into a creature with a love of human flesh with a counterpart chef from the same carnivorous race).

All of these return visits show that Troughton had a place in his heart for the show right up until his untimely death; but let us not forget his other, now largely overlooked, roles.

Doctor Who was neither saint nor sinner to Patrick Troughton. What the Doctor has done for him is to keep him in the minds of the young forever, as the immortality of *Doctor Who* will keep his work alive and, perhaps, tempt some people into finding old Troughton gems on TV and DVD.

'It now seems so long ago that I played the part of the Doctor that there is really very little I can add to what has already been written. And, of course, I've played so many different parts in the last forty years.'

Patrick Troughton from 'Doctor Who Indulged My Passion for Clowning'
Doctor Who – A Celebration, Two Decades Through Time and Space
Peter Haining

Before moving on to the life and career of Jon Pertwee, I do wish to labour the fact that Patrick Troughton's life and career is dreadfully understated. Unfortunately, the biggest culprit of this was Troughton himself, not wishing to do too many interviews. But also it is the BBC's fault by erasing so many episodes of his Doctor Who and also destroying – or not recording – so many of those early live TV series such as *Robin Hood*, *Gunpowder Guy* or *Kidnapped*. In many ways, Patrick Troughton is the forgotten actor, let alone the lost Doctor. One thing I have saved to mention here is his fantastic performance as Adolf Hitler in the Gateway Theatre production of *Eva Braun*. This was in 1950, when feelings about the Nazis still ran high, but he did it and he did it well.

Patrick Troughton isn't quite overlooked nowadays; he has a legacy through his family. His daughter's son is now Harry Potter's nemesis Dudley Dursley (Harry Melling). His son David Troughton – apart from being an accomplished Shakespearean actor – appeared in *Doctor Who* during his father's time, in stories 'The Enemy of the World' and 'The War Games', also playing a more substantial role as the dashing King Peladon opposite Jon Pertwee's Doctor in 'The Curse of Peladon', and Professor Hobbes in David Tennant's excellent story 'Midnight'. David Troughton's brother Michael is an actor and teacher, most notable for playing opposite Rik Mayall in *The New Statesman* as Sir Piers Fletcher-Dervish.

The Patrick Troughton Theatre opened at Mill Hill School in 2007 to celebrate one of its most accomplished former actor students and, along with his family and many *Doctor Who* fans around the world, Troughton's legacy is somewhat secured. That and, of course, the latest Doctor Who, Matt Smith, singling him out as a huge influence on his own interpretation of the Doctor.

'For who would bear the whips and scorns of time.'

Hamlet

William Shakespeare

CHAPTER FOUR
JON PERTWEE

'Dr Who is me – or I am Dr Who. I play him straight from me.'

Jon Pertwee from *The Making of Dr Who* by Malcolm Hulke
and Terrance Dicks

LIKE PATRICK TROUGHTON and William Hartnell, Jon Pertwee was one of the great British character actors of the 20th century. His ability to throw his voice and adopt a multitude of characters made him a man in high demand, especially on radio in the 1950s and 60s. He was incredibly versatile and as much in demand as Kenneth Williams, or indeed his character acting cousin Bill Pertwee (who later played Hodges in *Dad's Army*).

John Devon Roland Pertwee was born on 7 July 1919 in Chelsea, London. He was educated at Frensham Heights School, Rowledge and Sherborne School, Sherborne, Dorset.

The name Pertwee is of French-Huguenot origin, actually being Perthuis de Laillevault. He was the son of the famous playwright, novelist and actor Roland Pertwee. Roland's friend Henry Ainley was Jon Pertwee's godfather. His son, Anthony Ainley, would become an actor and play opposite Jon in 'The Five Doctors' as the Master, while Anthony's brother Richard would become Tom Baker's drama teacher, while he was coached as an amateur by William Hartnell.

Jon's dad was also good friends with A A Milne, and Jon was invited to tea one afternoon where he met Milne's son Christopher Robin. After tea, Christopher took Jon upstairs where he was introduced to the boy's toy animals: Piglet, Owl, Kanga, Roo and Christopher's favourite – Winnie the Pooh. Jon was also allowed to ride on Christopher Robin's donkey – Eeyore.

Despite having a famous father and interesting acquaintances, Pertwee's upbringing was not a happy one. For a start, he didn't see his mother until he was 15. She had an affair when Pertwee was an infant and his father kicked her out of the marital home. She moved away with her lover, and Pertwee and his elder brother Michael were left with a father who was neatly wrapped up in his own world, with little time for them. (Pertwee also had a stepbrother called Michael, who he called Coby, which was short for his surname.) The three boys were close brothers but if anyone got left out it would be Jon.

Jon spent much of his formative years under the care of his uncle Guy, but he was also very close to his grandmother, who helped to look after him.

Despite feeling left out by his father, Pertwee didn't think of any other career but acting. Laurence Olivier was one of Pertwee's early acquaintances. Towards the end of his life, Pertwee used to quote a true story that proved Olivier was indeed the greatest actor that ever lived. He explained that one day he was invited to a party while Olivier was visiting his house. He asked the actor to accompany him, but Olivier wasn't keen. Pertwee refused to take no for an answer and begrudgingly Olivier went along. Once at the party, Pertwee sat Olivier down with a sandwich and some tea. Believing that he would be all right, Pertwee left him alone. He then explained that Olivier hated anyone creeping up behind him but unfortunately somebody did. An old lady came up behind him on the sofa, put her hands over his eyes and said, 'Guess who?' Olivier shot up in the air and the poor woman was propelled backwards over a chair. An enraged Olivier stormed over to the host and demanded, 'Who was that woman?'

The host replied, 'That was my wife.'

Seamlessly Olivier declared, 'What an extraordinary woman.'

Acting was the family business, so Pertwee took it for granted that he would follow in his father's footsteps. In fact, Jon had four great-aunts, the Moore sisters, who were also on the stage. He always explained in interviews later that this complacency led him to always joking with the cast between takes, to many a director's disdain. However, it didn't start out that way. At boarding school there was a shortage of young lads who wanted to become actors. His peers considered him a 'poofter', so he was picked on for a while.

It wasn't all doom and gloom though. When he was old enough to drive, Pertwee bought a 250cc SOS trials motorbike and went for a ride. At a T-junction he lost control, went over a wall and into a vicar's garden. 'Well done!' the vicar said. 'You're just in time for tea!' So acting and fast bikes were part of his teenage make-up and neither ever left him.

Some people look upon the above story as a joke, but in fact it wasn't – Pertwee did indeed fly into the garden and was offered tea. Years later, the actor was passing the very same place with his son Sean and showed him the spot where he hit the wall, because it had never been repaired.

Pertwee joined RADA at 18, where he trained alongside Duncan Lamont – who would appear alongside Jon in the *Doctor Who* story 'Death to the Daleks'. Jon's time at

RADA came to an end when he was expelled for refusing to play the part of a 'Greek wind' in a production. This caused a bit of embarrassment for his father as he was one of the school governors.

He then spent some time – while still at school – at a travelling circus riding the wall of death, which he maintained was very easy to do. What wasn't easy to do – and something he of course refused to do – was to put a real-life lion in the act with him. Because the circus had a very old toothless lion, they thought it would be good for Pertwee to take it for a spin on the wall of death! A preposterous idea, but it was suggested.

The rest of the 1930s saw Pertwee working in a travelling theatre company and the occasional stint on radio, which gave him a lot of experience as an actor.

Much of Pertwee's output from the 1930s and 40s is now lost. Programmes were performed live and too few were recorded on 78 rpm records. At one stage Pertwee was performing 15-minute stints on radio every day for months on end. This made him quite wealthy, but sadly there are only a smattering of examples of this work preserved today.

What we do know of Pertwee's early career is that his father helped him. One of Pertwee's early theatre runs was in *To Kill a Cat*, which his father wrote. Also, his 1939 movie *The Four Just Men* was scripted by his father who also took a small part in it. The movie also has the added distinction of being the first in which Pertwee actually spoke.

Speed was still a passion of Pertwee's, despite his growing popularity as an actor, and he competed at Goodwood for the odd motor car engagement right up to the outbreak of the Second World War. He then joined the Royal Naval Volunteer Reserve (RNVR) and became an officer. Like Patrick

Troughton, he too escaped death at sea. Pertwee was one of a small group of people who got transferred from HMS *Hood* shortly before it was destroyed in under ten seconds by the *Bismarck*. '1,762 men went down in one bang,' he told Michael Parkinson in 1982. It was a very lucky escape on that occasion, and he experienced several other close calls with death during the war.

Another little-known episode from Pertwee's war was his tattoo. He recalled in interviews that one day he had a 'run ashore' – a naval term for having a good drink on land – got extremely drunk, and woke up with a large tattoo on his right forearm. He remembered nothing about having it done. It can be seen in several moments of his time on *Doctor Who*, including his very first *Spearhead from Space*. And when he was asked to roll his sleeve up for an injection in his second serial, *The Silurians*, he choses the left arm, keeping his souvenir of a drunken night out well hidden.

Pertwee and Troughton met several times during the war years, as he told Peter Haining, '[Troughton] had a strong dislike of the standard issue tin hat that the Navy made the people on motor torpedo-boats wear. So instead he wore this old family tea cosy on his head. It was a gaudy-looking thing and must have annoyed his Commanding Officer no end – but he still went on wearing it!'

Troughton would wear a tea-cosy hat while playing the Doctor, in such sea-based stories as 'Fury from the Deep', and for him it became normal sea-going apparel. But Troughton wasn't the only eccentric would-be actor that Pertwee met during the war. There was also Robert Newton, a legendary character in the RN, always managing to acquire quality booze and disappearing to drink it and then sleep it off. Pertwee admired the man, especially in how he managed to get away with his insubordination (Newton was, like Pertwee, also expelled from RADA). However, he was eventually arrested and punished by the RN who sent him on a trawler, but even then he managed to delay the ship's departure in order to acquire smoked salmon sandwiches and quality booze (in wartime!), so he and the crew could enjoy a good meal on the ocean waves.

A little-appreciated episode in Pertwee's war was when he was transferred to the Naval Intelligence Department (NID) in Whitehall. Towards the end of his life, Pertwee toured his one-man show *An Evening with Jon Pertwee* in which he briefly mentioned his tour in NID, but no real detail about the job. NID was actually the department where Ian Fleming (the man who would write James Bond) worked. In fact, the real-life James Bond – Fleming's main inspiration for the character – also worked there: Patrick Dalzel-Job who, as part of 30 Assault Unit (a crack team of commandos created by Fleming), was instrumental in gathering intelligence concerning V Rocket installations behind enemy lines in Europe. Pertwee remembered that James 'Jim' Callaghan was there as a 'tea boy' (long before becoming the British Prime Minister), which caused him much amusement years later.

Pertwee wasn't one of the most distinguished officers in NID; he recalled during his one-man show that he had to dispose of Winston Churchill's cigar ends after Cabinet meetings with the Joint Planning Staff (JPS, which included author Dennis Wheatley) and NID. He would sell the cigar ends and make a bit of extra cash.

Although he eventually landed a desk job in NID, Pertwee admitted towards the end of his life that his severe back problems originated from his time in the RN and some of the close-shaves he had with danger. Indeed, his war was not easy, and the desk job in NID shows that he had genuine injuries but his input was still vital.

Towards the end of his career in the Navy, Pertwee joined the broadcasting section, where he met Lieutenant Eric Barker and seriously began his career in radio. This led to two series that made him a household name – *Waterlogged Spa* and *The Navy Lark*. He took on many trademark voices in the latter show, including an eccentric postman that endeared him to the nation, with the catchphrase, 'It doesn't matter what you do, as long as you tears them up' (referring to people's letters).

For a while, Pertwee worked alongside another great mimic in *The Navy Lark*, Ronnie Barker, who played Fatso Johnson in the show. Pertwee and Barker became firm friends. Barker later said of Pertwee, 'Jon was always such fun to work with. We had a lot of laughs and he was always one of the prime instigators. But he was very professional and very talented and I thoroughly enjoyed working with him.' (*Jon Pertwee: The Biography* by Bernard Bale, Andre Deutsch, 2000).

When Barker left and Pertwee was asked who they should put in his place to do the other voices he'd done so well, he suggested himself, and went on to do over a hundred different voices for the show in the end.

The Navy Lark ran for 18 years, making it the longest-running comedy show in the world at that time (only to be surpassed later by *The News Huddlines*), but it wasn't the only success that Pertwee worked on during that time; he also appeared in the theatre alongside Frankie Howerd in *A Funny Thing Happened on the Way to the Forum*, which Howerd continued to have great success with on TV (*Up Pompeii*) and film (both *A Funny Thing...* and *Up Pompeii*), Pertwee's role in the movie being taken by Phil Silvers.

Pertwee's first starring role in a film was in *Will Any*

Gentleman...? (1953), coincidentally alongside William Hartnell. But that wasn't the only *Doctor Who* tie-in that came from the movie. During filming, Pertwee met Jean Marsh whom he later married on 2 April 1955. Jean would become William Hartnell's companion in the longest *Doctor Who* story ever, 'The Dalek Master Plan' (12 episodes). Unfortunately, she was killed towards the end of the story and, sadly, her marriage to Pertwee didn't last long either. They separated in 1958, before divorcing in 1960. Pertwee remarried shortly afterwards to a German lady he had met on a skiing holiday, Ingeborg Rhoesa. They married on 13 August 1960 and had two children, Sean and Dariel.

Pertwee's career as a character actor continued on radio (most notably in *The Navy Lark*), television and films throughout the 1950s and 60s. Indeed, there are some forgotten gems, such as *The Ugly Duckling*, starring Bernard Bresslaw as Henry Jekyll and Teddy Hyde, with character actor David Lodge putting in an appearance too.

On Sunday, 1 November 1964, Pertwee appeared in the British Forces Broadcasting Service (BFBS) 21st anniversary gala night, at the Victoria Palace Theatre in London. Although Pertwee appeared alongside people such as Ken Dodd, Jimmy Edwards, Charlie Chester, Larry Adler, Ted Ray and Tommy Trinder, to name but a few, the ultimate stars of the show were The Goons (Spike Milligan, Peter Sellers and Harry Secombe), who performed a whole episode of their madcap but groundbreaking show. Pertwee was a friend of both Sellers and Milligan, but in later life he would fall out with Spike over who was the bigger fan of the pantomime *Aladdin*!

It was occasions such as the BFBS gala night where Pertwee was in his element, surrounded by talented like-minded people who, despite some dreadful experiences during the war, took a comedic influence from those troubled times and shaped the face of British comedy for the next 50 years. *The Goon Show* was barrack-room humour and *The Navy Lark* was not dissimilar. Character actors such as Peter Butterworth (who played fellow Time Lord the Meddling Monk, alongside William Hartnell), was actually a prisoner of war in the real-life escape that inspired the 1950 film *The Wooden Horse* – although he didn't get a part in the movie because he 'didn't look convincingly heroic and athletic'. Butterworth, who was in many of the *Carry On* films, served as a lieutenant in the Royal Navy and was captured in the Netherlands in 1940. He escaped through a tunnel from the prisoner-of-war camp Dulag Luft, near Frankfurt, in June 1941, then covered 27 miles in just three days before a member of the Hitler Youth captured him. Afterwards, he joked he could never work with children. Two other escape attempts never got beyond the camp grounds.

Several years after the BFBS gala night, while playing on Broadway in *There's a Girl in My Soup*, Pertwee was offered the lead role in a brand-new BBC comedy series. The leading role was written with his comic talents in mind: the role was Captain Mainwaring, the show *Dad's Army*. Pertwee turned down the part, and it went to Arthur Lowe, whose interpretation would become legendary. Pertwee later said that he didn't really know what he was being offered back home at the time, that he was too wrapped up in the part he was playing. Suffice to say, if he had taken the part, he most certainly wouldn't have gone on to star in *Doctor Who*.

Pertwee wasn't sore about losing out on *Dad's Army*, he knew that he wouldn't have had the opportunity of being the Doctor if he had taken the role, and he also found Arthur Lowe's interpretation of the part hysterical.

In 1970, while filming horror spoof *The House That Dripped*

Blood (1971), fellow actor Christopher Lee wanted to know who Pertwee was sending up in his on-screen characterisation. The horror actor told Pertwee that some of the characteristics seemed familiar but he couldn't put a name to who it was. Pertwee told Lee that he was actually sending *him* up. Lee found this hysterical; however, the director of the movie cut out much of the fun and the film received indifferent notices as a consequence.

While recording *The Navy Lark* in 1969, Pertwee had a conversation about *Doctor Who* with Tenniel Evans (who would later play Major Daly in Jon's *Doctor Who* adventure 'Carnival of Monsters'). Evans told him that there was a rumour that Patrick Troughton was leaving the show and that he was ideal for the part. Pertwee was interested enough to call his agent, who, although unconvinced that he was right for the part, contacted the BBC to see what the situation was. He found that Pertwee was on the short list of actors to take over from Troughton and had been for some time.

Pertwee was offered the job. He accepted, and only then were there problems concerning his interpretation of the lead part.

The BBC wanted Pertwee's Doctor to be a bit of a joke-telling minstrel to begin with, building further upon the Pied Piper-like antics of Patrick Troughton. However, Pertwee said that, although his children enjoyed watching Troughton, he thought his friend had gone a little over the top. Pertwee was keen to play the part straight and bring in some real science. He also wanted to incorporate fast cars, power boats, motor bikes and Aikido. After long conversations with producer Peter Bryant, Pertwee got his way and not only did he make the transition from black and white to colour but also attracted a more adult audience into the bargain.

In truth, it wasn't as easy as all that. It was director Barry

Letts who told Pertwee to play the role straight – as himself – and this presented problems to the actor because he didn't know who he really was. When his wife started to get him to do various things around the house, he discovered a love for anything mechanical and risk taking (as his stunt man Terry Walsh would come to appreciate!), which brought him a deeper understanding of the type of thing he most enjoyed doing and, consequently, a greater understanding of himself.

It is true that Pertwee brought in some humorous moments for the younger viewers, but there was always a very serious side to his personality too. Just as in life, Pertwee's Doctor didn't suffer fools gladly. He despised ignorance and wanton destruction, displaying a heart-on-his-sleeve need to always do the right thing. He was constantly at odds with the Brigadier who always wanted to blow things up.

So, at the turn of the 1970s, *Doctor Who* took a major jump away from its roots, not just from the black and white children's classic to colour family entertainment, but also by explaining where the Doctor came from, his planet and his people. Although Pertwee's Doctor would be Earth-bound for some time, the mystery of where he came from was explained, albeit having its roots in the last ever Patrick Troughton story 'The War Games'. He was a Time Lord from the planet Gallifrey, who had his appearance changed (from Troughton) and was exiled to Earth because he stole the Tardis and roamed through time and space as a maverick. Soon a fellow Time Lord would became a regular cast member, to be the Professor Moriarty character to the Doctor's Sherlock Holmes. The character was called the Master and was played by the excellent, seasoned actor Roger Delgado. With his devil's beard, Mediterranean good looks and stern eyes, Delgado was the perfect balance to Pertwee's flamboyance.

All of this was a brave move by the BBC. They were destroying the romantic unknown past of the Doctor, which must have been a great gamble on their part. They were explaining the 'Who?' in *Doctor Who*. Would they get away with such a thing? Surely that was an important ingredient in making the show successful? To keep the audience guessing.

There were many changes imposed by Pertwee's Doctor, which then seemed radical but are largely taken for granted today. Nowadays, we are used to the Doctor running everywhere and using many gadgets, but it was Pertwee who really started all that off with his dashing interpretation of the title role. His was the James Bond Doctor, but there was no falseness with his interpretation. Also Pertwee's love of character acting is sprinkled throughout *Doctor Who*. In some memorable scenes in the story 'The Green Death', he not only disguises himself as a Welsh milkman in order to get into a high-security establishment, but also as a cleaning woman! They are wonderfully comic moments from an actor who established himself with wonderful comic voices on the radio. Although it is interesting to note that, in a scene from an earlier *Doctor Who* episode, where he provided a voice for a radio broadcast, it was later rerecorded by another actor because his voice was so recognisable.

'The Green Death' was significant for another reason too. It provided the first fragrance of romance between the Doctor and one of his companions: Jo Grant, played so lovingly by Katy Manning. Jo falls in love with a hip young Welsh scientist and decides to leave the Doctor and go up the Amazon and get married (see 'The Green Death'). The Doctor attends the happy couple's leaving celebrations, but he is clearly upset at losing Jo, whom he always had a soft spot for. The final scene sees the Doctor sneaking out of the party and, in silhouette, driving his beloved car 'Bessie' away, in what is the greatest unrequited love scene in the show's history. Katy Manning has fond memories of Pertwee, who really took her under his wing while filming the show, and this affection really comes across in every scene they played together.

Pertwee enjoyed the more serious storyline, which complemented his interpretation of the Doctor perfectly. He loved the odd pretentious moment too, such as passing comment on a manor house wine cellar while waiting for a 'ghost' to turn up ('Day of the Daleks'). But where Pertwee really succeeded was when he was allowed to get cross at interplanetary narrow-mindedness; then he was in his element. His most serious scenes balanced his more comic ones, so much so that, when Tom Baker first took over the role, some young fans found the lack of seriousness an issue.

It is interesting how most of the actors up to Peter Davison were passionate about the underlying messages in the scripts and how they could be translated in a positive way to the younger viewers amidst the action, monsters and the ever-building mythology of the show. A basic theme of good transcending evil has always prevailed in *Doctor Who*, and the Doctor has been a very enigmatic character as a result. To a degree we can thank William Hartnell for laying down some ground rules here.

Returning to Pertwee, it is no surprise that his favourite story was 'Frontier in Space' and the Draconians (creatures from the same story) his favourite foe. This story started off with epic aspirations, being part of a twelve-episode 'Space War' story that took the Daleks into the kind of mega-scale story they enjoy in the new series today. Alas, the epic didn't really come off, but what fans reflect upon and enjoy today are two quality classic stories with a continuity thread from the end of one to the beginning of the other ('The Planet of the Daleks').

The first story said farewell to Roger Delgado's Master, although not intentionally. Shortly after filming the story, Delgado went to Turkey to do some filming for his first comedy film role, the never-released *Bell of Tibet*. Unfortunately, he was killed in a car accident, through no fault of his own. When Pertwee heard of his friend's death, he was terribly upset and did all he could to try to get some compensation for Delgado's wife, Kismet. No matter how hard he tried he couldn't do it. He was appalled and realised how much he had taken his life into his own hands by playing with so many cars, bikes and powerboats throughout his life.

The impact on the show was catastrophic as well, depriving the Doctor of what was planned to be a grand showdown with the Master; where it would be revealed what relationship they truly had with each other (the consensus of opinion being that they were brothers).

When Pertwee heard that Barry Letts and Terrance Dicks were leaving the show soon afterwards, he decided that it was perhaps time for him to leave too. The team had really been broken up, especially with Delgado gone. Head of Drama Shaun Sutton quickly stepped in to ask if he would reconsider, which he did. Pertwee agreed to do two further seasons of *Doctor Who* if the BBC would increase his salary. Pertwee was shocked when Sutton shook his hand and said, 'Thanks for everything, sorry to see you go!' There were no negotiations at all. Pertwee was out of a job. He felt hurt but was told there was no flexibility in the budget, so that was it.

Ever the professional, Pertwee shot the stories that would complete his current season with equal vigour as his earlier episodes. The next story after his resignation was 'The Dinosaur Invasion'. This story introduced the Doctor's space-age flying car The Whomobile, which he even drove through Piccadilly Circus one fine day, to the London police force's horror!

During his last season as the Doctor, Pertwee received a touching letter from a mother of a little girl who was a big fan. The mother explained that the girl was going through a tough time and was emotionally disturbed. Pertwee wrote to the little girl and sent her a signed photo. The change in the girl's behaviour was amazing. She took the photo of Pertwee everywhere with her. It was comforting for her. The mother and daughter both kept in touch with Pertwee for many years and, when the little girl grew up and had two children of her own, Pertwee became their godfather.

Halfway through recording 'Planet of the Spiders', his last *Doctor Who* adventure, Pertwee filmed his regeneration scene. He lay still on the floor for what appeared to be an extremely long time, to be replaced by – changed into – Tom Baker. Many of the cast and crew said that Pertwee was a different man afterwards. He didn't join in with the jokes on set, but took himself away to read and reply to his fan mail instead. Although ever the professional on screen, Pertwee knew he was at the end of his time as the Doctor, and was doing nothing more than preparing himself to move on. He had no idea at the time that the part would never leave him – for all the best reasons – he really thought it was the end at the time. Like his predecessors, he didn't entirely want to go, but knew it was the right thing to do for his career.

When asked years later by Terry Wogan if he missed the Doctor, Pertwee said, 'I miss *Doctor Who* from time to time; but I enjoy Worzel too.'

And, of course, Pertwee had another enormous success following *Doctor Who*: *Worzel Gummidge*. Based on the novels by Barbara Euphan Todd, Pertwee took a country accent and much make-up to become the eccentric scarecrow of Scatterbrook Farm and won the hearts of children all over again. Worzel Gummidge was always an acting highlight for Pertwee, indeed he loved the original stories when he was a child and had listened to the radio series after the war.

Worzel Gummidge was produced by Southern Television for ITV and written by Keith Waterhouse and Willis Hall. It co-starred Una Stubbs as Aunt Sally and Geoffrey Bayldon (better known for his own hit children's TV show *Catweazle*).

The show lasted four series in its original format between 1979 and 1981, 30 episodes in total (season two cut slightly short by industrial action, as Pertwee was keen to point out in interview).

There were many guest stars in the series, including Billy Connolly, Barbara Windsor, Bill Maynard, Joan Sims, Bernard Cribbins and Pertwee's cousin, Bill Pertwee.

There was one Christmas Special entitled *A Cup O' Tea and a Slice O' Cake*, and Pertwee and Stubbs performed a musical version of the series in 1981 at the Birmingham Repertory Theatre.

Two new series were commissioned by Television New Zealand, but only Pertwee and Stubbs agreed to fly across to film the episodes (22 in total). Pertwee didn't like the scripts very much but then again Keith Waterhouse wasn't involved.

One interesting point about these last two series was the early credited contribution from Peter Jackson (*Lord of the Rings*, *King Kong*) who worked on special effects, but of course this meant little at the time.

Like *Doctor Who*, *Worzel Gummidge* spawned TV tie-in paperbacks, Christmas annuals, toys, games, videos and even records, and was an enormous success, but this time there was no one else associated with the role, Worzel was Pertwee and

Pertwee was Worzel and it's been that way ever since – some 30 years.

What made Worzel Gummidge so endearing? Pertwee had much to do with it. His ability to mix both extreme humour and pathos in one scene, and chaos and heart-warming love in another, reflected the personality of every child in the country. They could identify with him. Pertwee took the role to heart so much in one famous scene he even cried real tears on cue.

Pertwee continued *The Navy Lark* through his *Doctor Who* years, and from 1972 to 1978 (i.e. just before *Worzel Gummidge* started) he hosted *Whodunnit?* with Patrick Mower. *Whodunnit?* was a celebrity quiz show not unlike *Cluedo*, where the panel would see some visual clues and a piece of film and decide who killed who and in what capacity. However with the word 'Who' in the title, there was the natural tie-in to the longest-running SF show. Not only that, but Mower would solve every weekly case.

Before *Worzel Gummidge* and towards the end of his *Doctor Who* days, Pertwee found it possible to appear in the movies a little more. His role in *Against the Desert* (1973) is a bit obscure because it was never released. However, the year after he left *Doctor Who*, he had a role alongside Peter Ustinov, Helen Hayes, Derek Nimmo, Joan Sims, Bernard Bresslaw, Roy Kinnear and Derek Guyler in Disney's successful movie *One of Our Dinosaurs Is Missing*.

More movies followed, including a remake of one of his favourites, *Ask a Policeman*, which had originally starred Will Hay, Graham Moffatt and Moore Marriott. Pertwee would work with comic duo Cannon and Ball in a more sedate version called *The Boys in Blue*. Again, great character actors worked alongside Pertwee in the movie, including Jack

Douglas, Eric Sykes and Roy Kinnear. Never a patch on the original movie, it endures today as a light family film.

Of course, Pertwee played in some of the greatest British comedy films, the Carry On movies. Pertwee appeared in *Cleo* (1964), *Screaming* (1966), *Cowboy* (1966) and *Columbus* (1992); however, he thought he was being offered a part in a serious movie with the last one and was slightly deflated when he found himself in another Carry On. Although he always seemed a little embarrassed about being in the Carry On films during interview – my personal opinion – he took his cameo parts extremely well in all of them, playing alongside the likes of Sid James, Kenneth Williams, Jim Dale, Harry H Corbett, Charles Hawtree, Joan Sims, the list goes on and on.

On 20 March 1994, Pertwee fell foul of Noel Edmonds on his Saturday-night *House Party* by receiving a Gotcha Award. A Gotcha was a spoof award given to a celebrity by Noel in some embarrassing predicament without their knowing that they were being set up and secretly filmed. Pertwee's set-up involved his taking part in a spoof radio show in which he was meant to pass comment about his favourite music. However, the wrong music was played, spoof callers – part of a live phone-in – inadvertently insulted him, and the studio started leaking water. The endearing thing about Pertwee's Gotcha was how amiable he was throughout. When Noel turned up at the very end, Pertwee was oblivious to the fact that he had been set up, and was very pleased to see him. The whole piece – slightly shy of ten minutes in length – is a delightful insight into Jon Pertwee, the man; indeed, he appears not as grumpy as he is sometimes made out to be!

Pertwee's last TV appearance was on Cilla Black's *Surprise, Surprise* in which he appeared in costume as the Doctor to present a small boy with a life-sized Dalek. Again, he is the endearing elder statesman, who can still perform for his audience, especially starry-eyed youngsters.

Jon Pertwee died in his sleep of a heart attack. He was on holiday at Timber Lake, Connecticut, with his wife, taking a break from his one-man show *Who is Jon Pertwee?* He was 76. Following instructions in his will, Jon was cremated with an effigy of Worzel Gummidge attached to his coffin.

Pertwee managed the first great transition for *Doctor Who*, taking the programme into colour TV, giving more insight into the Doctor's own race of Time Lords and bringing in more adult content.

To many people, Pertwee is the 'definitive' Doctor, embodying the lust for adventure and serious intent that was at the very heart of the show and is still prevalent today in the new series, as Tom Baker, who considered Pertwee a friend, qualifies: 'I was a great admirer of such a stylish actor. He was not only a great performer but he was so good to work with. He made everyone feel at home.' (*Jon Pertwee: The Biography* by Bernard Bale, Andre Deutsch, 2000)

In November 1982, Pertwee summed up his interpretation of The Doctor against the backdrop of his whole career quite succinctly: 'The impact it made on my career was immense. I saw the Doctor as an interplanetary crusader and it was this dashing Pied Piper image that appealed to me. I could spread my cloak, take the Earth under my wing and say, "It's all right now… I'll deal with this."'

'Men – *our* kind of men – Earth men – never have had enough time to tackle the important questions.'

Methuselah's Children

Robert A Heinlein

CHAPTER FIVE
TOM BAKER

'… I was working on a building site, broke, and with no prospect of work when I was offered the part of the Doctor. It was just the most extraordinary thing…'

Tom Baker

WHEN TOM BAKER shook his curly hair, opened those big staring eyes and applied more than a trace of English eccentricity, a new Doctor was born.

Well, not quite. It took at least Baker's first story, 'Robot', for him to win over the faithful, i.e. for the fans to get used to him as the new Doctor. Like Pertwee before him, Baker embedded a little humour into the most scariest moments and, like Hartnell, he ensured that fans never saw him – the actor Tom Baker – doing anything as human as smoking or drinking, he was almost angelic in that respect. He instinctively knew the importance and power of the role – the Pied Piper enigmatic nature of the role (where did he come from, where did he go, what was his motive, how did he come to be the creature he was, why did he not do human things, and didn't he have some kind of magic about him?) was fascinating and infectious.

There was a natural fun type of eccentricity about Tom

Baker and this fitted nicely into his interpretation of the Doctor. But who was Tom Baker? Where did he come from?

Thomas Stewart Baker was born in Scotland Road, Liverpool, on 20 January 1934 to a Jewish father (John Stewart Baker) and a Catholic mother (Mary Jane).

Being in the Navy, Baker's father was hardly home, but he did instil his Jewish values in his son, while his mother brought him up a staunch working-class Catholic. No wonder then that he left school at 15 to become a monk and live a monastic life for six years (fending off erections and perverts along the way!).

After losing his faith, he left the order to do his National Service in the Royal Army Medical Corps, serving from 1955 to 1957. Some say it was here that Baker got the acting bug, but he believes that the acting spirit was always inside of him.

In the early 60s, Baker fell in love and married Anna Wheatcroft. The marriage lasted five years and produced two sons. He would later lose contact with his first family, but acting soon became his main passion and he took many small roles as animals (or parts of animals, such as the back of a cow!). Baker's success was not overnight.

Baker featured mainly on stage in the late 60s, but he did get roles in two episodes of *Dixon of Dock Green* and a film version of *The Winter's Tale*, which seems to have faded into obscurity, or maybe mediocrity.

In 1971, bored with playing parts of animals on stage – to Laurence Olivier's amusement – Baker turned down the opportunity of a tour of America, believing that he could get better parts in the UK with everyone abroad. The opportunity soon arose, playing alongside Laurence Olivier, Joan Plowright, Derek Jacobi and Jeremy Brett in *The Merchant of Venice*. Baker was desperate for a speaking role and found the only part open to him was that of the Prince of Morocco.

Unfortunately, the director wanted a dwarf to play the part, but an undaunted Baker strode in to the audition and said, 'Sorry about the height, I was brought up a Roman Catholic.' And suddenly the Prince of Morocco was a taller man.

Baker has fond memories of working with such great actors as Olivier and Brett. He admitted in his autobiography *Who on Earth is Tom Baker?* (HarperCollins, 1997) that they made him more extravagant as an actor. Olivier persuaded him to take risks in *The Merchant of Venice* and developed a bit of a soft spot for him, later telling Baker that his eyes were perfect for the stage, that they could penetrate the back rows of any theatre. In *The Musical Murders of the 1940s* (Greenwich Theatre), nearly 15 years later, it was obvious when he was on stage during darker moments, because, even though cast in dark shadows, there was only one actor in the company who towered over everybody else, and that was Tom Baker. His height, teeth, hair and eyes gave him much character on both stage and screen and he really came to public prominence in 1974 when he became the Doctor.

Elizabethan plays have been a staple in Baker's career. 'A marvellous Elizabethan play' (Baker's words) is *A Woman Killed with Kindness*, which Baker starred in alongside Derek Jacobi after *The Merchant of Venice*. But it was Olivier who suggested Baker for his first film role, as Grigori Rasputin in *Nicholas and Alexandra*. Olivier took a part himself, but it was Baker who stole the film. His performance begins humble but chilling. The eyes say it all initially, exposing a chilling depth behind a very calm exterior. But then he becomes more passionate, more angry. 'I spent two years in a monastery and then I walked home again,' he states in the movie, and one cannot fail to spot the connection with Baker's own life. Indeed, his intensity and conviction of beliefs clearly come from his deep understanding of religion. The role of Rasputin was perfect for Baker, and Olivier was absolutely right to suggest him for the part.

This powerful role led to Baker being nominated for two Golden Globe Awards, one for Best Actor in a Supporting Role and another for Best Newcomer.

So, after sacrificing a trip to America, Baker had created an opportunity to play alongside some of the cream of British acting, with plaudits too.

Baker's next key role in cinema came in 1973: *The Golden Voyage of Sinbad*. Baker played Prince Koura, a black-hearted wizard who attempts to thwart Sinbad in his quest. 'Every voyage is a new flavour,' Sinbad says, and *The Golden Voyage* is one of the most memorable adventures in Sinbad film history. Although the plot is basic, the movie is a classic piece of fantasy. Lavish locations, sets and costumes provide a magnificent backdrop to Ray Harryhausen's wonderful stop-motion animation.

Caroline Munro is the beautiful love interest alongside John Phillip Law's excellent Sinbad who, through their heroic deeds, make Baker appear even more blackhearted and sinister.

With the use of vintage trick photography, Baker's serious, intelligent performance enhances the impact of the overall movie. 'He who is patient *obtains*,' he tells his sea captain as they pursue Sinbad towards the fabled Fountain of Destiny.

Prince Koura is one of Baker's most sinister roles, and one that endures and captivates children to this very day. In fact, being only a year before he took over the role of the Doctor, *The Golden Voyage of Sinbad* captured the magic of Baker's acting skills that were quintessential to *Doctor Who*. He never overplays the role, keeping enough back to be sinister without being overtly scary.

One scene is of particular note, which nicely blends Baker's acting skills with Ray Harryhausen's creations; it is where Koura employs his sorcery in making a ship's female figurehead come to life to do battle with Sinbad and his crew. Throughout the suspenseful scene, Baker uses mime and his own physical props (large piercing blue eyes) to show his character's inner turmoil. When the scene is over, Baker's character has physically aged; such is the price of summoning the demons of darkness.

In another scene, Baker plays with a tiny winged demon that he has brought to life with drops of his own blood. Using mime and the playful way one talks to a pet budgerigar, he makes the incredible seem plausible. Perhaps all of this helped convince the BBC that he could indeed be the next Doctor Who.

The Golden Voyage of Sinbad is a film that encapsulates the dying embers of the out-and-out swashbuckling movie, which indeed the first Douglas Fairbanks Jnr movie in the series so blatantly was. With a very early appearance from Martin Shaw (from TV show *The Professionals*), *The Golden Voyage of Sinbad* is an important milestone in fantasy cinema.

If the part of Prince Koura prepared Baker for the part of the Doctor, it certainly wasn't the most important element; that fell to an earlier BBC Play of the Month entitled *The Millionairess* (1972). Baker worked alongside Maggie Smith in this production, blacking up for the part of an Egyptian dignitary (not unlike the Arab Prince Koura perhaps). But it was the director – Bill Slater – not Maggie Smith, who would become the crucial person in Baker's future as the Doctor.

One Sunday evening, a couple of years after *The Millionairess*, Baker wrote to Slater and asked him if there were any regular parts going at the BBC for an actor like him. He posted his letter that Monday morning, the same day as Slater, soon-to-be Head of Series, had a meeting with *Doctor Who* producer Barry Letts.

Baker didn't know that Jon Pertwee had quit the show and

that other actors were being considered for the part (in his autobiography, Baker mentioned that Graham Crowden and Richard Hearn had at least been considered for the part).

The casting meeting between Letts and Slater drew no conclusions, so they decided to reconvene later that week and because of Slater's workload that meant Wednesday.

On Tuesday, Baker's letter arrived at the BBC. After several late meetings, Slater went home with Baker's letter and read it getting into bed with his wife, Mary Webster. It was 11.15pm. Having discussed his day with his wife over supper, it was suggested that perhaps Baker would be a good choice as the Doctor. Mary suggested that Slater call Baker, despite the time. He did. Baker answered. Slater asked him if he could get to TV Centre for a 6.30pm meeting the following day. Baker said he could. That was it. Everybody went to bed.

The following morning Slater had his casting meeting with Barry Letts. He suggested Baker for the role and told Letts that the actor was coming in at 6.30.

When Baker walked in – on time – Slater took him to Head of Drama Shaun Sutton's office, where Slater, Sutton and Letts talked things over with the nervous actor. After nearly an hour, Slater said, 'We've got an idea, you see, Tom. Do you think you could come back and see us tomorrow?'

Baker agreed. The following day, Baker went to work on a building site and then went and got changed, had something to eat and turned up slightly late at the BBC, but soon found himself back in the same office with the same people. There was a brief silence before Baker was asked, 'Would you like to be the new Doctor Who?'

Baker had been so depressed and skint that he had written a begging letter to Slater, who was now offering him the biggest role in television. All Baker could do was nod, and nod again and again. And then he was asked to keep his joyous news a secret for ten days, which somehow – fearing the part might be taken away from him – he managed to do, until, of course, he walked into the BBC Headquarters at Wood Lane with a friend as chaperone to attend a press conference announcing him as the new Doctor. Everybody wanted to touch him or shake his hand and he just rode the crest of the wave, knowing that he could now jack in the job as general labourer because he was suddenly a renegade Time Lord.

None of his predecessors had enjoyed so much celebrity on taking the role, but the show had built up huge interest and fan loyalty over the previous ten years, and the announcement of a new Doctor was big news.

While celebrating in the West End with his friend, Baker picked up the second edition of the *Evening Standard* and saw his face plastered over it. 'Oh bliss. Fuck off anonymity, hello everybody,' Baker declared in his autobiography, and the relief was that joyous.

Although Baker had played some great roles and acted with some of the most important professionals of the 20th century, work had dried up, he had become depressed, he had taken a labouring job and then – *Doctor Who*.

Perhaps all that praying in the monastery years previously had finally paid off, or maybe the good lord served best those who helped themselves.

Although Baker would make the part his own with his jelly babies and floppy hat, his multi-coloured over-long scarf came about by accident. James Acheson, the costume designer, had provided too much wool to the knitter, Begonia Pope, and she used it all up. It was Baker's wish to use the final ridiculously long scarf, which is probably the most iconic piece of *Doctor*

Who costume in the show's history; if you refer to somebody's scarf as 'a Doctor Who scarf', you quickly get the impression of something colourful and a little outrageous.

When Baker finally took to the controls of the Tardis, he found that Barry Letts – who had effectively given him the job – had wanted to leave the show with Jon Pertwee. Letts did, in fact, stay for a while, directing the story 'The Androids Invasion'. Elisabeth Sladen who played Pertwee's feisty journalist companion, Sarah Jane Smith, was still very much part of the show as well, which must have pleased Baker (it wasn't a mass exodus after Pertwee's exit!). Also, for Baker's first season, Ian Marter became the Doctor's companion and the three actors developed a good rapport both on and off camera. Baker even went to Italy to write a script with Marter, which sadly didn't come to anything.

Baker was keen to meet the show's iconic characters. Sladen reminisced about her time with Pertwee and the Daleks, and it was soon known that the infamous pepper pots were to make a comeback in a six-part story called 'Genesis of the Daleks'. This was to become one of the greatest stories in the show's history, introducing the Daleks creator Davros, so brilliantly played by Michael Wisher.

Baker got very absorbed by the character of the Doctor. The fan mail poured in, and he met children walking down the street who all accepted him as their friend; and strangely this was fine by their parents too. The Doctor was not a stranger, he was a man to be trusted. It was as though the role placed the actor in a protective bubble, away from suspicion, accusation and scorn: if you are the Doctor, you are a friend to all children. And, as a Marvel movie so aptly states, 'With great power comes great responsibility.' Baker became another man. He refused to be seen doing anything remotely human-like when children were around. He wouldn't eat or drink, smoke, anything like that. He would sign autographs 'The Doctor', knowing that the children saw the character, not the actor, so, like his predecessors, he turned up at various events in costume and played to the younger audiences who poured nothing but total love upon him in return.

For one story – 'The Deadly Assassin' – Baker was concerned about the violence of a fight scene and, on his way back from a *Doctor Who* Exhibition in Blackpool, he found himself watching the show with a young family in Preston. He simply knocked on the door and asked, 'Do you watch *Doctor Who* here?' Whereupon he was let in with a big smile to sit and watch the show with the family, which included two young lads who were simply amazed that the Doctor could be in two places at once – on screen and in their front room. 'What a wonderful hour or so that was,' Baker reminisced years later. Again, proof of the unique power of the Doctor.

But did that power go to Baker's head?

Baker freely admits that, by the time the story 'The Stones of Blood' was screened (four years into his career as the Doctor), he was arguing with the director. At this stage, he was the only important person in the show, as all of his peers had left. He knew better than others and he had the responsibility to the younger audience. Yes, he did get difficult, but, then again, so had William Hartnell all those years ago, and he had quit because he felt the children's element was going out of the show.

And so we can see a very important coincidence. Something shared by the actors who play the Doctor. And it's there from the original series to the new series: the Doctor has a responsibility to the youngest of viewers, those who live and breathe the show, those who believe he is real. In some cases, children know the names of the actors, but that doesn't mean the character isn't real to them also. In their young minds, the Doctor lives his adventures on screen, a separate person to the actor associated with him. There's the show's magic encapsulated.

Patrick Troughton always used humour during scary scenes so that the children didn't get frightened too much; Pertwee would ham it up during action scenes, or when a particularly menacing monster came wandering in; Baker could defuse tension by offering a jelly baby, and so it goes on. In fact, a great scene from a David Tennant story called 'The Girl in the Fireplace' has him returning from a Regency night out on the tiles with his tie round his head, waxing lyrical about having a great time and completely – or so it seems – missing the deadly peril his companions are in.

There is a responsibility that comes from being the Doctor, and Tom Baker faced that full on, so much so, in fact, he is still considered to be one of the very best Doctors. But off screen was he one of the very best husbands?

While still a very young man, he married Anna Wheatcroft, a nice lady from a respectable family. Baker had two sons with her, but the marriage fell apart after five years and the actor-to-be soon lost touch with his young family. Towards the end of his reign as the Doctor, Baker married his co-star Lalla Ward. The marriage lasted two years, but Baker lived the life of a single man, drinking with Francis Bacon and Jeffrey Bernard – to name but two – in Soho, and failing to settle down to domestic life, which Lalla really wanted him to do. The break-up of this second marriage is something Baker still feels guilty about and, although Ward has now happily remarried, the two never see each other any more, not even at *Doctor Who* signings and exhibitions.

Baker's third marriage was successful, though, in the respect that it has so far lasted approximately 25 years. Sue Jerrard worked on the production team of *Doctor Who* and Baker became friends with her before he married Lalla Ward. But, after that marriage failed, Baker found more solace in the company of Jerrard, rather than his drinking pals.

By the time Baker called it a day with the Time Lord (seven years in total, making him the longest-serving Doctor to this day), he was a household name. Although a respected actor beforehand, he was now so much in the public eye he was instantly recognisable, but not necessarily typecast, as time would prove. Perhaps playing other parts at the same time as starring in *Doctor Who* helped this situation somewhat.

The Book Tower was a long-running children's programme made for the ITV regions (ATV). By accompanying a narrated story with dramatic scenes and music, it tried to encourage more children to read. And the programme became extremely successful.

The eerie theme tune was based upon Bach's Toccata and Fugue in D Minor, which was arranged by no less a figure than Andrew Lloyd Webber.

The programme was presented by different people over the years, including one-time Carry On star and former Ice Warrior, Bernard Bresslaw. But it was Tom Baker who started the ball rolling on 3 January 1979, presenting the first 22 episodes. Baker brought his own charm to the part, along with the mystery of the Doctor, who he was still playing at the time.

Of course, with Baker as the ever-popular Doctor, children who probably wouldn't normally watch such a programme were tuning in and fulfilling the show's original remit of introducing them to books. *The Book Tower* would endure over ten years, with 11 seasons, before finishing on 30 May 1989.

Some would think that after *Doctor Who* Baker's career would have started winding down, but series such as the revised *Randall and Hopkirk (Deceased)*, with Vic Reeves and Bob Mortimer, showed his continued worth as an actor.

Baker played Wyvern against Reeves (Hopkirk) and Mortimer (Randall), with Emilia Fox (Jeannie). The show ran for two seasons (2000 and 2001) and had many little tie-ins to the original 1960s TV show of the same name (including, in episode one, Spooner Drive, in praise of former scriptwriter Dennis Spooner who also penned some early episodes of *Doctor Who* and *The Avengers*).

Baker had become noticeably older since audiences had last seen him on screen, but he was wonderfully eccentric and cherished his friendship with the comic duo.

Comedy was the watchword for Baker around this time, as he provided the tremendous voice-over for TV series *Little Britain*.

With his own quirky sense of humour, it shouldn't be surprising that Baker gets on with people such as Reeves and Mortimer, Lucas and Walliams, and indeed the whole of the *Blackadder* cast too. There's something of the alternative comedian in Baker. Even Ian Hislop was a little surprised by Baker's comments when chairing *Have I Got News For You*, again something he took to quite naturally, but failed to get asked back to chair again.

When the dust has settled on the female 'eye-candy' of David Tennant's Doctor, Tom Baker will again be referred to as the Doctor personified. His teeth, curls, big staring eyes were all the evidence one needed that there really was a maverick alien roaming around the universe looking for justice and excitement.

As he had played the Time Lord for seven years and was so instantly recognisable and popular in the role, one would have thought that Tom Baker would have been horrendously typecast after leaving the show. But he wasn't, and he didn't need to return to the building site to earn a crust. Although he admitted on a BBC news item that he had 'no immediate plans' after quitting the role, he went on to say that he had done the best he could with the part and that it was somebody else's turn to have a go.

Baker's resignation came two weeks after the announcement that robot dog K9 would be leaving the show. Asked if the show could go on without them both, Baker said, 'It will just go on and on and on,' in what was a slightly flippant interview that seemed to intimidate the female presenter somewhat (because Baker was slightly abrupt, bordering on the provocative with the woman). That said, Baker did admit that *Doctor Who* had changed his whole life and had created some of his fondest memories in his acting career. But one cannot but marvel at another mass exodus: just as Barry Letts and Terrance Dicks had wanted out after Pertwee quit, suddenly Baker and co-star/wife Lalla Ward would leave together, with the only continuity being three companions introduced into the series at the end of the season and, of course, producer John Nathan-Turner. That said, Baker's final scene will go down as one of the most visually stunning – and slightly poignant – regeneration scenes ever, after David Tennant's departure perhaps; then again the whole of Baker's final story was very good ('Logopolis'), not unlike Jon Pertwee's last story in that respect ('The Planet of the Spiders').

Tom Baker returned to the theatre, first at the Mermaid playing Long John Silver in *Treasure Island* and then in *Feasting with Panthers* at the Chichester Festival. Although perfectly suited to the theatre, he came back to the BBC to play Sherlock Holmes in the four-part adaption of Sir Arthur Conan Doyle's *The Hound of the Baskervilles* (1982), thanks to Barry Letts who produced it; then he was back in the theatre for *Hedda Gabler* and the 1982–83 RSC production of *Educating Rita*.

A couple of odd one-offs occurred in 1986, when he took small roles in *Roland Rat: The Series* and *The Kenny Everett Television Show*. However, there was one role of note: his part in *Blackadder II*. Although only in one episode of the hit comedy, entitled 'Potato' (Season 2, episode 3), his part is memorable. Baker plays the legless (physically and alcoholically) Captain 'Redbeard' Rum, a mad old sea captain who pledges his heart to Nursie before venturing off with Blackadder, Baldrick and Percy, to sail around the Cape of Good Hope.

Rum is a drunkard charlatan who cannot even find the coast of France let alone the Cape of Good Hope. He does, however, manage to run Blackadder and his trusty sidekicks aground on a volcanic island with cannibal natives. Rum's fate is to be put into the cooking pot, not dissimilar to Captain Cook and his crew after discovering Australia. Indeed, Blackadder brings a boomerang back from his travels for Queenie (played so brilliantly by Miranda Richardson), implying that Blackadder got there many years before Cook.

Baker took on the role of Captain Rum with red-faced relish. His blend of humour and eccentricity fitted the series perfectly.

Years later, Baker mentioned his role in *Blackadder* while narrating an episode of *Little Britain*: 'With nothing on telly but repeats of *Doctor Who*, *Medics* and that episode of *Blackadder II* I'm in, Lou and his friend Andy choose a video tape.'

Baker's cameo in *Blackadder* is proof that even the smallest roles can be indelible on the minds of a watching audience. In one respect, Captain Rum was the quintessential Tom Baker role: loud, eccentric – slightly hammed – and enormous fun.

Another quality acting role came along shortly after *Blackadder*, in the acclaimed TV drama *The Life and Loves of a She-Devil*; but that's where the serious stuff seemed to dry up for Baker.

He returned to a semi-regular role in *Monarch of the Glen* for several series, even managing to once again grace the cover of the *Radio Times*, but, having assumed the dubious mantle of the oldest living Doctor Who, he decided to slow down a little.

And what about big movie roles? Baker was offered a part in Peter Jackson's *Lord of the Rings* trilogy, but not the part of Gandalf as some people suggest. However, when he learned that he would have to spend time away in New Zealand, he turned down the opportunity, something the jobbing actor on a building site would never have dreamed of doing.

As well as his autobiography, Baker is also an author of a macabre children's novel entitled *The Boy Who Kicked Pigs* (Faber and Faber, 1999). Filled with dark humour, the story is about Robert Caligari, who is an evil 13-year-old who kicks pigs because of an unfortunate experience with a bacon sandwich. The slim tome is illustrated by David Roberts, and in size and style of illustration the book reminds me of Eric Morecambe's children's classic *The Reluctant Vampire*.

Nowadays, threatening retirement, Baker is still known as the voice of *Little Britain* and as a British institution. If he was a little 'precious' while being the Doctor, then he must be forgiven, for he *was* the man children would instantly trust, and follow without question – the Pied Piper of children's TV. He was – and still is to many – the quintessential Doctor Who and a man who encapsulates the individualism and eccentricity that only the very best British character actors can muster. Louise Jameson (companion Leela in *Doctor Who*) summed up for me the Tom Baker she knew in the series as opposed to the Tom Baker she knows today: 'Things weren't too brilliant between us to begin with. He was unsympathetic to writers and actors, but he lived, ate and slept the programme. He took it very seriously. He felt a great responsibility towards the children who watched the show and never smoked around them or anything like that.' Louise went on to discuss Baker's presence: 'You know when he's in the room even when he's not showing off, and that voice of his is beautiful. He's mellowed over the years, and I'm grateful for the friendship we share nowadays. We go out and have lunch, or take a walk in the countryside. He's a great friend and a great actor and, if anyone thinks he's awkward, I ask them to meet up with him today.'

Tom Baker once told of a visit he made to a hospital ward where children had been maimed by drunk drivers and other road accidents. He saw crushed limbs and kids at death's door, and he was asked to go there as Doctor Who. I think it is very clear where Tom Baker's responsibilities lay during his time in the Tardis and the reason why he was such a perfectionist. Like Pertwee before him, he was asked to approach children in extreme physical and mental anguish, and he responded beautifully to that responsibility. The role has given such emotional fulfilment to the actors who have played him.

'And this whirligig of activity went on for all my time as Doctor Who. Suddenly the crowd who'd found me boring found me fascinating…'

Who on Earth is Tom Baker? An Autobiography
Tom Baker

CHAPTER SIX

PETER DAVISON

'I was Peter Davison's wife in *Molly* [1995]. And Peter is great fun. Not quite serious enough!'

Louise Jameson

PETER DAVISON WAS born Peter Moffett on Friday, 13 April 1951 in Streatham, London, son of Sheila and Claude (his father was an electrical engineer from British Guyana).

Davison soon moved with his parents and sisters (Barbara, Pamela and Shirley) to Woking in Surrey, where he was educated at Maphill School. He was later educated at the Winston Churchill Secondary Modern School, where he failed to excel in anything until he wrote a speech on philosophy – which he knew little about – and won a Rotary Club public-speaking contest that grammar school children normally won. Peter's headteacher then recommended that he go on to stage school.

He had been interested in amateur dramatics, and was a member of the amateur dramatics society the Byfleet Players, but he managed to secure a place at the Central School of Speech and Acting. In 1972, he acquired his first job at the Nottingham Playhouse. Although he suffered from first-night nerves – forgetting his lines – he recovered and went on to spend a year with the Edinburgh Young Lyceum Company, working up to a series of Shakespearean productions including *Two Gentlemen of Verona*, *Hamlet* and *A Midsummer Night's Dream*.

Davison changed his name from Moffett so he wasn't confused with Peter Moffatt, the actor and director with whom he would later work.

In 1975, Peter appeared in an episode of the Thames TV children's SF series *The Tomorrow People*, entitled 'A Man for Emily'; the spoiled Emily character was played by future wife Sandra Dickinson.

When one looks back at this role today, one cannot be anything other than deeply shocked. With big white curly wigs and screechy Southern American accents, the episode can best be described as horrific. The couple were married on 26 December 1978.

Davison and Dickinson would play opposite each other again – albeit briefly – in Douglas Adams's *The Hitchhiker's Guide to the Galaxy* (1981), with Peter playing a heavily made-up Dish of the Day that tries to sell itself to his clients (Dickinson and others) at The Restaurant at the End of the Universe. In fact, when John Nathan-Turner called Davison to ask him if he would become the new Doctor Who after Tom Baker announced his departure, Dickinson was very supportive of her then husband, even to the point of requesting that she be one of his companions, so clearly their relationship was a strong and supportive one to begin with.

Davison and Dickinson composed the theme song to the children's programme *Button Moon* and had a daughter, Georgia Moffett, who was born in 1984 and would grow up to be the Doctor's daughter (not just Peter Davison's, but Doctor Who himself, during David Tennant's stint as the Time Lord). It would not be all plain sailing for Georgia, as her parents would split when she was eight, she would have a child at 17 and, despite her incredible good looks (inherited from her slim blonde mother), would stay clear of men until her mid-twenties, when she started to date David Tennant (see Chapter 13).

Davison's first major TV role was as Tom Holland in the 13-episode *Love for Lydia* (written by H E Bates) starring Jeremy Irons. This was followed by the highly successful *All Creatures Great and Small*, a programme that focused on the trials and tribulations of being a vet in North Yorkshire and based on the books by James Herriot (played by Christopher Timothy in the series). The programme also made a household name of Robert Hardy who played the pompous Siegfried Farnon; his younger and much-maligned brother Tristan was played by Davison.

All Creatures Great and Small was the turning point in Davison's career, not just in giving him a regular job, but also allowing him to develop a character in a popular BBC show. This was only enhanced when Timothy had a car accident and was restricted from doing location shots for a while, as Davison's character was given these scenes instead, which added to his experiences as an actor.

It was during *All Creatures Great and Small* that John Nathan-Turner, then just a production unit manager, recognised Davison's talent and noted him as somebody to watch.

Davison was only 29 when he became Doctor Who, the youngest person to play him at that time (only to be outdone by Matt Smith, who would land the role at the tender age of 26).

His first story 'Castrovalva' was frustrating for many fans, as the Doctor was hardly himself after his regeneration. However, the story did build into something quite interesting with the continued presence of the Master, who returned to the show in Tom Baker's last two episodes.

The next story 'Four to Doomsday' fared well, as did the period piece 'Black Orchid', where the Doctor actually got to play cricket (Davison's Doctor wore a cricket jumper as part of his regular costume, so the inevitable had to happen). It was the ingeniously plotted Great Fire of London story 'The Visitation' that really won the hearts and minds of the seasoned *Doctor Who* fan though, a story hailed as a classic to this very day. But it was not voted the best story of the season; that accolade went to 'Earthshock', which showcased the return of the infamous Cybermen. The story had a memorable and shocking climax, showcasing the death of one of the Doctor's young and faithful companions. The end credits were silent as a consequence, with no title music, which added to the sense of loss felt by the Doctor and his companions. Unfortunately, the following story, 'Time Flight', was a disappointing end to an otherwise memorable first season for Davison.

After 'Castrovalva', Davison was accepted as the Doctor. His sincerity and youthful get up and go was instantly appealing and struck the right balance with his evil enemy the Master, who cropped up throughout Davison's era.

Davison's second season saw the return of the Brigadier, played once again by Nicholas Courtney, and the Black Guardian, once again played with menace by veteran actor Valentine Dyall (who originally played the character opposite Tom Baker's Doctor). Again there were strong stories throughout, most notably 'Arc of Infinity' (shot in Amsterdam and featuring future Doctor Who Colin Baker as a Time Lord guard), which marked the return of the powerful Time Lord Omega (first seen in 'The Three Doctors'). However, it was 'Mawdryn Undead' (featuring the Brigadier) and 'Terminus' (the last story for companion Nyssa) that were the most noteworthy stories. One story that didn't work out so well was 'Snakedance'. This story marked the return of the incredibly scary Mara from Davison's first season ('Kinda'). However, both 'Snakedance' and 'Kinda' were two of the worst scripts of Davison's era. A great shame as the Mara were incredibly scary enemies in both stories. What probably didn't help matters with regard to 'Snakedance' was the laughable giant snake that appeared at the climax of the story. Perhaps this was the first real sign that *Doctor Who* budgets were getting even smaller than the shoestring they normally operated under. Whatever the case, it is unfortunate that the Mara haven't made a more memorable comeback in *Doctor Who*; who knows what reaction they would get with a half-decent script.

Davison's stories seldom over-reached the modest BBC budget; however, towards the end there was more criticism of poor special effects. For example, 'Warriors of the Deep' was a great comeback story for the Sea Devils and the Silurians, but was a little tainted by a giant monster that looked like the winning prize in a *Blue Peter* competition. The story had great sets (by Tony Burroughs) and a half-decent script, but the poorness of the monsters started *Doctor Who* on a downward slide that finished with the show's demise.

Davison would only play the Doctor for three years. This is commonly thought to be the influence of the second Doctor, Patrick, who advised the young actor to quit after three years due to typecasting. Both Davison and Troughton did do some TV interviews together around the time of 'The Five Doctors', and indeed Troughton did mention typecasting then, so this perception does ring true. It appears that Davison thought that three years was long enough and sentimental headlines said things like 'Dishy Doctor says Ta-Ta to Tardis'. Despite being the first young Doctor, Davison created a credible character, deeply moral and sincere, which endeared him to many children.

Davison probably had the last decent season of the original *Doctor Who* series, which culminated with the regeneration story 'The Caves of Androzani'. Not since the Tom Baker story 'The Deadly Assassin' did we witness the Doctor being blown up, covered in muck and virtually taken to the brink of his physical abilities. Not only that, but he loses the battle this time and actually dies – well, regenerates!

'The Caves of Androzani' was a pastiche of *Phantom of the Opera* and, during David Tennant's era, was voted the best story ever by *Doctor Who Monthly* readers. It seems that Peter Davison quit while he was still ahead of the game and, judging by what happened directly afterwards, and the deteriorating quality of special effects of the monsters in his last season, his decision to leave was probably not wrong, albeit for different reasons.

Despite rarely being considered the very best Doctor Who, Peter Davison simultaneously fails to get much criticism and was a worthy follow-up to Tom Baker, who was quite a tough act to follow. Perhaps in that respect history later repeated itself, with the youngster Matt Smith following the extremely popular David Tennant. But then again, Tennant – if we are to believe the *Children in Need* Special *Doctor Who* episode 'Time Crash' – had the utmost respect for Peter Davison's Doctor, replicating him with his dodgy trainers and 'make me look more intelligent' glasses.

'Time Crash' was the first TV comeback for Davison's Doctor. First broadcast on 16 November 2007, the fifth Doctor meeting the tenth had a bit of the Troughton/Pertwee confrontation about it. Tennant poked fun at the stick of celery on Davison's lapel ('Look at me, I'm wearing a vegetable'), but then settled down to declare at the end that 'I loved being you' and 'You were my Doctor'.

Although not a major return for Davison's Doctor, he did enjoy the opportunity of putting on his cricket jumper and his stick of celery again, saying afterwards, 'It is an honour for me to be able to make the connection between the fifth and the tenth Doctor.'

It's a shame a Doctors' reunion story, such as 'The Three Doctors' or 'The Five Doctors', hasn't been forthcoming in recent years. But with more Doctors to accommodate (and inevitably some dying off), it would become a bit of a logistics exercise to pull off. Indeed, ideas for a 30th anniversary story were scrapped, even though a script, 'The Dark Dimension', had been written. Instead, there was a *Children in Need* sketch entitled 'Dimensions in Time', to commemorate the shows 30th anniversary, in which Davison's only contribution was blowing up a Cyberman. Not a very satisfying celebration for the actor or the fans.

Doctor Who never affected Davison's career in an adverse way; it has been as much a part of his career as programmes such as the trials and tribulations of brotherly love in *Sink or Swim* (1980–82), a very popular situation comedy, where Davison played the sensible older brother pulling his kid brother out of trouble every five minutes. The title music was The Hollies' 'He Ain't Heavy, He's My Brother', which basically summed up the whole programme.

The 1980s had many easy-viewing situation comedies, including another one starring Davison, this time for the ITV regions. *Holding the Fort* (1980–82), which was written by Laurence Marks and Maurice Gran (*The New Statesman*, *Birds of a Feather*). Three series were broadcast (20 episodes) over three years. The basic situation for this comedy was role reversal. Davison was a passive househusband looking after the baby, while his wife was a captain in the Woman's Royal Army Corps. Matthew Kelly completed the regular cast and was there to fulfil Davison's love of football, drinking and pacifism, thus leading to chaos. It was mild stuff, but that was the 1980s, gone were the gritty situation comedies of the 1970s, such as the brilliant *Steptoe and Son* and *Porridge*. Even cop dramas got more sedate after *Callum* and *The Sweeney*, with *The Professionals* and *The Bill*. And dare I suggest that football players had a little less blood and muck on them in the 1980s than the 1970s, which has led to the overprotected (and overpaid) cry babies on the field of play in the new millennium.

Davison played in more than his fair share of situation comedies, but he also seems to be the master of the two/three-year stint at TV dramas, such as *Campion* (1989–90) and *The Last Detective* (2003–07), two of his most popular shows, which showcase his ability to act the straightest of roles as well as the more comic ones. *Campion* was adapted from the Albert Campion novels written by Margery Allingham. Two seasons of the show were made by the BBC starring Davison alongside Brian Glover (as his manservant Magersfontein Lugg) and Andrew Burt (as policeman friend Stanislaus Oates). Interestingly, Davison sang the theme tune to the first season but had it replaced with an instrumental version for the second. 16 episodes were recorded in total and the show told the story of a credible detective with very human failings. A great shame that Davison wasn't allowed to continue the show and build it into something quite legendary, but the actor has never overstayed his welcome.

Davison hasn't done too much work in cinema. However, in

1994, he did appear alongside Sean Bean, David Thewlis and Jim Carter in *Black Beauty*. Davison played the good-natured Squire Gordon, with his delicate wife and beautiful children. Very much the English gentleman, Davison fits this gentle family film perfectly.

Although horse-anoraks see some technical flaws in the movie – as any military enthusiast would with a war film – many younger viewers loved the film, with the horse narration throughout echoing the sentiment of the original novel perfectly. It was a nicely made film, and a good solid part for Davison, and one does wonder why he didn't get more credible film roles afterwards. There was of course TV movie *Molly* in 1995, where Davison played alongside Louise Jameson (*Doctor Who* companion Leela) as husband and wife, but film roles are few and far between.

But after *Doctor Who* there was plenty of work for Davison. Directly after completing his last season as the Time Lord, Davison started work on the show *Anna of the Five Towns*, which was set in the Midlands. Work for this was completed at the beginning of May 1984, and he then went on tour in the theatrical production of *Barefoot in the Park* with his pregnant wife.

Barefoot in the Park was a very physical role for Davison as he had to do a lot of running up and down stairs, especially when he had to do two shows a day.

Lots of bread and butter roles followed, including a part in *Jonathan Creek* and other TV detective programmes. But perhaps his most complete and famous role in recent years has been as Dangerous Davies in *The Last Detective*.

Based on the books by Leslie Thomas, *The Last Detective* succeeded where other detective/police series have notoriously failed (for example *Anna Lee* and, to a degree, *Rebus*). Most of this is due to Peter Davison being a very good TV counterpart to the original novels. His natural sincerity means he could play the role quite lightly and still portray a character with much depth. '[I'm] more a detective than a policeman,' Davies says, but do people – especially his colleagues – go along with that?

Battered by life, Davies walks around with seemingly the world's problems on his shoulders. His melancholy is deeply felt and the show is a memorable one as a consequence.

The Last Detective was not a violent show, which instantly made it, and the main character, endearing. Comedian Sean Hughes's inclusion in the show enhanced the more uncharacteristic laidback style, and one cannot help but like the show. It's a well-worn shoe, comfortable and reliable, so fantastic TV fodder, and a show instantly missed after its demise by its faithful audience. A lost gem but not a total classic.

Like Patrick Troughton before him, Peter Davison has been content to work hard at a huge range of roles for television. Yes, he was once Doctor Who, but he was also once Tristan Farnon, Dangerous Davies and a whole list of others characters too.

Davison made it very clear – as did Patrick Troughton, Jon Pertwee and Tom Baker before him – that there was life after *Doctor Who*, although every one of them seemed to worry about the typecasting that plagued William Hartnell to his death.

Recently, Davison has starred alongside Jill Halfpenny in the musical *Legally Blonde* at the Savoy Theatre. One could argue that Davison wasn't suited to this role – especially if people only know him for his TV roles – but with theatrical credits as prestigious as *Spamalot* and *Chicago*, one can appreciate that there is more to this actor than initially meets the eye.

Peter Davison is closely linked to *Doctor Who* in the new millennium, not just with his cameo, but also with his daughter's role as the Doctor's daughter. No one could have foreseen that David Tennent and Georgia Moffett would fall in love, have a baby and then get married, but they did, and Davison was overjoyed for them both. Will Davison ever make a serious come-back as the Doctor? Only time will tell, but neither he nor his fans have ruled it out.

'I do feel I have managed to distance myself from the character [the Doctor] now – but if I got to the age of 65 and somebody offered it to me then, I'd do it till I dropped. It's a great form of retirement – you just keep going until you keel over!'

Peter Davison in conversation with journalists 1998

CHAPTER SEVEN

COLIN BAKER

'If you're ever on *Who Wants to be a Millionaire*, make sure Colin Baker is your Phone a Friend. He has the brain the size of a planet!'

Louise Jameson, in conversation with the author

'I LOVE WORKING with Colin,' Louise Jameson said. 'We do one-off plays together. We toured in a whodunit called *Corpse* with Mark McGann. We also did *Bedroom Farce* [2007] together.

'Back in the seventies, we played darts as a team (post Leela) in Oxford. And Colin had to get a double and a bull to win the game, and I foolishly said to him, "If you get it, I'll sleep with you." And he got it! I shot out of the pub and he chased me.

'Fast forward thirty years and we are in rehearsals for *Bedroom Farce*, and the stage is basically three bedrooms, and Colin said to me, "At last I've got you into bed!"'

Anyone who meets or works with actor Colin Baker adores the man. Intelligent, humorous and adorable with children (I speak as one who has introduced him to two), one quickly forms the opinion that he got the least out of being the Doctor, which is a shame as he had been a fan since the very first episode. With falling budgets, unimpressive storylines – for the most part – and the sword of Damocles over the head of the show, Baker's Doctor had a rocky ride. But Baker shouldn't be passed off as a lesser Doctor or lesser actor because of the quality of his stories. When I started this project, I wrongly thought that there was less to document about Colin Baker than most of the other Doctors, but I was very wrong, his list of credits is extremely long, with much theatre and TV work (see Part Two).

Baker is one of the most experienced jobbing actors in the country and has been working hard since the 1960s. He is one of those actors seemingly taken for granted, but those in the acting profession have great admiration for him, as do his many *Doctor Who* fans.

Colin Baker was born at the Royal Waterloo Lying-in Hospital, London (behind Waterloo Station), during an air raid on 8 June 1943. He escaped death while still a baby when a piece of shrapnel embedded itself in the side of his cot! Perhaps the luck of the Irish came in here (his mother being of Irish ancestry).

His family moved to Rochdale when he was two and he was educated in Manchester.

His first acting role came about by accident. The mother of a fellow pupil was a casting director and needed a child who could speak good French. Baker soon found himself playing a young French boy in a series called *My Wife's Sister* (1954), starring Eleanor Summerfield, Martin Wyldeck and Helen Christie.

After this flirtation with acting, Baker went on to attend St Bede's College, Manchester. He would appear in the college productions of Gilbert and Sullivan operettas *Yeoman of the Guard* and *Iolanthe* (the latter in the lead role). And after seeing an amateur production of the *King and I*, Baker joined the North Manchester Amateur Dramatic Society.

The new Who: Matt Smith, pictured here with Karen Gillan, who plays assistant Amy Pond.

© *Brian Aldrich*

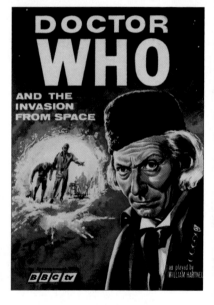

Above: The First Doctor, William Hartnell (*left*), with Richard Attenborough and Harry Ross in a still from the classic 1947 film *Brighton Rock*.

© *Rex Features*

Below left: A publicity shot for the series *The Army Game* (1957-62).

© *Rex Features*

Below right: One of the first – and rarest – books released to accompany the series: *Doctor Who and the Invasion from Space*.

Above left: For Hartnell, there was no escaping the roll of the Doctor.

Above right: Patrick Troughton, pictured here in a 1971 episode of *The Persuaders*, replaced Hartnell in Doctor Who. © *Rex Features*

Below: Troughton in one of his numerous roles in classic horror films.

Above left: The Third Doctor was played by one of Britain's great character actors: Jon Pertwee.

© *Rex Features*

Above right: A poster for *Doctor Who – The Ultimate Adventure,* which was staged at the Wimbledon Theatre, London in March 1989. Jon Pertwee starred in the first half of the run and Colin Baker in the second.

Below left: Another of Petwee's much-loved characters: Worzel Gummidge.

© *PA Photos*

Below right: Pictured with a Dalek in 1993.

© *Rex Features*

Above left: Tom Baker, one of the most popular Doctors ever, played the iconic role for 7 years. He is pictured here with his barbarian assistant, Leela, famously played by Louise Jameson. © *Rex Features*

Above right: Publicity shot from 1980. © *Rex Features*

Below: Baker returned as the Doctor for the five-part *Doctor Who* radio special, *Hornets' Nest*, in 2009. © *Rex Features*

Above: Old friends? Baker at the *Doctor Who* Exhibition in Earl's
Court, London, 2008.   © *Rex Features*

Below left: The great Laurence Olivier, who gave so many young
careers a boost, including Patrick Troughton, Tom Baker and Peter
Cushing, as well as being friends with Jon Pertwee and his father.

Below right: The Doctor and the Master: Tom Baker and Sir Derek
Jacobi, friends from the theatre in 1970 to their association with *Doctor
Who* in the Millennium.   © *The Stamp Shop*

Above: Peter Davidson was cast as the fifth incarnation of the Doctor (*left*). He has gone on to star in many of Britain's best-loved television series, including *All Creatures Great and Small* (*right*). © *Rex Features*

Below: Pictured with some of the actresses who have played the Doctor's assistant over the years: (*from left to right*) Louise Jameson, Carole Ann Ford, Caroline John, Sarah Sutton, Elisabeth Sladen and Janet Fielding. © *PA Photos*

Above: John Nathan-Turner, the show's longest serving producer, who cast Peter Davison, Colin Baker and Sylvester McCoy in the role of the Doctor.

© *The author*

Below: The Sixth Doctor, Colin Baker, pictured with two assistants, Nicola Bryant and Janet Fielding.

© *Rex Features*

Although he loved the theatre, he spent five years training to be a solicitor because his father told him that a steady career was better than being an actor. He became an articled clerk but never took his final exam. His father had a stroke and that prompted Baker to suddenly decide that he no longer wanted to pursue a career he didn't enjoy, so he auditioned for the London Academy of Music and the Dramatic Arts (aged 23). He was accepted and studied alongside David Suchet, who is now the definitive Hercule Poirot.

Baker left the Academy in 1961 and spent a short time with a touring company. He then spent three years in repertory theatre. He found the touring company hard work but told Terry Wogan in 1986 that he didn't get much work in rep, making irregular appearances.

Baker made his first appearance on TV in *Roads to Freedom* (1970), which was based on the novels by Jean-Paul Sartre. He played the part of a rapist, and sinister roles have seemed to follow him since.

A long list of TV and theatre credits followed *Roads to Freedom*, but perhaps most notable was his portrayal of Paul Merroney in the TV series *The Brothers*, alongside Kate O'Mara who would become famous to *Doctor Who* fans for her own part in the show's history as the evil Time Lord the Rani.

The Brothers was compulsive Sunday-night viewing between 1974 and 1976, clocking up 46 episodes. His portrayal of Merroney – a cold, pompous and ruthless accountant – made Baker a household name. He was even voted the most hated man in television as a consequence, something he was very proud of until someone punched him and knocked out one of his teeth. It seems some people equate being evil on screen with being evil in real life.

In 2002, the cast of *The Brothers* got back together again. It had been over 25 years since some of them had last met. Kate O'Mara reminisced that the actors in the show cared an awful lot about each other and used to socialise quite a lot, going out for meals and other social events. It was a very tight-knit team. Many actors, such as Louise Jameson, talk about the humour and pleasant times they have had around Baker, and many of the cast of *The Brothers* speak highly of him, despite the pressures – and punches! – which came from the show's success.

After *The Brothers*, Baker found it difficult to get work. In fact, *The Brothers*, more than *Doctor Who*, proved to be the bigger show for Baker to get over. Indeed, when it was announced that he was taking on the Doctor, one newspaper commented, 'Actor Colin Baker, once a J R Ewing-type television screen villain, is to take on the role of one of the small screen's most loved heroes, Doctor Who!'

Typecasting never seemed to bother Baker. When he took on the role of the Doctor, he spoke on *Breakfast* (BBC morning magazine programme), effectively saying that he didn't worry about such things and that he'd rather enjoy the experience.

In 1980, Baker appeared in Terry Nation's *Blakes 7*. The story was called 'The City at the Edge of the World'. Coincidentally, Baker played alongside another *Doctor Who* legend in that episode, Valentine Dyall (the Black Guardian). The episode was about the opening of a sinister vault and Baker was the obligatory bad guy, Baybon the Butcher (a sort of leather-clad Paul Merroney), exploiting the cowardly Villa (one of the regular cast) to open the vault for him.

Baker said of the role, 'Baybon was the second most dangerous man in the galaxy, which caused him great annoyance because he wanted to be the most dangerous. It was a great part, an over-the-top role.'

It's an important fact that Baker has played many 'bad guy'

roles, the Doctor being a bit of an exception; perhaps it's his training to be a solicitor that gave him his sinister side.

In 1983, Baker took his first role in *Doctor Who*. He played the part of Commander Maxil in the Peter Davison story 'Arc of Infinity'. He impressed and entertained the cast and crew both on and off camera throughout the filming to the extent that the director, Ron Jones, would suggest Baker as the next Doctor to producer John Nathan-Turner when Davison decided to call it a day.

This wasn't a bolt from the blue. Baker had wanted to take the lead role after Tom Baker resigned, but conversations never went further than those he had with his agent. This time, however, he had made an impression and he got the opportunity of taking on the role he had watched since the show began in the 1960s, although he claims the part never entered his mind then. 'When I read in the papers that Peter was leaving,' Baker said in 1983, 'and that they were looking for an older Doctor, or even possibly a woman, the idea didn't even cross my mind. So, when John Nathan-Turner rang and asked me to go and see him, I genuinely didn't have a clue what it was about!' Baker went on to explain that he thought he would be asked to open a fete not be offered the role of the Doctor.

When Baker found out the real reason for the call he was absolutely delighted, as he explained: 'It offers the most tremendous scope to an actor, and it really is in a category of its own. *Hamlet* talked about plays being "tragical-comical-historical-past-oral"; well, if you add "scientifical", you've got *Doctor Who*.'

Like every other actor who has taken the lead role since Jon Pertwee, Baker had to keep quiet about landing the role until the official announcement, which caused more than the odd embarrassing situation, as he explained in the

Doctor Who 20th Anniversary Radio Times Special: 'We were having dinner with friends one night and this chap said, "My wife wants to write to the BBC and tell them you'd be perfect as the next Doctor Who. Do you think she should?" I had to keep my face very straight as I said, "No, I shouldn't think so. Knowing the BBC, they've probably already made up their minds."'

Baker got off to a very shaky start as the Doctor with the story 'The Twin Dilemma', one of the very worst *Doctor Who* stories ever in terms of story and costume design. The fact that Baker's doctor was a little erratic at the time – having just regenerated – turned the story, what there was of it, into a bit of a circus and didn't bode well for the future.

Baker had a clear idea of how his Doctor should behave. He remembered watching the show in its infancy and explained his perception of the Doctor shortly after taking on the part: 'I think he should have wit with a sharp edge to it, even a touch of anger underneath, and, watching some of the early Doctors, I realised that they do have their hard moments, when they show an apparent lack of concern for the people around them…'

Baker's interpretation of the Doctor was pretty faithful to this description, but there is a school of thought that believes that he played the role too brashly and his costume (an idea of John Nathan-Turner's) was the least impressive of all the Doctor Whos with its multicoloured (pied) patchwork quilt look. Perhaps this is partly true, but the programme – by the time Baker took over – was on the rack, getting tired and too expensive and that's probably a major factor in the slippery slope of the original series from there on in. It wasn't Baker's fault. In fact, when he sat up at the end of 'The Caves of Androzani' having just regenerated, his pomposity – or is it his self-assurance? – was quite inspiring and interesting. Then again, 'Androzani' was a classic story written by one of the most distinguished *Doctor Who* writers ever – Robert Holmes.

One of Baker's very best stories was one alongside his 'American' sidekick Peri and Patrick Troughton's Doctor and his companion Jamie. 'The Two Doctors' is an absolutely classic *Doctor Who* adventure, with quality location filming and some old enemies coming back for a big dust-up! What was also refreshing about this story was the introduction of the alien chef – Shockeye – who has a taste for human flesh and abducts Peri in order to slaughter and eat her. With Jacqueline Pearce (a former *Blakes 7* regular) as yet another evil influence in the story, the classic adventure restored some dignity to the show and really allowed the actors to prove what they could do with a half-decent script and location. It was a great shame that the BBC had no faith in the track record of the show at that time because 'The Two Doctors' showed that there was still life in the old boy yet. Coincidentally, the story was written by Robert Holmes, reinforcing the idea that a half-decent set of scripts would have ultimately saved the show from being dumped (and of course the return of classic *Who* monsters the Sontarans).

Baker had some good times working on *Doctor Who*. With 'The Two Doctors', he worked with one of his favourite Doctors, Patrick Troughton, which provided many an opportunity for practical jokes. In one scene, the Doctor (Baker) had to wake Peri up by splashing water on her face. The scene went well but Nicola Bryant was asked to do the scene again whereupon Baker threw a whole jug of water over her. It was a few moments before she realised that she had been set up!

Bryant got on very well with Baker but it was hard to keep a straight face on location in Spain, as Baker confessed: 'There was an awful lot of joking between Pat [Troughton] and I on that Spanish shoot... we were both a bit badly behaved and took the piss out of each other unmercifully. I used to call him a geriatric and he got his own back by calling me "fatty".'

It wasn't long before John Nathan-Turner called Baker to tell him that the show was to be suspended. Baker called the news 'pretty devastating' but his wife was about to have a baby and he realised that a job was just a job at the end of the day; the BBC had effectively given him paternity leave. Having lost a baby before to cot death, Baker recognised that keeping perspective was the most important thing, but worse things for Baker's Doctor were just around the corner.

Doctor Who came to a bitter end for Colin Baker on Thursday, 19 December 1986, when the BBC announced that he was to leave the show. He flatly refused to shoot a regeneration story to make way for the next Doctor. John Nathan-Turner tried to persuade Baker to shoot the scene but he wasn't having any of it, he felt let down and consequently didn't want to know.

The *Sun* newspaper would write some heavy headlines blasting BBC controller Michael Grade who apparently didn't want Baker to continue in the role.

In 2004, Baker played alongside Louise Jameson and Peter Duncan in *Corpse*, a humorous play that Baker enjoyed. Later, in 2005, he played alongside Richard Bremner's lead in *Dracula*, where he played the part of Van Helsing, in what was a very good interpretation of Stoker's original story; both plays were very atmospheric and macabre and enjoyed good reviews.

Although Baker was free from *Doctor Who* at this time, he was still billed as 'starring former *Doctor Who* Colin Baker', something that didn't bother him too much. Just like the show's producer, he was keen to see a packed theatre and, if the Doctor could draw more people in, then that's what needed to be exploited. This was in contrast to William Hartnell who wanted to shake off the Doctor image when he rejoined the theatre after leaving the programme. *Doctor Who* wasn't an albatross around Colin Baker's neck, he was totally at ease with it – and still is today – but, for Hartnell, it really was a Jonah.

Despite the backstage bust-ups, *Doctor Who* was never far away from Baker: the stage play *Doctor Who – the Ultimate Adventure* opened on 23 March 1989. Initially, Jon Pertwee played the Doctor, but he didn't take it on tour; instead, it was left to Colin Baker who made a good fist of it after the dust had settled on his TV departure. Although there were problems with some visual effects and certain shows did not sell out, the young fans – the target market – loved it. Daleks and Cybermen terrorised the Doctor but there was enough time towards the end of the play for the Doctor to remember – in a very sentimental way – the companions who had left him behind and went on to do better things. This included Sarah Jane Smith, who, when she did return to the show in the new millennium, explained to the Doctor that she had waited for him to come back and that she thought he was dead. So the Doctor got it all wrong there.

Colin Baker and Sylvester McCoy get rough rides as Doctor Whos because of the problems they had with budgets and scripts, but their careers as actors gave them the ability to rise above 'the silly bits' and show some Dunkirk spirit in their interpretations of the Time Lord. In 1986, Baker told Terry Wogan that, if the budget of *Doctor Who* was inflated to cope with bigger SF shows, it would probably lose its appeal. Hindsight would prove Baker to be wrong here, but I would suggest that if somebody at the BBC had actually given a damn it would have fared better during Baker and McCoy's time. One could also suggest that, despite being a lovely man and, the right man at the right time, producer John Nathan-Turner had spent too long in control of the show and may have got a little stale. That said, he had done so much good for the show over the years it is hard to deal out any harsh criticism of the man; he weathered many storms within the BBC.

The BBC tried many ways of reshaping *Doctor Who*, from threatening to get rid of the Tardis to putting a female in the lead role. In the end, they sacked a perfectly good Doctor because they couldn't work out what they wanted to do and therefore only half-heartedly supported the programme.

To this day, Baker continues to keep the show close to his heart. He may have left to rejoin the theatre, and become a school governor (and look after the education of his four daughters), but, as time has shown, *Doctor Who* is still very much a happy part of his life now.

He has many strings to his bow. He is a book reviewer, a lyricist and the writer of a children's musical, *Scrooge – A Ghost of a Chance* (written with composer Sheila Wilson and performed in over a hundred schools). He has also contributed regular weekly columns to the *Bucks Free Press*, which culminated in an anthology of articles in his first book *Look Who's Talking* (Hirst Books, 2009). Colin Baker will continue to surprise and delight his many fans around the world.

'A great reason for the programme's continuing success has to be the fact that every four or five years you have a new generation of kids growing up… The time I liked the least was when the Doctor became the person the establishment rang up and said "Help us out, Doctor!"'

Verity Lambert *Doctor Who – A Celebration, Two Decades Through Time and Space*

Peter Haining

CHAPTER EIGHT
SYLVESTER McCOY

'Then up and spoke the Cameron,
And gave him his hand again:
"There shall never a man in Scotland
Set faith in me in vain.'

'The Saying of a Name'
Robert Louis Stevenson

SYLVESTER McCOY WAS born Percy Kent-Smith in Dunoon, Argyllshire, on 20 August 1943. McCoy's father was from Pimlico, London, and was an acting petty officer in the Royal Navy. Unfortunately, McCoy never met him. Within six weeks of meeting his Irish mother, Molly Sheridan (which included a two-week honeymoon in Ayrshire), he was blown up in a submarine in the Mediterranean. McCoy's father was only 23 years old when killed and his mother never recovered from the trauma, receiving medication for the rest of her life as a consequence and, as McCoy would later claim, spending a lot of her life in an institute for the emotionally distraught. He spent his formative years being raised by his mother, grandmother and aunts, and he attended St Mun's, a local Dunoon school.

McCoy never started out with the intention of being an

actor. His first vocation was the priesthood. Between the ages of 12 and 16 he trained at Blair's College, Aberdeen, to become a priest – the same choice of career as the young Tom Baker and, like Baker, he decided that it wasn't the career for him. He left and completed his education in Dublin and Scotland, then went for a holiday in London, where he stayed and worked in an insurance company until it went bankrupt.

It was around this time that he became a hippy and took a job at the Roundhouse Theatre, London, where he reputedly was one of the most unlikely bodyguards of The Rolling Stones, as he explained: 'The roundhouse in the 60s and 70s was a wonderful place where lots of avant-garde plays were put on, and lots of rock concerts. I was a bouncer for The Rolling Stones one night.' So, more of a fluke than a serious vocation then!

It was at the Roundhouse that McCoy met actor Brian Murphy (later to star in TV comedy *George and Mildred*) who was out of work and selling show tickets. One day a producer came in seeking an actor to replace someone who had let him down, whereupon Murphy suggested McCoy (wrongly presuming that he was an out-of-work actor too) by saying, 'There's a guy in the box office who's crazy...' It seems this craziness has followed McCoy ever since, as a perception if nothing else.

The producer was Ken Campbell and, through his wacky roadshow, McCoy began to develop his own unique routine. Another actor who enjoyed the roadshow alongside McCoy was Bob Hoskins. Murphy also joined the fray and devised the name Sylveste McCoy in a play called 'An Evening with Sylveste McCoy', in which McCoy would stuff ferrets down his trousers and set fire to his head.

Sylveste McCoy stuck because journalists thought that was

indeed the actor's real name, but McCoy lengthened it to Sylvester McCoy because he favoured a 14 letter name to a 13 (some superstition in there, no doubt).

McCoy remembers his tour with the Ken Campbell Roadshow as one where he 'learned to do the impossible with total conviction', and it was surely his apprenticeship to the world of acting.

In 1976, McCoy did a bit of serious acting in *Twelfth Night*, which also starred McCoy's future nemesis Davros – actor Terry Molloy. He followed this with *She Stoops to Conquer*, albeit, at that time, still under the name Sylveste.

Big Jim and the Figaro Club was an early sitcom success for McCoy; although it was only meant to be a BBC Bristol one-off, it was shown on BBC2. The club were a group of builders who lived and worked around a seaside town in the 1950s. The show was broadcast between 1979 and 1981 and apparently captured the 1950s feeling so much people loved it.

McCoy played the deranged 'Turps', a character that brought him his first true character actor plaudits, although, again, he was still billed under the name Sylveste McCoy at the time.

Throughout the 1970s and 80s, McCoy took madcap roles in children's programmes such as *Vision On* and *Eureka*, often as an eccentric professor-type character; appropriate then that his *Doctor Who* companion Ace would nickname him 'professor' when he took the part of the Doctor; and his often madcap antics fitted the show perfectly.

In 1985, McCoy played one of his finest roles in the six-episode serial *The Last Place on Earth*. The serial was a dramatisation of Roland Huntford's book *Scott and Amundsen*, which studied, in detail, the infamous race to the South Pole.

The programme, like the book, shows where Scott made some vital errors, which caused a bit of an outcry when the book was first published. The mini-series is faithful to the book and a largely overlooked classic nowadays, not unlike Paul McGann's *The Monocled Mutineer*, which was also castigated for the politics of an historic event (but more of that later).

McCoy played the part of the heroic Bowers, one of Captain Scott's most trusted men, and the serial showcases one of McCoy's finest – and most poignant – performances.

In mid-1986, McCoy and Timothy Dalton performed together with Vanessa Redgrave in a season of Shakespearean plays at the Theatre Royal, Haymarket. The duo discussed the rareness of regular quality parts in the acting profession. A year later McCoy was cast as the seventh Doctor and Dalton was cast as James Bond in *The Living Daylights* (1987).

'And to Koppelberg Hill his steps addressed,
And after him the children pressed,
Great was the joy in every breast.'

The Pied Piper of Hamelin
Robert Browning

An incredible coincidence is that one of the strongest themes in *Doctor Who* history, *The Pied Piper*, became the catalyst for McCoy getting the part of the Doctor in the first place. *The Pied Piper* was a colourful theatre production written for McCoy by Adrian Mitchell, with a very 80s 'Pied Piper Rap' in it (performed by McCoy).

McCoy learned that the part of the Doctor was available again while performing *The Pied Piper* and duly went for it.

This wasn't the first time he had gone for the role of Doctor

Who, as he had also done so when Davison had given up the part, but that time he had lost it to Colin Baker. This time things would be different.

At the same time as approaching producer John Nathan-Turner for the part, a producer who knew McCoy got in touch with Nathan-Turner and told him that McCoy would be a great Doctor. Although Nathan-Turner suspected conspiracy here – which it wasn't – he went along to see McCoy in *The Pied Piper* (6 January 1987) and came away suitably impressed.

On obtaining the part, McCoy sent out an introductory signed letter to the first fans that wrote to him, along with a colourful flyer publicising *The Pied Piper* at The National Theatre (29 October 1987–20 January 1988) and a one-page biog on Doctor Who headed paper entitled 'The Real McCoy', where he is asked at the conclusion if he had a favourite Doctor, to which he replied, 'We are all the same person, so why should I!'

An interesting aside regarding McCoy's introduction to playing the Doctor is a low-budget movie called *Three Kinds of Heat*. Mere months before taking on the role of the Doctor, McCoy appeared in the movie which also included Mary Tamm (companion and fellow Time Lord Romana from Tom Baker's era as the Doctor) and Trevor Martin (one of the very few stage Doctor Whos).

McCoy's Doctor Who was not a write-off despite what some critics claim. Although there was a diminishing budget, some quality stories were made, such as 'The Curse of Fenric', 'Silver Nemesis', 'Delta and the Bannermen' with the legendary Ken Dodd, and 'Dragonfire', with its scary *Raiders of the Lost Ark* melting-face scene.

McCoy certainly brought back much mystery to the part of the Doctor, with his flirtation with being Merlin the Magician. But it was his token Dalek story that impressed many. 'Remembrance of the Daleks', which has had the rare opportunity of being released as a special-edition DVD, was the first story to show a Dalek travelling up stairs. It also returned the Doctor to his Earth origins at 76 Totter's Lane, the junk yard in the very first episode back in 1963.

There was much to like about McCoy's Doctor, including his final story 'Survival', which brought the whole original series to a climax with Anthony Ainley's last outing as the Doctor's nemesis the Master.

McCoy was always thrilled to be Doctor Who. He wrote in his introduction letter to the fans, 'My new appearance takes place on UK TV screens in September 1987 for 14 action-packed episodes. 1988 is *Doctor Who*'s 25th anniversary so there is plenty to look forward to.'

And indeed there was, until the programme was terminated through no fault of McCoy's. The show, in its old incarnation, had just run out of steam…

… but McCoy's career hadn't. In 1996 he appeared in an episode of *Rab C Nesbitt*, just as future Doctor Who and fellow Scot David Tennant would. McCoy's episode was entitled 'Father', and he played Rab's mentally ill brother Gash Snr.

McCoy also appeared as Grandpa Jock in John McGrath's *A Satire of the Four Estates* (1996) at the Edinburgh Festival. It appears that McCoy doesn't forget his Scottish roots and one would like to see the two Scottish Doctors (McCoy and Tennant) get together in perhaps a non-Who project sometime in the future.

Another interesting part for McCoy was as Snuff in the dark and macabre BBC Radio 4 comedy series *The Cabinet of Doctor Caligari*.

McCoy has had a series of near-misses on the larger scale of things. When Spielberg was planning on directing *Pirates of the Caribbean: The Curse of the Black Pearl*, McCoy was attached to the role of Governor Swann. Also McCoy was second choice to play Bilbo Baggins in the Peter Jackson *Lord of the Rings* trilogy.

McCoy took the part of the lawyer Dowling in the BBC production of Henry Fielding's novel *The History of Tom Jones, A Foundling*. He also appeared in the RSC's *The Lion, the Witch and the Wardrobe*, as well as *King Lear* (2007), playing the fool to Ian McKellen's Lear, a performance that allowed McCoy to play the spoons!

In 2008 he performed *The Mikado* (Gilbert and Sullivan) with the Carl Rosa Company. He only performed with the company briefly, for the show's one-week run at the Sheffield Lyceum.

Sylvester McCoy never started out with the intention of being an actor. Like his hippy beginnings, his life kind of happened around him, both impressive and diverse. He even – like so many Doctor Whos – brushed shoulders with Laurence Olivier. It was a non-speaking part in the Frank Langella 1979 production of *Dracula*, but, yet again, the great actor had a presence in the life of a Doctor Who. Perhaps the great 'Larry' was the Doctor that got away.

'After bidding farewell to the second supporting party, Captain Scott and his four companions, Wilson, Oates, Bowers, and Petty Officer Evans, entered on what might be called the last phase of the polar journey…'

No Surrender
Harold Avery

CHAPTER NINE
PAUL McGANN

'… but abide the change of time…'

Cymbeline

William Shakespeare

PAUL McGANN IS an underrated actor. Although – as far as TV is concerned – having the shortest reign as the Doctor, he has done many *Doctor Who* audio recordings and dramas, and has been seen to be around the show and, ostensibly, fans, since appearing in *Doctor Who – the Movie* in 1996. In fact, because of the amount of work he has done with audio, radio drama and even comic strips, there is a school of thought that considers him the longest-serving Doctor Who.

McGann's Doctor is significant, because, despite only one outing within the series, he was part of some legendary milestones in the show's history. He was the first Doctor to kiss a companion, he had the first new Tardis interior (something in line with the series from Christopher Eccleston's relaunch), and the first feature-length one-off episode (OK, it *was* called a movie but it was a continuation of the TV legacy unlike its earlier movie counterparts).

Many *Doctor Who* fans have wondered why McGann has never been offered an opportunity to do a few seasons as the Doctor. Even now there is nothing to stop him. He wasn't a failure in the role. He signed a contract that was to last longer than his one-off special. And what harm would there really be in going back to the eighth Doctor after Matt Smith?

Paul McGann is the Doctor everybody wants to see a little more of but probably won't get the chance.

So how has his career been affected by the programme? It is something he once did on screen, as much as he once did a film called *Withnail and I*. It was a one-off but nevertheless one that gave him much prestige. Yes, he has continued to have an interest in the show – through audio plays and readings – but his TV contribution is not a major one and the audio dramas are only truly appreciated by the insatiable fans, not the general public at large (and consequently not tackled in this book with any seriousness).

Paul McGann was born on 14 November 1959 in Liverpool. He was the third of six children. In 1958, his mother Clare gave birth to twins Joseph and John, but John died shortly after birth. Joe, along with his three younger brothers, Paul, Mark and Stephen, are all actors. His sister – Clare – works behind the scenes in TV.

McGann's first significant role in television was as Mo Morris in the BBC series *Give Us a Break* (1983). He was the fresh-faced snooker ace in a show that capitalised on the TV snooker boom of the early 1980s, where charismatic players such as Alex 'Hurricane' Higgins and Jimmy 'Whirlwind' White captivated huge TV audiences. The show had its moments as early-evening light entertainment, but soon ran out of steam.

In 1986, McGann took on the role that would be a

significant milestone in his career, *The Monocled Mutineer*. Based upon the 1970s novel by William Alison and John Fairley, McGann played Percy Toplis, a vagabond, deserter and criminal.

The show was highly praised at the time and McGann received many plaudits; however, the show was blasted by the Conservative Party as left-wing in its interpretation of a sensitive action during the war (the Etaples Mutiny), which Toplis was apparently involved in.

The *Monocled Mutineer* was never repeated on the BBC; however, it has since been released on video and DVD. It showcased the very best of the young Paul McGann and allowed him to show his worth, and like other BBC series of that time, such as the mini-series *House of Cards*, it is remembered fondly by those who watched it.

McGann is generally known to a younger audience for his part in *Withnail and I*. Noted as a student film (i.e. that it is primarily student audiences that watch it), it follows two out-of-work actors, Withnail (Richard E Grant) and Marwood, aka 'I' (McGann). With drink, drugs and more than a hint of homosexual angst, the film is student self-indulgence to excess. The movie is set in the 1960s and is meant to be based upon the director's (Bruce Robinson) own formative years.

McGann enjoyed making the movie but only really got to see it 20 years later at the anniversary screening on the South Bank.

McGann has called the film 'an extraordinary piece of work', because it is a film of words, a film where the actors have to act and not hide behind props and special effects. To a degree, McGann is right. To me, the film lacks a little substance in its plot, but that's not to say that the performances are lacking, they are not. In fact, Richard E Grant, a famous teetotaller, was made hideously drunk by Robinson to assist the reality of the part he was acting!

Withnail and I is a carefree buddy movie. The characters are frustrated unemployed actors lusting for the spotlight while living in squalor. The film is a kind of high-class version of 80s comedy *The Young Ones*. Grant is very dramatic and camp, while McGann is the fresh lamb being led to the slaughter – but somehow surviving.

Although both McGann and Grant loved filming the movie and over 20 years later have much good to say about it, it is a film for a certain generation (late teens/early 20s), which, if it counts among your favourite films at that time, you will reminisce about fondly, but not watch religiously, for the rest of your life. For this reason, *Withnail and I* will always be classed as a cult movie and just a little too genreless to be labelled a great film. People either love it or hate it, and personally I probably fall into the latter category.

McGann's other significant work is a classic SF movie, *Alien 3* (1992). There was much anticipation regarding the conclusion to the *Alien* trilogy. The first two movies in the series were nothing short of SF classics and fans believed the third film would fit nicely into this prestigious sequence. In fairness, with the previous movies having the indelible touches of Ridley Scott and James Cameron, respectively, the third film had a tough acts to follow and, unfortunately, it failed to deliver.

Alien 3 was probably the most disappointing – or simply the worst – movie in the *Alien* franchise. There was a big media build-up regarding how good the computer-generated aliens were in the film, but the public's complaints that they couldn't see the creatures too well because of the dark corridors and recesses they hid in put paid to that accolade.

And what of Paul McGann's part in the movie? McGann is

an outcast, a deranged prisoner. Unfortunately, his part was severely edited in the final movie, thus making it difficult to analyse his character properly. That said, to see such a laidback actor become an alien-addicted psychopath showed yet another side to his versatility. What is worth mentioning here is 'The Assembly Cut', which is a segment of the movie restored for the Blu-ray set of the *Alien* series, and showcases a more rounded interpretation of McGann's character, but still nothing like the Director's Cut of *Aliens*; so it simply adds to the frustration.

Alien 3 was probably a worthwhile project for McGann to be part of for experience sake, but it didn't give him the artistic licence he would have hoped for.

Doctor Who – The Movie (1996) is the third outing for the Time Lord on the big screen (well, actually, it was a TV movie with a much bigger budget than the show was normally accustomed to).

The target market was clearly the American one (it was made by Fox after all), but, unlike the early *Star Trek* movies, the baggage of the TV series encroached too much and, as a consequence, only a true fan of the show would be impressed by references to the Daleks, and understand the history of the Master and Time Lords.

Combine the above with a very average script and you have the downside of the film encapsulated. The upside is Paul McGann and Daphne Ashbrook (Dr Grace Holloway), who really do hit it off on screen.

McGann is the young, dashing Doctor, full of energy and passion, but not in a James Bond type of way. Yes, he does steal a kiss from Grace but it's more euphoric than anything else, showcasing the innocence of the movie.

Since Sydney Newman laid down the law in 1963, the Doctor doesn't do guns, which probably explains why McCoy's Doctor is gunned down so easily at the start of the movie. The Doctor might be streetwise as far as Daleks are concerned but not wise to run-of-the-mill thugs from the US of A.

Doctor Who – The Movie set the scene perfectly for Russell T Davies. The Tardis interior changed very little from McGann to Eccleston, and the love interest – although an undertone – was certainly built upon from the movie into the new millennium series.

Paul McGann reinvented the Doctor. Unfortunately, many influential people failed to see this and the fans were deprived of what would have been a very invigorating and influential interpretation of the Doctor. It is of course acknowledged that McGann has played the Doctor in other media (audio and drama series), but it doesn't alter the fact that he didn't get the opportunity to develop the character through a series of TV adventures. If we are to simply judge him on his first appearance alone, then we must concur that he would definitely be up there with William Hartnell and Christopher Eccleston as one of the great debut Doctors, because his first story includes an excellent acting performance from the lead actor.

Has *Doctor Who* had an adverse effect on McGann's career?

No. McGann still dabbles with the show, he still attends the conventions and meets the fans, all of whom have much respect for him. Indeed, he manages to play many other parts without people remarking that 'he used to be Doctor Who'. One of those great key roles being in *Hornblower* (1998–2003). *Hornblower* was one of the very best period mini-series made by the ITV regions. Ioan Gruffudd starred as the main character, Horatio Hornblower, the hero of CS Forester's classic Napoleonic adventure stories. Gruffudd was supported by an excellent cast, which included Robert Lindsay (who McGann appeared alongside in *Give Us a Break* all those years ago) as Admiral

Sir Edward Pellew, Paul Copley (Matthews), Sean Gilder (Styles) and, for four out of the eight episodes, Paul McGann as Lieutenant William Bush.

What is most endearing about McGann's role is the dignity and total dedication to his friend and commanding officer Horatio Hornblower.

Lavishly shot and wonderfully acted, *Hornblower* was a classic series that sadly didn't get the opportunity to showcase the bigger – better – novels in CS Forester's series, mainly because of the cost of each episode.

Paul might not have been the McGann to play the Doctor, as his brother Mark also went for the part, but his interpretation of the Doctor has bridged the most significant moment in the show's history: the journey from the original series to the new one. Although his career has been largely unaffected by the show, he has chosen not to leave it behind him, making him a most popular and endearing personality.

CHAPTER TEN
PETER CUSHING

"'Interesting, though elementary,'" said he as he returned to his favourite corner of the settee.'

The Hound of the Baskervilles
Sir Arthur Conan Doyle

DOCTOR WHO WAS not Peter Cushing's most accomplished or famous role. For that you must look to the Hammer Horror movies and his classic performances alongside Christopher Lee as Professor Van Helsing and Victor Von Frankenstein. Also, as a devout Sherlock Holmes fan, his performances as the master detective on television and on film must number among his most complete work. Then there is his acclaimed role as Winston Smith in the 1954 TV version of *Nineteen Eighty-Four*, and of course, Grand Moff Tarkin in the first ever *Star Wars* movie in 1977.

Doctor Who is such an after-thought in the career of Peter Cushing, it's almost a non-event, but for several reasons there is merit in taking a closer look at – albeit in a smaller way – the acting career of this much underrated actor.

Peter Cushing was born in Kenley, Surrey, on 26 May 1913. His first job was as a surveyor's assistant – or glorified tea boy

– at Purley Urban District Council. This job was organised for him by his father who didn't want him treading the boards like other members of his family; he was keen on Cushing taking a 'real' job.

Acting was in Cushing's blood. He was in amateur dramatics while a surveyor's assistant and he left after winning a scholarship to the Guildhall School of Music and Drama – despite his father.

After this he took a job in the repertory theatre in Worthing, primarily as an assistant stage manager, but the determined youth decided to go to Hollywood and see if he could make something of himself there.

In 1939, he managed to get his first film role in *The Man in the Iron Mask*. Cushing earned a few more bit parts, most notably in Laurel and Hardy's last great movie *A Chump at Oxford* (1940).

Soon Cushing got homesick and took a variety of jobs in America and Canada to get his passage home, where he failed his medical to go into the Armed Forces. However, acting beckoned again and Cushing became a member of the Entertainment National Service Association (ENSA) and went on tour to entertain the troops.

In 1946, while appearing in a play, *Born Yesterday*, he was spotted by Laurence Olivier and invited to take a part in his first major motion-picture role as Osric in Olivier's *Hamlet* (1948). Coincidentally, Patrick Troughton made his second movie appearance in this film, and was also spotted by Olivier. Twenty years later, Olivier would spot and encourage Tom Baker and give him his first major break in a movie as Rasputin. And let us not forget that Olivier was a friend of Jon Pertwee and his father. Indeed, *Doctor Who* has much to thank the great Olivier for.

Incidentally, Cushing himself wrote to William Hartnell after seeing him on stage in *Seagulls Over Sorrento*. He was very praiseworthy and even took a role in the play in 1956 when it made its transition to radio.

Cushing toured with Olivier and the Old Vic Theatre Company and, from there, went on the circuit. In 1954 came Cushing's first landmark role, as Winston Smith in the TV adaptation of George Orwell's classic *Nineteen Eighty-Four*. The show was shot live twice in one week, but unfortunately the BBC only kept the second version, which Cushing maintained was the inferior version as far as his performance was concerned. Nevertheless, plaudits were his. Scripted by Nigel Kneale, there is a starkness; a depressing undercurrent, that mirrors the unsettling feelings experienced when reading Orwell's original novel. It is an exceptional interpretation of the book, only outdone by John Hurt's movie (Richard Burton's last) in 1984.

Three years later, Cushing appeared in another Nigel Kneale-scripted production, this time a movie, *The Abominable Snowman*. This film was well crafted, leaving a lot to the imagination of the viewer. Filmed in black and white, it has the stark loneliness and eerie sense of danger that another great snowbound movie *The Thing from Another World* had, several years before it.

Later that year, Cushing's first Hammer Horror was released, *The Curse of Frankenstein*, playing alongside Christopher Lee as the monster. Cushing's Victor Frankenstein was reckless and unfeeling, a perfect evil in a cinema of few out-and-out horrors. Indeed, the colour Hammer Horror movies saw the end of the gothic movie and the birth of the multicoloured gore we endure today.

With *The Curse of Frankenstein*, Cushing would meet up

with a previous acquaintance, the now established character actor Patrick Troughton, who had crafted an impressive – more impressive than Cushing – career on television.

In 1958, cinema history was made with Hammer's *Dracula*. This was Christopher Lee's first outing as the prince of darkness and his performance left audiences shocked into submission. Cushing, alongside his friend, played Professor Van Helsing (a role future Doctor Colin Baker would also play) and set the Hammer industry on fire. 1959 saw Cushing play his fictional hero Sherlock Holmes in a lavish interpretation of Sir Arthur Conan Doyle's masterpiece *The Hound of the Baskervilles*. Cushing and Lee would never need to play another role again, twinned as horror icons forever afterwards. But over the next ten years, Cushing – nicknamed 'props' because of his use of a variety of props in his various roles – typecast himself into Hammer Horror-type roles, with several exceptions, two of note being almost back to back in 1965 and 1966 respectively: *Doctor Who and the Daleks* and *Daleks' Invasion Earth: 2150 AD*.

With William Hartnell unable to take on the role, Cushing played the grandfather figure in these full-colour children's movies based upon the still young hit TV series.

Unfortunately, these movies haven't stood the test of time too well. With too many hammed comedic scenes, the movies are pale counterparts – although more expensive – in comparison to the earlier black and white TV versions. Yes, children did get to see the Daleks in colour, but this wasn't ground-breaking stuff. It targeted the very young side of the *Doctor Who* audience, while the ten-year-old-plus side still had to get their kicks from the likes of *The Day the Earth Stood Still* and *Destination Moon*, absolute classics but not *Doctor Who*.

Although a third film was discussed, it never came to fruition. Notable performances from the *Doctor Who* movies are few and far between. Perhaps Bernard Cribbins as policeman Tom is an exception to the rule as far as a quality performance is concerned, but even he would upstage himself in terms of *Doctor Who*, when he joined the regular cast in the new millennium alongside David Tennant's Doctor for the odd hair-raising adventure.

Cushing is not a convincing Doctor by any stretch of the imagination. His white wig and obviously fake moustache set him up as an unfunny and decrepit Groucho Marx, let alone *Doctor Who*. Little wonder then that it would be 30-odd years before a third *Doctor Who* movie was attempted.

In 1970, Cushing's world fell apart when his wife Helen died. He was so emotionally destroyed by her passing he contemplated suicide, as actor and friend Christopher Lee has substantiated. Some years later, on a special edition of *Jim'll Fix It*, Cushing was 'fixed' when a rose was named after his beloved wife, the Helen Cushing.

In 1976, Cushing played another ageing professor in the children's favourite *At the Earth's Core*. The reason why this is significant is because his make-up for the part is not dissimilar to that he wore as the Doctor in the two *Doctor Who* movies ten years previously.

The following year saw Cushing reach another milestone in his acting career, taking fourth-place billing, above Alec Guinness but behind Mark Hamill, Harrison Ford and Carrie Fisher, in the first ever *Star Wars* film.

Playing the evil dictator Grand Moff Tarkin, Cushing would again immortalise himself in cinema history. Indeed, after his death on 11 August 1994, he would appear alongside Christopher Lee once again, albeit cut and pasted from old film stock, in yet another *Star Wars* movie, such was the importance of his role.

Although *Doctor Who* did very little to influence, effect or win extra plaudits for Peter Cushing, it is interesting how his career followed a similar path as to that of the first two *Doctor Who* actors, playing in theatre, TV and cinema, having his first film role given to him by Olivier – a film in which no less a figure than Patrick Troughton would appear – and being cast in horror, fantasy and adventure movies his whole career.

Although *Doctor Who* fans have a special place in their hearts for Peter Cushing, Cushing's career overshadows his small flirtation with the show. As Christopher Lee later said, 'He should have been knighted years ago.' And maybe he was right. To this day, Peter Cushing is an instantly recognised face in British cinema history and is both respected and renowned the world over for his major influence in the *Star Wars* franchise if nothing else. His final screen appearances were with his best friend Christopher Lee in a TV series about the making of the Hammer Horror movies. Christopher Lee sums up his friendship quite succinctly: 'He was greatly loved, which is a rare thing nowadays. I respected him immensely as an actor... We shared a lot of laughter on and off set, from the day I first met him to the very last.'

There are few true friends one makes throughout life and Peter was one of them to Christopher Lee: 'If anyone had overheard our telephone conversations they wouldn't have believed that it was us two talking. There's nobody alive today with whom I can share certain things – phrases, words, telephone conversations, clippings from newspapers. He's gone. And of course Vincent [Price] is gone.

'It's difficult to explain, but Peter could send me a clipping

– I could send him a clipping – and without putting a letter to it we would know what the other one meant. Now all that's gone forever in my life.

'But you know, he wanted to die from 1970 onwards. When his wife died. She was his entire world. The only thing that kept him going after that was the work. He buried himself completely in his work.'

Peter Cushing is 'The Forgotten Doctor' today because his is the only career that has overshadowed the work he did as the great Time Lord. It was an insignificant moment in comparison.

'It was no surprise to me to learn that the first *Doctor Who* film came into the top twenty box-office hits last year, despite the panning the critics gave it… a lot of people have accused me of lowering my standards in some of the pictures I've done, but I've never felt I'm wasting myself. You have to have a great ego to want to play *Hamlet* all the time and I just haven't got that ego.'

Peter Cushing

CHAPTER ELEVEN
THE ONES THAT GOT AWAY

"'Farewell maister Doctor, yet ere you goe...'"

The Tragical History of Doctor Faustus
Christopher Marlowe

TREVOR MARTIN AND David Banks are also forgotten Doctor Whos, having played the part only on stage. Martin played the Doctor in *Doctor Who and the Daleks – Seven Keys to Doomsday*, at the Adelphi Theatre, London, in 1974. Producers didn't want to cast either outgoing Jon Pertwee or incoming Tom Baker in the role, opting for Martin who had played a Time Lord before in Patrick Troughton's last adventure 'The War Games' (he was one of the three Time Lords who sentenced the Doctor to exile on Earth).

Seven Keys to Doomsday was well received by reviewers but parents were worried about a real-life doomsday. With IRA bombs disrupting London life, the show was not well attended. Concerned parents cancelled bookings and the show was taken off after only four weeks. Trevor Martin didn't really get the opportunity for the role to have much effect on his career. He has signed some prints for a *Doctor Who* shop and appears in non-fiction books like this one, albeit briefly, but *Doctor Who* was little more than an interesting aside in his career.

Also, when one looks at photographs from the production today, he is a dressed like William Hartnell with similarly swept-back hair, the only addition being a huge clown-like bow tie, which was less than endearing.

Wendy Padbury starred alongside Martin (companion Zoe to Patrick Troughton's Doctor), and with a script penned by Terrance Dicks, the show certainly had some pluses, but it simply wasn't given a chance due to poor audience levels.

David Banks understudied the role of the Doctor and played him twice during Jon Pertwee's run in *Doctor Who – The Ultimate Adventure* in the late 80s. He didn't get a look in when Colin Baker took over the stage show from Pertwee, but at least the production was much more successful than the *Seven Keys to Doomsday*.

David Banks is probably best known to *Doctor Who* fans as the ultimate voice of the Cybermen, from Peter Davison's 'Earthshock' to Colin Baker's 'Attack of the Cybermen'. In that regard, Banks is one of the show's unsung heroes. His own book about the Cybermen, called simply *Doctor Who – Cybermen*, is a fond favourite with fans of the show, a first-edition hardback commanding a respectable £25–£35 on the collectors' market in nice condition, with signed copies being offered for at least double that. As a theatre Doctor and not just one of the great Cybermen, Banks's place in *Doctor Who* mythology is firmly secured.

Perhaps the other uncredited Doctor is Richard Hurndall. Hurndall played William Hartnell's Doctor in the 20th anniversary TV special 'The Five Doctors'. Although a short life on screen, Hurndall's Doctor is a non-Doctor in the respect that it's an interpretation of a previous Doctor (William Hartnell), not a new one. So, perhaps along with Martin and Banks, Hurndall is a Doctor in limbo, somebody who took on the part as somebody else's Doctor but is largely unappreciated in the broad canon of their careers.

That said, one could argue that Peter Cushing could fall into this category as well. Was he the first actor to 'cover' the first Doctor? Indeed, he had a granddaughter and was a grandfather figure in the film. In that respect alone, the interpretations of Hartnell's Doctor – three if we include Trevor Martin's likeness in costume and hairstyle – makes him the most copied Doctor and, therefore, perhaps the definitive Doctor. At the very least, his indelible performance still strikes a chord throughout the show's 50-year journey, and that's impressive.

So there are four forgotten Doctors, men who took on the role but do not fit into the mythology of the show. They are not one of the 11 named actors, they are the ones that got away but, as far as I'm concerned, still worthy of mention here. One can split hairs and discuss TV comedy and charity stints from other actors, but I won't be drawn into that. This book is about the men who *really* played Doctor Who, those on TV, film and stage, and this chapter is just a gentle reminder of some of those who may escape our attention.

CHAPTER TWELVE
CHRISTOPHER ECCLESTON

'What a piece of work is man.'

Hamlet
William Shakespeare

CHRISTOPHER ECCLESTON AND Billie Piper are responsible for bringing *Doctor Who* back in the new millennium and making it a household name all over again.

It seems, in retrospect, that Eccleston was given a hard time for not sticking to the show longer than an introductory year. Rumour has it that he only signed a one-year contract, but it is clear that he would have been offered a renewal due to the popularity of the show. Indeed, he told *Doctor Who Monthly* that he emailed Russell T Davies upon hearing that the show was making a comeback, and he wanted to be considered for the main role because of Davies's involvement. But what happened during that first year for him to suddenly change his mind? It surely wasn't the pressure of work; Eccleston was an experienced actor. What it could have been was a slight fear of the love, adoration and total euphoria of the legions of *Doctor Who* fans. Eccleston wasn't a SF fan; he was a level-headed Northerner who played football and hung out with the lads while growing up. He didn't know about the intensity of anoraks, especially those interested in *Doctor Who* and particularly those fans – both new and old – who would be overwhelmed by the show's reinvention and his interpretation of the Doctor.

Eccleston has been given a hard time by the fans who consider him a 'lightweight' (a phrase used by one of the ex-Doctors in my presence on hearing that Eccleston had quit) for leaving without much of an explanation. His track record was impressive and he certainly had enough quality work behind him not to be swallowed up and typecast by the show.

There was an element of Jon Pertwee about his interpretation of the lead role: he could be deadly serious, he could get angry, but he could also be warm-hearted and amusing. Eccleston brought the action back into the show; something I'm sure Paul McGann would have done if given the chance.

Eccleston's Doctor provided a blueprint that David Tennant would build upon. He introduced the programme to a whole new generation. Yes, those children would shout 'Exterminate' in the playground, but they would also chant 'Mummmmmmyyyy, are you my mummy?'

Older fans still enjoyed the programme too. What really worked for them was the faithful blue police box – the Tardis. A more sinister, but the same old, theme tune, and, most of all, the Time Lord with two hearts and more love and compassion for the human race than any other alien in SF history.

Again, like Pertwee, many of Eccleston's stories centred around the Earth, but, unlike Pertwee, Eccleston had to deal with modern girls and modern families, resulting in more than one amusing 'domestic' incident. So was the Doctor romantically linked again? The Doctor actually dances with Rose Tyler (Billie Piper) and we appreciate that she is in love with him, but that love is, as ever, strained and unfulfilled. It's Jo Grant all over again, but this time the Doctor doesn't drive off in Bessie. He stands his ground, he lets the relationship move on until, during David Tennant's Doctor, he loses her and has his heart – or hearts – broken by their parting ('The Parting of the Ways').

There has been much to learn about the Doctor emotionally since the programme came back. The return of Sarah Jane Smith (during the Tennant era) was a bitter-sweet moment. She admitted that she had been in love with him and waited for his return. She tells him that she thought he had died, and he delivers the killer blow, saying that he had lived, but everybody else had died. And there lies the rub, the doomed romantic that is the Doctor, the Time Lord who wants a relationship with a human woman but knows it can't happen, knows that it wouldn't last long, because she wouldn't live as long as him (echoes of *Highlander* here). And so it seems the Doctor simply breaks the hearts of many an adventurous woman on his travels. It is part of his curse. So suddenly we understand more about him emotionally; in fact, more than we came to realise throughout the whole of the original series. Put the CGI and other great things about the new show to one side, and look at the emotions that have streamed out of the Tardis doors since its comeback.

The Doctor has disciples nowadays, a group of eclectic companions who follow him religiously. It's not just the odd companion that comes and goes; it's a group of people who come in and out of his life to join his clan, to dance to his merry tune. The Doctor is still the Pied Piper, his cave – the Tardis into which no one apart from the initiated can follow – is still the land of magical dreams. When Eccleston poked his head back out of the Tardis door at the end of the first episode and asked Rose Tyler if she was coming with him, she instantly ran straight in, so powerful was the Doctor's charm. So let us not forget that it was Christopher Eccleston who started the ball rolling with all this depth within the new-look series. A lot of ladies swooned with such a dishy Doctor at the helm of the Tardis, just as they would again when Tennant did his four years.

But with only one solitary year as the Doctor, did the show have any impact on Eccleston's career or him personally? Possibly not. He found work immediately after *Doctor Who* and with equal plaudits. Christopher Eccleston is a jobbing actor and one who will turn his hand to a wide variety of roles. Where his predecessor would find it difficult to let go, he didn't. He was cold enough to stand back and say, 'I've done enough.' So how did it all start for Eccleston, and how has his career developed over the years?

Christopher Eccleston was born on 16 February 1964 in Little Hulton, near Salford, Lancashire. He was educated at Salford Technical College and, by his own admission, was not a model student, being too much in love with Manchester United Football Club and television to take his studies seriously. In short, Eccleston was a working-class boy with working-class dreams.

At the age of 19, he had to make a decision: either continue with the football, which he wasn't exactly brilliant at, or take his acting seriously.

Inspired by *The Boys from the Blackstuff*, Eccleston went to train at the Central School of Speech and Drama. He wanted to pursue his love of gritty roles centred around the Midlands and North of England (*Kes, Saturday Night and Sunday Morning*). However, it was Shakespeare and Chekhov that he worked at first, the staple of any serious future acting career.

At the age of 25, Eccleston joined the Bristol Old Vic for *A Streetcar Named Desire*. This was perfect casting for him, and his confidence grew, and he went on to perform in several other plays around this time.

Like his *Doctor Who* predecessor Tom Baker, Eccleston found some periods of unemployment and worked on a building site to earn his money, but his big break did come. In 1991, he took the lead in the film *Let Him Have It*. Eccleston played Derek Bentley, a slow-witted guy who falls in with a group of small-time criminals. The film then takes on the true-life story of how Bentley was hanged (28 January 1953) for a crime he didn't commit. Bentley was held by a policeman after an abortive break-in and called out to his 16-year-old friend Chris Craig, 'Let him have it,' meaning surrender the gun Craig was carrying. Craig apparently read this statement the wrong way, believing that Bentley had asked him to kill the policeman, which he duly did. Craig was imprisoned while the unarmed 19-year-old Bentley was hanged.

Eccleston plays Bentley wonderfully, showcasing the young man's ordinariness and innocence against a society that had no time for him.

Shortly before being hanged, Bentley dictates a letter to his guard (Michael Elphick). Eccleston shows, through the despair of the character, how simple and inexperienced he really is. The guard knows this, praising Bentley for his letter, which the doomed man just manages to sign at the bottom.

Let Him Have It is a powerful and poignant story. Although Bentley has now been pardoned and indeed his whole case has had a radical influence on the British legal system, the film serves as a testament to the levels of influence and corruption there is in the criminal world and why hanging wasn't always

– or shouldn't have been – the answer (we can't bring the poor fellow back from the dead and say sorry).

Eccleston's next career highlight was *Shallow Grave* (1994). This was his first work with director Danny Boyle, his second being *28 Days Later*.

Shallow Grave would be Ewan McGregor's first film. Eccleston plays an accountant called David and the role shows clearly that he can be something other than rough and ready. It was a good 'growing' film for him as an actor. But there was better to come.

Later the same year, he took the part of Nicholas Hutchinson in the BBC drama *Our Friends in the North* (released 1996). Over nine weeks, Eccleston gave a performance second to none, working alongside Daniel Craig, Malcolm McDowell and Larry Lamb, in a landmark in 1990s television.

Our Friends in the North had the public divided. Some people thought the show was contrived and patronising, while others saw it as inspired and a pastiche of modern-day Britain. Perhaps the show was too honest, perhaps it hit home too much. Eccleston certainly believed in his part and played his extremist – egotistical – role to the hilt, which leaves a bitter taste and rightly so.

Hard-hitting roles suddenly became Eccleston's staple, none so impressive as his parts in *Hillsborough* (1996) and *The Second Coming* (2003).

Hillsborough is Jimmy McGovern with his heart on sleeve. Sometimes he can lose direction but not so here. Eccleston took his part well. You don't have to be a fan of Liverpool Football Club – or even a football fan – to feel the weight of the terrible tragedy that took place at Hillsborough in that FA Cup semi-final.

Hillsborough was proof – if proof were needed – that current tragedies could be dramatised without facing public outcry. There was a genuine need by society to understand what had happened at that football match and ensure that it never happened again. Eccleston likes being involved with high drama, and also with important dramas of real-life issues that shaped the society we live in today. *Let Him Have It* was the first time we saw this, *Hillsborough* a worthy second. After that dreadful match, fences were taken down at matches and crowds respected the decision, bringing a greater awareness and responsibility to the game of football – a game Eccleston once considered for a career. Yes, this dramatisation meant much to Eccleston and it clearly showed in his powerful performance.

In 2001, Eccleston appeared alongside Nicole Kidman in *The Others*. Directed by Alejandro Amenábar, this chilling ghost story of a mother-of-two's realisation that her house is haunted is both intriguing and captivating.

Grace (Kidman) has plenty of psychological baggage to bear inside her unsettling house, and the return of her husband (Eccleston) from the Second World War compounds that. Then she finds that her daughter Anne has been conversing with the dead.

The Others succeeds because of the unease and tension the director brings to the movie, with the aid of the key actors. The children's aversion to sunshine combined with the choice of lighting and colour bring an extra dimension to the film, even though the story is a tried and proven one.

The Second Coming (2003) was written by Russell T Davies, and by the end of the production he would appreciate Eccleston's abilities more fully.

Steven Baxter (Eccleston) comes to realise that he is the son of God and is full of the power of miracle. But is the modern world ready for him?

Shown over two episodes on ITV (after being turned down by Channel 4 and the BBC), it provided a rare taste of pure serial quality. *The Second Coming* is a perfect representation of how the modern world couldn't cope with the reality of Jesus Christ being something other than just part of an ancient faith.

So Eccleston approached Russell T Davies when he heard that he was to be the producer of *Doctor Who*. He wasn't a fan of the show himself but had seen it in passing while growing up. But it was Davies and the work they had achieved before *Doctor Who* that attracted Eccleston to the part and he played the Doctor for as long as any other serialisation; just for a one-off season. On taking the role of the Doctor, Eccleston explained (to Jonathan Ross) that the Doctor was known as 'a posh part' and that he was 'not going to be everybody's cup of tea'. He also explained to Ross that when he pictured the Doctor he saw Patrick Troughton (a Doctor favoured by Matt Smith). And also explained that Jon Pertwee and Tom Baker were the other two Doctors he was most aware of.

One could say that Eccleston had a bit of a chip on his shoulder regarding the 'posh' accent of the previous Doctors; indeed, he mentioned that a Mancunian now had the prime BBC slot – himself – while two Geordies had the prime ITV slot – Ant and Dec.

Eccleston's Doctor could handle himself. He looked the part. He was no longer a cosmic hobo, an eccentric professor, he was now a down-to-earth, no-nonsense fixer of hostile extra-terrestrial life, a kind of Jon Pertwee figure in street clothes.

His first story 'Rose' sees him battle against an old *Doctor Who* foe the Autons (Nestine Intelligence). Fast paced and filled with incident, it was the perfect introduction to the new-look show. Billie Piper, aka Rose Tyler, was the perfect modern girl to be the new *Doctor Who* companion, so suddenly the show was off on a brand-new rollercoaster.

Some viewers thought it amusing that the show had come back, and so successfully too. Some old fans were flabbergasted that the show was now considered 'cool' (or as certain children called it 'sick', meaning cool!), when it used to be strictly for anoraks. But it was well made, it had a quality budget, production team and, of course, a quality selection of regular actors. When John Barrowman turned up in 'The Empty Child', women swooned. With all tastes catered for through Eccleston, Piper and Barrowman, *Doctor Who* was suddenly sexy.

One of the great achievements of the new series was the self-contained story. In the old days, *Doctor Who* was made up of a set of 25-minute episodes (normally spread over a month – 4 episodes), but, nowadays, the stories were started and finished in no more than two 50-minute episodes (many being one episode long). The reason for this was explained by the show's producer – Davies – because essentially life was lived at a much faster pace in the new millennium, people were not prepared to wait four weeks to see a whole story. Life had moved on since the heady days of Tom Baker. Of course, Davies was right, but the season finale, which took in many recurring themes – some sub-themes – throughout the season, made for a strong and satisfying conclusion. The very fact that the Daleks were involved – many of them, in fact more than ever before – was an added thrill.

The season finale, 'Bad Wolf' and 'The Parting of the Ways', was a breathtaking piece of television. *Doctor Who* was getting five stars right across the board from critics and, when Rose Tyler is captured by the Daleks, and the Doctor – not unlike a chivalrous knight in shining armour – tells her that he is coming to get her amid a horde of Daleks, top viewing figures were achieved. Russell T Davies had pulled off the perfect comeback, the cast were household names, the show had completely regenerated into something quite new and special, but Christopher Eccleston had announced that it was time to go.

Virtually everyone was shocked.

After Eccleston had left *Doctor Who*, it was announced at the Cannes Film Festival that he was to star in a Linda La Plante-produced SF romantic comedy, *Double Life*. Directed by Joe Ahearne (who directed the actor in *Doctor Who*), one could have thought that Eccleston's career had changed direction from the gritty, earthy type to SF junky, but this wasn't true. Later in 2005, Eccleston appeared on stage at the Old Vic Theatre in London in the play *Night Sky*.

It was also announced on 20 December 2005 that Eccleston would star as Christopher Marlowe in Peter Whelan's *The School of Night*, but the production was cancelled on 6 January. This setback didn't deter Eccleston from the Elizabethan genre. In May 2006, he appeared as the narrator in the Lowry Theatre (Salford) production of *Romeo and Juliet*.

What is also worth mentioning here is the work Eccleston has done for actors with learning difficulties and his affection for his hometown. It is a side of him that he rarely flaunts, which is a shame as he is quite a misunderstood person in that respect. Indeed, his depth of feeling – as an actor and human being – made him the BBC Breakfast narrator of the tsunami disaster, for which he flew out to Indonesia to comment first hand on what was happening (December 2005).

From his hometown, Eccleston travelled back across the Atlantic to take part in *New Orleans, Mon Armour* (2008) and NBC's *Heroes*. He returned home to give an outstanding performance as rock genius John Lennon in the BBC4 film *Lennon Naked* (2010). Made as part of Fatherhood season, the film focused on how Lennon's childhood haunted his adulthood.

Eccleston instantly captivated his audience with perfect voice and mannerisms. Lennon's very public reunion with his father (played by Christopher Fairbank) showcases the anger Lennon felt towards him. The contradiction to all this was the way Lennon actually treated his own son. Although happy to castigate his own father, he couldn't see how, or wasn't prepared to do anything, to save his own son from the same hurt of a broken marriage and the scars of a fatherless youth.

Eccleston's portrayal of John Lennon was of a man so wrapped up in his own troubled mind – but rushed through life due to the popularity of his music – he couldn't see or discriminate the moral dilemmas of his life.

Lennon Naked was one of the very best interpretations of the icon of a generation that was John Lennon. The script was specific, the music was the original songs and there was even real footage of The Beatles to link the key moments in his life.

It appears that *Doctor Who* hasn't affected Eccleston's career in a bad way. If it has done anything, it has opened a previously closed door of SF, which now stands proudly open to provide a little respite from those more serious roles he undertakes.

But let us return to the reason why Eccleston left *Doctor Who*. In June 2010, Eccleston finally gave his reasons for leaving the show: 'I didn't enjoy the environment and the culture that we, the cast and crew, had to work in. I wasn't comfortable.'

This is explanation enough, as it exposes the very private – but very talented – actor that Eccleston is. John Barrowman implied in his books that David Tennant fitted into the family of Doctor Who more than Eccleston had. This isn't a criticism, it's a statement of fact. It takes nothing away from what was a fabulous performance from Eccleston, as he qualifies himself, '… the most important thing is that I did it, not that I left. I really feel that, because it kind of broke the mould and it helped to reinvent it. I'm very proud of it.'

The BBC released an apology for saying that Eccleston had found the series gruelling and feared being typecast, which indeed he didn't and wasn't. Christopher Eccleston's role as Doctor Who was courageous and important to the ongoing development of the show in the New Millennium and I for one thank him for that.

> 'I durst the great celestial battles tell,
> Hundred-hand Gyges, and had done it well.'
>
> *Elegia I*
>
> **Christopher Marlowe**

Above: Sylvester McCoy starred as the next Doctor. He is pictured here with his assistant Melanie (played by Bonnie Langford). © *Rex Features*

Inset: Promotional material for a 1988 production of *The Pied Piper* starring McCoy.

Below left: Paul McGann had only one outing as the famous Time Lord – in the 1996 film *Doctor Who – The Movie*. © *Rex Features*

Below right: McGann has had an extraordinarily and varied career so far. Perhaps his most celebrated role was alongside Richard E Grant in 1987's *Withnail and I*. © *Rex Features*

The forgotten Doctor, Peter Cushing. Although he played the Time Lord in two films in the 1960s (*above*), Cushing will always be remembered for his numerous roles in Hammer Horror films, such as 1959's *The Mummy* (*below*).

© *Rex Features*

Above left: Russell T Davies, the man behind the 2005 revival of Doctor Who.

Above right: In April 2011, fans were saddened to hear of the death of the actress Elisabeth Sladen, who played Sarah Jane Smith, one of the Doctor's longest serving and most popular companions.

Below: Sladen pictured at the 2009 Welsh BAFTAs with two other Doctor Who regulars: Bernard Cribbins and Catherine Tate. ©*Rex Features*

Above: Christopher Eccleston was cast as the Doctor for a new generation. He left after one season, much to the disappointment of many fans.   © *Rex Features*

Below: Pictured with Billie Piper – who played assistant Rose Tyler – during a break in filming in Cardiff in November, 2004.   © *Rex Features*

Above left: Scottish actor David Tennant was chosen to replace Eccleston in 2005. He was a phenomenal success in the role. *© Rex Features*

Above right: With Billie Piper in 2006… *© Rex Features*

Below left: …and Catherine Tate, who played the fiery Donna Noble.

© Rex Features

Below right: Sharing a joke with Freema Agyeman, who played medical student Martha Jones. *© Rex Features*

Above: Tennant at the BAFTA Cymru Film and Television Awards in 2007, where he won the Best Actor award for *Doctor Who*. He is pictured with Eve Myles, the Best Actress winner for her performance in the *Doctor Who* spin-off, *Torchwood*.
© Rex Features

Below left: Tennant in the title role of the Royal Shakespeare Company's 2008 production of *Hamlet*, with Patrick Stewart. It was while he was with the RSC that he announced his departure from *Doctor Who*.
© Rex Features

Below right: Promotional material from *Hamlet*.

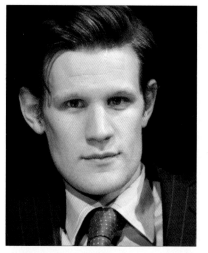

Above left: Matt Smith was chosen to play the Eleventh Doctor, the youngest actor to have ever played the Time Lord.

© *Rex Features*

Above right: Before stepping into the Tardis, Smith has acted in the West End production of *Swimming with Sharks*, which starred Christian Slater and Helen Baxendale.

Below: Although Tennant's shoes were big ones to fill, Smith proved an instant hit with fans.

© *Rex Features*

Matt Smith and Karen Gillan filming their first series of Doctor Who (*above*), and at a promotional event (*below*).   ©*Rex Features/Brian Aldrich*

CHAPTER THIRTEEN
DAVID
TENNANT

'Time travel is increasingly regarded as a menace. History is being polluted.'

Life, the Universe and Everything
Douglas Adams

DAVID TENNANT WAS born David John McDonald on 18 April 1971 in Bathgate, West Lothian. He grew up in Ralston, Renfrewshire. His father was Alexander 'Sandy' McDonald, the local Church of Scotland minister. David had two older siblings, one brother (Blair) and one sister (Karen), six and eight years his senior, respectively.

The young David attended Ralston Primary School and Paisley Grammar School, before earning a bachelor's degree from the Royal Scottish Academy of Music and Drama.

He always had aspirations to become an actor (from the age of three) and, not unlike many other children growing up in the 1970s, he wanted to be Doctor Who. He managed to meet Tom Baker in Glasgow, at a book signing, and his single-mindedness seemed to persist right through to the role he made his own – just like his multicoloured-scarf mentor – for a whole new generation after the show was relaunched in the new millennium.

When joining Equity, David found that he couldn't use his own name, as there was already an actor called David McDonald so, inspired by a writer at *Smash Hits* magazine and soon-to-be front man of pop group The Pet Shop Boys, he used the surname Tennant.

It wasn't long before Tennant started to get roles on Scottish TV, one of his most notable being an over-the-top transvestite barmaid in *Rab C Nesbitt*. From this unusual start, Tennant got noticed by the BBC and began to receive roles, albeit small ones to begin with.

Ever keen on the theatre, Tennant kept the pace by treading the boards alongside his TV and occasional film work. His energy and natural enthusiasm for his career shone through at all times and he became quite prolific. Years later, actors such as John Barrowman and Billie Piper would comment about Tennant's fun side, despite the hard workload on *Doctor Who*; this was sometimes discussed in comparison to Tennant's more serious predecessor Christopher Eccleston, which was a shame – and just a little unfair – as Eccleston was a different type of actor.

In 2000, Tennant appeared in the first episode of the new *Randall and Hopkirk (Deceased)*, alongside Vic Reeves, Bob Mortimer and Tom Baker. The episode was called 'Drop Dead' and Tennant played emotionally unwell character Gordon Stylus who even wears a wedding dress in the episode.

Tennant's next significant role was in *Foyle's War* (2002). He played Theo Howard in a story about an investigation into a young evacuee's death from a booby trap in a summerhouse, after a conscientious objector dies in his cell after losing his appeal at court. Two unrelated subjects they may appear to be, but a judge appears to be the catalyst for much of what went on.

Foyle's War was significant on a personal basis as well as professional, as actress Sophia Myles also appeared in Tennant's episode (who would later play Madame de Pompadour in the *Doctor Who* story 'The Girl in the Fireplace'). Although never in the same scene together, Tennant did catch up with the actress on set, and they started dating before playing alongside each other in *Doctor Who*.

Tennant's short films for the BBC, such as *Sweetnightgoodheart* (2001) and *Traffic Warden* (2004), showcased, in ten-minute bite-sized chunks, his capacity for comedy and farce, as well as his ability to play the romantic lead, anticipating *Casanova* (2005), his breakthrough TV role.

Casanova was the start of his journey to *Doctor Who*. Released in 2005, it was written by the man who would bring back the enigmatic Time Lord, Russell T Davies. The show was directed by Sheree Folkson and produced by Red Production Company for BBC Wales in association with Granada Television. The show was three episodes long and told the story of the flamboyant 18th-century Giacomo Casanova, based upon his 12-volume memoirs. The comedy drama also featured Peter O'Toole as the old Casanova, looking back over his life, and Matt Lucas.

The show's veracity and off-beat humour made it an unusual hit, showcasing Russell T Davies's talents and bringing him into a contract with Executive Producer Julie Gardner that would lead to *Doctor Who* that very same year.

Tennant's next role of note was *Harry Potter and the Goblet of Fire* (2005). It was in this film that we saw Tennant's darker side, perhaps anticipating traits in anger at least of his tragic *Hamlet* still four years away. Tennant played Barty Crouch Jnr, who is disguised as Professor Moody to begin with. He transforms from the professor to his normal self in a scene that appears much more painful than a Time Lord's regeneration. Crouch is a highly charged, sweating, delinquent, with no redeeming features. Tennant said of his role, 'It's fun to be a baddy. To do a bit of moustache twisting.' And he certainly played the role with passion.

Although his part was minor, there was a fair bit of Harry Potter name dropping in one *Doctor Who* episode 'The Shakespeare Code', where the Doctor admits to being a fan himself: 'Wait till you read book seven. I cried!' he said almost coyly. He then brought the episode finale to a climax by shouting out a Potter spell and saying 'Good old J K', as in J K Rowling.

Tennant adored his cameo in *Harry Potter and the Goblet of Fire*. He stated that he would never be in anything as big again. This wasn't exactly modesty, as Tennant was in awe of the size of the crowd at Leicester Square for the premiere, as he would be again for the premiere of the next movie *Harry Potter and the Order of the Phoenix*, where he stated that he now felt part of the Harry Potter family. But there was another family he was already a major part of.

In *Doctor Who* he did much running and jumping around, and if we look back at his humble beginnings as a TV actor, he was running around even then (see *Sweetnightgoodheart*). It's the adventurous, subtly romantic roles that seem to attract him and, in that way, he is a little typecast. Even his *Hamlet* was a bit of an aerobics exercise but a damn good one nevertheless.

Doctor Who was the right thing at the right time for Tennant. It enhanced his career by putting his talents firmly in the public eye, and he managed to do other work while still being the Doctor, in order to keep his career travelling in the right direction and not be bogged down by the Time Lord.

Tennant exploded on the scene as the Doctor. Although

undergoing a difficult regeneration, he manages to save the world yet again in his first story, 'The Christmas Invasion', albeit losing a hand in the process.

There was no lean period when Tennant took over the role. *Doctor Who* had only been on air for a year and people were still reeling from Eccleston's shock departure. Tennant was accepted and, from the moment that he told Rose Tyler's mother to be quiet, his popularity grew and grew!

Like Pertwee and Manning before them, Tennant and Piper truly got on, both on camera and off. Their friendship was obvious and something Piper mentioned herself in her autobiography *Growing Pains*. When John Barrowman joined the regular cast, the camaraderie became more intense and a special team started to form, including Piper's on-screen mother, father and estranged boyfriend. Put all that together with the return of Sarah Jane Smith and K9, and there was certainly a big and quite brilliant regular team working on the show.

During a break from *Doctor Who*, David appeared on Ainsley Harriott's *Ready Steady Cook* with his father Sandy (who took a non-speaking part as a footman in the Agatha Christie-inspired *Doctor Who* episode 'The Unicorn and the Wasp'). Their appearance on the long-running and popular cookery programme resulted in a great Scottish episode: haggis, with neeps and tatties became the order of the day for Sandy, with, of course, some quality Scotch broth. David's less adventurous chicken and rice won the day, however... perhaps because the audience was crammed with *Doctor Who* fans.

Naturally, Sandy got his own back throughout the show, talking about his son's formative years. There were a few interesting anecdotes from Sandy. It became clear that David had always wanted to be an actor, even taking the leading role in his very first school production, and then the divining moment when he took an important role in a TV anti-smoking advert.

Sandy had clearly thought about his selection of food for *Ready Steady Cook*. What he had selected were foods the 'poorer Scottish families' had to live upon in the past, and his love of his own country's culture was refreshing and interesting. The very fact that the money won on the show by David went to a hospice in Paisley (close to where he went to school) was the perfect end to a very endearing episode of the cookery programme.

Tennant knew by this time that *Doctor Who* had changed his life. Of course he was living a dream, his childhood dream. He even mentioned that the Cybermen would be back in his second season, along with K9. His natural enthusiasm for *Doctor Who* overshadowed his more fragile moments in the kitchen opposite his father. At one stage, the audience laughed at his best efforts, at which he declared, 'The audience are laughing at me!' But it was all done in good taste, and his dad was on hand to show who was the more competent cook, rather than best jobbing actor.

As Tennant's era as the Doctor continued, so did the plaudits. The transition from Eccleston to Tennant was seamless in as much as the quality continued. No one was on a learning curve. Stories such as 'Army of Ghosts' and 'Doomsday', which detailed the end of the Doctor and Rose's relationship, made way for more classics, such as 'The Shakespeare Code', 'The Family of Blood' (featuring Charles Dickens' great-great-grandson Harry Lloyd as Jeremy) and 'Planet of the Ood'.

Tennant embraced each story with relish. There's no

denying that he loved his four years as the Doctor. It's there in every performance. He lived the part, and his fellow actors, as well as the audience, picked up on that. Billie Piper described Tennant as 'David Ten-inch' with a laugh and a cuddle and John Barrowman (Captain Jack) spoke highly of him and his humour and companionship both on screen and off. It appeared that the good ship Tardis under the command of David Tennant was always in happy mode. John Simm (the Master) actually stated that part of the reason why he wanted to play the Master was to act alongside Tennant. High praise from the accomplished actor of *The Lakes* and *Life on Mars*; but he meant every word of it and 'The Sound of Drums'/'Last of the Time Lords' was one of the great stories of the new millennium *Doctor Who*.

But then again there was the story 'Blink', a masterpiece of gothic suspense that clearly showed you didn't need the Doctor in the show all the time!

Veteran actor Bernard Cribbins enjoyed his time reacquainted with the Doctor and the Tardis, going over the top in the space-gun scene in Tennant's very last story; and this concludes quite nicely the fun experienced by the actors in Tennant's era as the Doctor.

Along with *Ready Steady Cook*, Tennant appeared in another BBC2 show, *Who Do You Think You Are?* (27 September 2006). The programme explored both his Scottish and Northern Irish ancestry. Tennant's maternal great-great-grandfather, James Blair, was a prominent Ulster Unionist member of Derry City Council after the partition of Ireland. He was also a member of the Orange Order, which appeared not to sit well with Tennant, but he was fascinated by what he found out about his ancestors on the show.

When Tennant picked up the award for Outstanding Drama

Performance at the National Television Awards in October 2008, he also announced to an unsuspecting TV audience that he was to leave *Doctor Who*. There was an instant wail of disappointment from his many fans. But, perhaps, his way of dealing with his decision to depart was the right one. He didn't let rumours slip out, he spoke directly to camera – to the fans – by satellite link during the interval of the RSC's *Hamlet* and announced his departure and the reason why, giving them over a year to get used to the idea. It was the best and most noble thing to do.

Tennant adored playing the Doctor. On *The Graham Norton Show* (9 November 2009), he said that he enjoyed every minute of it, that he enjoyed getting up and going to work every day. He also explained that if he didn't leave now he would never leave and they would have to one day bring him out in a bath chair (which is almost the same thing as he said when making the original announcement of his departure at the television awards).

However, quitting the most successful show on television was a tough decision to make for Tennant. *Doctor Who* had been so incredibly popular during his reign and he didn't want the bubble to burst, for him or the show. Personally, he wanted to quit while he was in front and not have to face the day when he would say, 'Oh no, not Daleks again.'

It would appear that he did peak with his penultimate story 'The Waters of Mars', which broke viewing-figure history for a *Doctor Who* story in the United States. Also, Tennant's last story hit the 10 million mark in the UK over Christmas 2009 and on New Year's Day 2010.

Although bitterly disappointed, his fans accepted Tennant's decision to go. He had taken a few roles while playing the Doctor, including that of a man who recovers from a serious head injury in a road accident (*Recovery*, which I will discuss presently) and, of course, his stint in Stratford-upon-Avon playing, most notably, *Hamlet*, but he wanted to do much more. So he left.

Tennant returned to the real world with a bit of a crash. He found that – certainly in America – he had to audition again, which was something he didn't have to do in the UK while playing the Doctor. Indeed, the Doctor had his privileges and the BBC had been rightly criticised for picking the same actors for their programmes time and again. This didn't happen outside its protective bubble and Tennant knew and embraced this challenge.

Although filled with trepidation, Tennant made the brave step away from the show and, touch wood, so far, he has done well. Of course, he will always be the Doctor to a whole generation of *Doctor Who* fans, but, then again, the same thing applied to all his predecessors – and probably successors too! The last scene he filmed saw him hanging from a wire in front of a blue screen, not the emotional regeneration into Matt Smith's Doctor. He recalled in *Doctor Who Monthly* that, after his regeneration scene, he left the studio alone while Matt Smith continued filming. He went home and revised his lines for the following day. Such is an actor's lot.

When the final episode was completed, Tennant was given a box of *Doctor Who* goodies including his sonic screw-driver, something he considered so sentimental he refused to keep at home, as he feared burglary.

Being the Doctor was something Tennant adored and, like most of his predecessors, he quit while he was ahead; but he did face some bitter moments. While shooting the Christmas special 'Voyage of the Damned', his mother passed away. In an interview with *Doctor Who Monthly*, he admitted that, although the working day wasn't difficult, going home and learning lines on his own was 'trickier'. Surely an understatement from one of the celebrity patrons of the Association for International Cancer Research.

Tennant managed to fit in other work during short breaks in *Doctor Who*, probably the most important of which was *Recovery* (2007). He plays Alan Hamilton, a hard-working man with a loving family who is knocked over in the street by a van travelling at high speed. He suffers brain damage and the 90-minute TV drama documents his slow and painful recovery.

Sarah Parish plays Tennant's wife Tricia Hamilton in the drama, and she goes through every type of emotional rollercoaster as her husband fights to regain his mind, body, family and dignity. Tennant said of the story, 'You can't really imagine what it must be like to be married to somebody who becomes a different human being [through brain injury]', but that's indeed what happens in the drama. One minute Tennant's character is fine, the next he is playing with a woman's breasts at a party and not aware that he is doing anything wrong, to his wife's total shock and embarrassment.

Recovery showed Tennant as a serious character actor, not just a Doctor Who with lots of CGI behind him. Was that the way Tennant looked at it? No, probably not, but he knew he needed to play a variety of other roles in order to progress his career and continue to enhance his reputation as a quality actor. He was still quite young as an actor, with many years stretching out ahead of him in a variety of different roles, or so he would hope.

As we have seen throughout this book, especially with the first four Doctors. *Doctor Who* never goes away. In one shape or form, Tennant will return. He has already come back in a two-part story in *The Sarah Jane Adventures*, and there is talk once again about another *Doctor Who* movie, and no one is better placed to take on the role than Tennant. Once upon a time, Jon Pertwee talked about a *Doctor Who* movie, but the backers wanted an American actor to play the lead role, so time will tell.

So what about life after *Doctor Who* for now?

Even before his last episode was aired, Tennant had become the CBeebies *Bedroom Stories* reader over Christmas 2009 with five stories. More importantly, he was signed to star as Rex Alexander, a Chicago litigator who, following a panic attack, coaches clients to represent themselves in the NBC drama pilot *Rex is Not Your Lawyer*.

Christmas 2009 was a bumper one for David Tennant on the BBC. Not only was Part One of his final *Doctor Who* story aired, but he also took an amusing part in *Nan's Christmas Carol* (Catherine Tate) and then there was the BBC version of the RSC's *Hamlet*.

Including most of the original cast, the TV *Hamlet* was a lavish affair, with its spy cameras, two-way mirrors and exotic camera angles.

'How is it that the clouds still hang on you?' Patrick Stewart's first words to Tennant's Hamlet sum up the stark loneliness of the self-wounding prince we first meet. But then Hamlet denies his sorrow with passion, only to spill his bitter-torn heart on the floor when alone.

Tennant's Hamlet is full of emotion and a passionate, if not sometimes vicious, delivery. He brings out the child in the young prince. The way he embraces his good friend Horatio directly after his first soliloquy is childishly over-happy in comparison to the devastated prince-alone two heartbeats earlier.

The reason Tennant received rave reviews for his stage *Hamlet* in Stratford-upon-Avon was because *Doctor Who* fans suddenly saw what the actor was capable of and, like the critics, they were blown away.

It was right that the BBC showed *Hamlet* the same Christmas as Tennant's last *Doctor Who* story. It showed clearly that the show couldn't keep an actor of his calibre in the same suit forever. He was capable of so much more. And he needed stretching. *Love's Labour's Lost* was good, but a small role; *Hamlet* was an exceptional lead.

For me, the modern glitzy sets, suits and ties, stifle the performance. There is always a dark, depraved, starkness about the period *Hamlet*, and Tennant demanded this with a classical interpretation. In short, the modern look took something away from the period piece but not the performances.

While other actors seem happy to gently walk through their lines with polite perfection, Tennant painstakingly lived – and indeed thought through – every word.

Hamlet was Tennant's giant leap away from *Doctor Who*. It shouldn't have been too much of a surprise. For 15 years, Tennant trod the boards, appeared in a variety of TV character roles and indifferent film parts, but it was *Doctor Who* that made him a household name, and *Hamlet* – and possibly *Recovery* (2007) – took him forwards as a potentially great actor who was, once upon a time, Doctor Who, an actor the adult female audience would follow without question (an adult Pied Piper no less).

Work continued to come in 2010 for Tennant. He provided a voice in the film *How to Train Your Dragon* and was reunited with the *Casanova/Doctor Who* Red Production Company for a four-part TV serial *Single Father*, which he was more than delighted with. His performance was very strong and, at time, a little sinister, which surprised some fans who were used to his more upbeat roles – including the Doctor.

Although his *Doctor Who* Christmas specials were repeated around New Year, Tennant's profile was, as one might expect, not as high as it had been the year before. However, Tennant hit the headlines again on 4 January 2011 when he and girlfriend Georgina Moffett announced that they would marry in about a year's time. This news was not a big surprise to some *Doctor Who* fans, who knew that the couple had been dating seriously since they met on the show. It was great news and started the year off well, even though it was a little confusing: the Doctor was actually marrying the Doctor's daughter – could Time Lords do that? Marry the daughter of a previous incarnation? There was more good news: on 1 April the *Daily Mail* announced the birth of a daughter, Oliva, to Tennant and his fiancée. The couple were understandably overjoyed, but it didn't stop Tennant from working in 2011. He played Peter Vincent in the movie *Fright Night* and starred opposite the multitalented Catherine Tate in Shakespear's *Much Ado About Nothing* at London's Wyndham Theatre.

The popularity of *How to Train Your Dragon* was confirmed when it was nominated for the Oscar for Best Animated Film. Perhaps Tennant's most important role around this time was in *United*, which was broadcast on 24 April, Easter Sunday. It was a drama based on the 'Busby Babes', the legendary Manchester United squad that was the youngest side to ever win the football league, which was decimated in the tragic 1958 Munich air crash. As usual, Tennant played his role, Jimmy Murphy, with his heart on his sleeve. Some found that the scenes of the crash itself could have been clearer, but Tennant did well in showing Murphy's determination of getting Manchester United through the disaster and taking the team to the FA Cup final.

After *United* was aired, two adverts were shown: one

advertising a new drama with Christopher Eccleston, and another featuring John Simm, who had starred alongside Tennant in *Doctor Who* as The Master. It was a clear sign that all three actors had moved on for the show untarnished by his passionate claws. Nevertheless, the previous day Tennant took part in a special tribute to Elizabeth Sladen, who had died of cancer the previous Tuesday (19 April). So although he had moved on and the role of the Doctor was now in the hands of Matt Smith, the show was never that far away from Tennant's thoughts. In his moving tribute he said, 'I just can't believe that Liz is gone. She seemed invincible.' He went on to say that she 'enchanted' his childhood and adulthood as Sarah Jane, and sharing the Tardis with her was an honour.

2011 proved to be a sad year for *Doctor Who* fans. On 22 February they endured the death of another stalwart of the show, Nicholas Courtneym. Although 81 years-old and battling cancer for some time, the loss of the actor who had played alongside nearly all the Doctor's was a great loss to the *Doctor Who* family. Courtney was a popular man at conventions and signing sessions, and very quickly, dealers of *Doctor Who* merchandise sold out their signed photograph stock of his character, the ever faithful Brigadier Alistair Gordon Lethbridge-Stewart. It was a great shame that both Sladen and Courtney couldn't survive to celebrate the 50th Anniversary of the show in 2013, but at the very least, they will be remembered and loved as a major part of the continuing success of the programme.

Tennant also embraced his Scottish roots in 2011, albeit by taking the part of an Englishman. He appeared in the movie *Decoy Bride*, which is set in his native land and also starred Kelly MacDonald and Alice Eve. The film tells the story of a famous woman who wants to marry her 'cute' boyfriend on a remote island in Scotland to avoid the paparazzi – but, of course, things don't always go to plan. It is a nicely made and heart warming movie.

So what of the young Matt Smith, the actor who was set to follow David Tennant as Doctor Who?

He certainly had a mountain to climb. He wasn't the sexy hero, so deadly serious and heroic; or so comic and reassuring. He was a 26-year-old actor with much less experience, but still with plenty of plaudits. The ladies who liked the 'eye candy' of David Tennant saw the 26-year-old Smith spit during his first scene in the Tardis – as it plunged towards Earth – and instantly dismissed him.

The Doctor was enigmatic. He didn't eat, drink, swear – or spit. Also, this chap looked a little geeky, or was he a little too Preppy?

Audiences were passing judgement before they even saw the man perform properly. It was as though the odd couple of minutes they saw of him in the Tardis as it plummeted to Earth were enough for them to know exactly what this Doctor was going to be like, and they didn't like it.

As *Doctor Who* has shown us over the years, you can write off an actor but you can't write off the character. No matter how good the last actor was, the Doctor – those essential ingredients – still existed and each actor had those ingredients firmly sown within him.

So, with some misgivings – from the fans' point of view – Matt Smith took over. The show moved on, David Tennant became history, and on 3 April 2010, with an awesome new opening sequence and music, a new executive producer and travelling companion, *Doctor Who*, the programme, not just the Doctor himself, regenerated into another entity entirely.

'There are more things in Heaven and Earth…'

Hamlet
William Shakespeare

CHAPTER FOURTEEN
MATT SMITH

"'… I wished him [Matt Smith] great success, and he left. As soon as he disappeared down the hall, I turned to the others in the office and said, 'I feel as if I just cheated on David [Tennant].'"

I Am What I Am

John Barrowman

PERHAPS ONE THING Matt Smith had going for him was the fact that, to all intents and purposes, he was an unknown actor and the youngest person ever, at 26, to play the Doctor. That said, he had to follow the most popular Doctor to date (according to *Dr Who Monthly* readers). So no pressure then!

As we can't hop forward in time to see how the show affects Smith's career as an actor, what we can do is analyse his immediate contribution to the show against his previous work and understand how seriously he – and the rest of the production team – took the new Doctor.

As far as the show was concerned, favourite aliens were brought back for Smith's first season as a kind of safety net. Fans young and old would at least tune in to see the Daleks, Silurians and Cybermen. And then there were the Weeping

Angels from one of the most popular episodes in the show's history 'Blink' (voted the second best story of all time by *Doctor Who Monthly* readers). Steven Moffat, creator of the Weeping Angels, was now executive producer, and the one thing he promised audiences was greater chills, not unlike the gothic days of former producer Philip Hinchcliffe (during Tom Baker's first seasons). It didn't quite work out that way. Smith's first season wasn't all chills and darkness; but it did have a feast of monsters in its two-part grand finale, which included Daleks, Cybermen, Sontarans and the promise of an appearance – but never seen – of old favourites the Draconians. These things would help the ratings if nothing else, but surely Matt Smith wasn't ruled out as a credible Doctor because of the success of David Tennant?

Of course not. The part is greater than the actors that have played it; but even Patrick Troughton thought no one could follow William Hartnell. And, of course, millions of fans thought no one could follow Tom Baker (and some still don't!); but actors do follow, and all of them have a blue police telephone box and a familiar theme tune. Along with two hearts and a fondness for red-headed human females – on *Jonathan Ross* in March 2010, when asked about Karen Gillan, Smith said, 'She's a ten' – there's always proof that life goes on after the death of a Doctor. So how did Matt Smith occupy his first 25 years on Earth and suddenly find himself at the controls of the Tardis to succeed David Tennant?

Matthew Robert Smith was born in Northampton on 28 October 1982. He attended Northampton School for Boys, where he became Head Boy.

Unlike many of his predecessors, acting wasn't his first love, it was football. Smith started out playing for his local team Northampton Town in their under 11s and under 12s squad.

He then progressed to Nottingham Forest and played in their under 12s, 13s and 14s. He finished his short football career playing for Leicester City's under 15s and 16s where he gave up due to a back injury.

While other people give up acting for a second career, Smith gave up football for an acting career. Having kept his hand in, he did well to fall into work. This was largely due to his drama teacher, who signed him up as the tenth juror in *Twelve Angry Men*. Smith said of his drama teacher, '[Mr Hardinham] encouraged me and I found it [acting] was something I enjoyed. I did an A Level in drama, without any particular aspirations at the time of becoming an actor.'

Smith then turned down the opportunity to go to a drama festival afterwards – something his drama teacher had arranged – but he was persuaded to join the National Youth Theatre in London.

His first role was in *Murder in the Cathedral* (2003), for which Lyn Gardner of the *Guardian* singled him out as giving '... an exceptionally mature performance as the Archbishop'.

The following year, he would play in *The Master and Margarita* and *Fresh Kills*, both of which would earn him plaudits, *Fresh Kills* being his first professional performance.

The National Youth Theatre's interpretation of *The Master and Margarita* ran from 23 August to 11 September 2004, and was adapted for the stage by David Rudkin at the Lyric Theatre, Hammersmith, and directed by John Hoggarth.

Smith was one of a 36-strong cast, and the production was three hours ten minutes in duration, which was overlong by anybody's standards. A handful of actors were highlighted for their performances, such as Tom Allen who played the sinister black magician Woland, supported by the 'seriously camp' Smith as Bassoon.

Smith played the 16-year-old Eddie in *Fresh Kills*, a gay-interest production, which *Variety* gave a rather poor review. Although Smith wasn't mentioned, the cast were accused of making 'heavy work' of the American working-class accents. Years later, Smith would adopt a Southern American accent for his narration of the audio book *The Runaway Train* (*Daily Telegraph*, 24 April 2010), which he did uncannily well.

On the Shore of the Wide World was a co-production by the National Theatre and the Royal Exchange Theatre, Manchester. At two hours 40 minutes, the company should have had plenty of time to convey the meaning of the piece, but audiences left a little baffled. *Variety* mentioned Smith once, saying that his character Paul Danzinger was 'crudely conceived'. Of course, not all reviews are good and Smith had to accept that, if you can't stand the heat, you should get out of the kitchen. But he didn't get out, and took the part of Lockwood in Alan Bennett's *The History Boys* at the Lyttelton Theatre, London.

The play, which focused on the lives of a group of bright young sixth-formers in a Northern school looking for a place at Oxford or Cambridge, was another long one (two hours and 45 minutes) but it was universally well received by theatregoers and critics alike.

Within the quality cast, Smith excelled, and it was no coincidence that later that year he landed his first TV role in *The Ruby in the Smoke*.

Smith co-starred alongside Billie Piper and, although a little scatter gun in its interpretation of Philip Pullman's original novel, the actors took their parts well, as they would the following year in *The Shadow in the North* and *The Secret Diary of a Call Girl* (Smith appearing in only one episode of the latter show).

It seemed that Smith worked very well with Piper, which is a little ironic considering that they missed each other in *Doctor Who*.

Smith's first West End role came in 2007 with *Swimming with Sharks*, acting alongside Christian Slater and Helen Baxendale at the Vaudeville Theatre, London. Smith took the part of Guy, personal assistant to devilish movie maker Buddy Ackerman, and received much praise.

He was shortlisted as an 'outstanding newcomer' in the *Evening Standard* Awards after his performance as Danny Foster in BBC2's political drama *Party Animals* (2007), which together with *Swimming with Sharks* really highlighted him as a young man with promise, and soon *Doctor Who* beckoned.

When Smith learned that he was to be David Tennant's replacement as the Doctor, he said that he paced around the room for three days. 'It does weird things to you,' he confessed in a promotional interview.

He went on to admit that keeping the whole thing a secret was extremely hard, and that he had to tell someone – his father – who was 'flabbergasted' and started to talk about Tom Baker! But his grandfather could remember even further back.

On the *Jonathan Ross* show (26 March 2010), Smith explained that he told his family that he was to be the new Doctor on Christmas Eve.

Just for a moment, imagine the joy of telling your parents that you've just landed the biggest part on television, that you will be immortalised in TV history. Put all the past behind you, those small roles, those character-building roles, those roles that were good and respected in the business – 'But now I'm Doctor Who.'

When the dust settled, Smith had about six months to build the character of his Doctor Who. A time he called 'empowering' (*The One Show*), when nobody knew the secret, not even an actress who asked him point blank what his next role would be.

Smith decided that he would 'be brave' with the part, and try to put as much enthusiasm into it as his predecessors. In fairness, there was no point in copying the very popular David Tennant, his Doctor had to be a complete break from what children had come to know as Doctor Who.

At the time of his promotional interview, Smith had only read two scripts but was incredibly excited about his future as the Doctor, not unlike those who had gone before him. He would later admit on *Jonathan Ross*, 'My Doctor becomes more assured as the series goes on'.

In one of Smith's first stories (Episode 6) 'Vampires of Venice', he pulls out what looks like an OAP bus pass that has a colour photo of William Hartnell on it. The moment lasts only a couple of seconds, but the true fan immediately picked up on it. The message was clear: the legacy was there, the show went on.

Doctor Who producer Steven Moffat took great care with the build of the new Doctor character, spending the first third of the opening story 'The Eleventh Hour', introducing his character and that of his companion Amelia 'Amy' Pond. The first episode was one hour long as a consequence, but Moffat's decision was vindicated when the *Daily Mail* reported that eight million people had watched it, making Smith an instant success.

It quickly became apparent that Smith liked spitting; he had done this as soon as he was regenerated from David Tennant's Doctor and now he was trying a variety of foods in his first story to see what he liked. After spitting most of it out, he settled for fish fingers dipped in custard. This was probably to suggest that regeneration gave a Time Lord cravings like a pregnant Earth woman!

Once Smith had won over the little girl serving him his fish fingers in custard – and over 35 per cent of the watching population – a fast-paced episode ensued and suddenly everyone was captivated by the new Doctor.

But the second episode didn't meet with as much praise from the fans' point of view. Although the reviewers were keen to give the show four or five stars, the story – what there was of one – confused most of the audience; but that was soon sorted by the third episode: the Daleks were back (God bless Terry Nation and the neurosis of Tony Hancock!), but this time the Daleks were making the tea and working for Winston Churchill.

The Doctor isn't fooled by their tricks and exposes the Daleks' mothership on the dark side of the moon. Suddenly, all hell breaks loose and Spitfires travel into outer space to attack the ship in a *Star Wars IV – A New Hope* type of way.

At the end of the story, a new-look Dalek is created and they escape to fight another day. A sinister crack on the wall appears throughout these early episodes to promise a grand finale of some substance. But for the moment it wasn't just the Spitfire attack that was evocative of the X-Wing fighter attack on the Death Star. Back in Smith's second episode, there was a chute that left them in an 'underground sewer' – a creature's mouth – but more than one fan made a connection to *Star Wars*, and then there was a further moment that mirrored – to many – Princess Leia's message inside R2D2 'Help me Obi-wan, you're my only hope'.

It was only when the Weeping Angels returned in their own

two-episode story that Smith truly arrived as the Doctor, emanating the dress and style of the first three Doctors. Yes he was – or rather is – a throwback to the old-style Doctor Who.

So much was expected of Matt Smith's Doctor, and the show was battered with so much criticism by the general public – not the critics! – it was almost as though they were in denial at the end of David Tennant's period as the Doctor, but Smith weathered the storm.

Smith's character is certainly more erratic than the others since the relaunch of the show, basing part of his character on Patrick Troughton's interpretation of the Doctor; but, as Smith revealed on *The One Show* (1 April 2010), he had based part of his character on Einstein too, building in a wacky eccentricity not uncommon to any great professor. It was also on *The One Show* that he apologised to 'six million viewers' for saying 'crap'. He was probably forgiven by most, due to the excitement felt for his first episode less than two days later (6.20pm, 3 April 2010) – D-Day indeed, when millions of children went to bed fearing the crack in the bedroom wall, even if there was no crack there.

With a new Tardis interior, sonic screwdriver, companion and an excellent variation of the theme tune, the Doctor was back again to do battle with the evil of the universe. With Moffat as the new producer, the scare voltage would be put up a notch, because that was what he did best. And the very fact that Matt Smith instantly made a success of the part, especially with the younger viewers, was proof positive that the programme would continue – as Tom Baker once put it – to 'run and run and run'.

Although Smith did many interviews in the run-up to the new series, and even toured the country like a politician craving votes to a multitude of fans, he couldn't have planned better publicity than being arrested at the airport for carrying an offensive weapon.

The *Telegraph* reported on 31 March 2010 that Smith was stopped while passing security at Heathrow Airport en route to Belfast. The X-ray machine showed what looked like a weapon in Smith's pocket when in actual fact it was his sonic screwdriver. Smith normally kept it on his person so he could practise with it wherever he went and had broken four before his first episode had been screened!

Smith politely told airport staff that he was the Doctor but they didn't seem to understand until he showed them some promotional *Doctor Who* memorabilia.

Only the Doctor could get arrested at Heathrow for having a sonic screwdriver, something that simply *has* to be written into the show someday.

'I have a wonderful journey in front of me.'

Matt Smith

So how did Smith cope with his first season as Doctor Who? Simply, he let the audience make up their own minds. There was resistance to begin with, because David Tennant was so popular. But as the weeks went on and the stories unfolded – along with the unfolding sub-plot – hearts and minds were won over and, everybody realised, it was the same old Doctor.

Smith's interpretation was old school, or rather public school, but that was the eccentric character we were used to. The Doctor's companion, Amy Pond, wowed many a teenage boy – and probably his father too! – and had that feisty presence we had come to expect from the Doctor's companions. Matt Smith and Karen Gillan were a great team, and people began to appreciate that. Along with some great scripts, which brought back Silurians, Cybermen and Daleks (to name but a few), the show proved yet again that time moves on and that there's always somebody ready to take your place.

The new version of the theme tune and opening title sequence were all extremely impressive, and showed that new ideas as well as interpretations were the order of the day.

The show had its heart-pulling moments, such as Amy's death and that of her fiancé (in an earlier episode), but nothing compared to the moment when Vincent Van Gogh was brought forwards in time to see how much his paintings were truly appreciated by people the world over; in fact, Van Gogh played a very important role in the overall theme of Smith's first series, painting the destruction of the Tardis itself.

The season climax featuring the Pandora box with Centurion sentry was both complex and chilling, but it was unfortunate that the show's budget denied us the opportunity of meeting the Draconians once again. They were apparently part of the union of the Doctor's enemies, but the budget wasn't there for us to enjoy them all over again (a shame as they were Jon Pertwee's favourite monsters).

When all was said and done, Smith and Gillan had pulled it off. Yes, there were things that didn't quite work (the *Star Wars* elements) and perhaps Churchill could have been in it a little more, as a kind of Brigadier figure (why not have a whole Second World War series?). But there were some great episodes, such as 'Amy's Choice', 'The Hungry Earth', 'Cold Blood' and 'Vincent and the Doctor', which scored highly. There was humour too in the 'The Lodger', where the Doctor actually got to play football (and allowed Smith to show off his teenage skills). And then there was the season finale, with some Tennant-style chase scenes and future promises to keep.

On Christmas Eve 2010 Smith appeared on *The Graham Norton Show*. Compared to his interviews at the beginning of the year – before his first *Doctor Who* season had aired – he seemed much more relaxed. Fellow guests included the comedy duo Matt Lucas and David Walliams, and Lucas confessed that he was a big fan of *Doctor Who*, explaining that that was why Tom Baker did the voiceover for their popular series *Little Britain*.

Smith's first *Doctor Who* Christmas Special (which aired on Christmas Day at 6.00pm) was called 'A Christmas Carol' and featured a Scrooge-type character played by Michael Gambon. Some fans of Dickens pointed out that Gambon's character also resembled the chemist Redlaw in another Christmas novella by the celebrated author: the lesser-known *The Haunted Man and the Ghost's Bargain*. In the novella, Redshaw raises his hand against a child, an event that also occurred in the *Doctor Who* special. Overall, the special was fine Christmas Day fodder.

Matt Smith had quickly established himself as the Doctor (something confirmed in issue 929 of *The Big Issue*, Dec 20 2010-Jan 2 2011), and his audience eagerly awaited his second season in the spring. It started with a strong two-parter ('The Impossible Astronaut' and 'The Day of the Moon'). In it the Doctor is killed off almost immediately and his family of companions (including a pregnant Amy Pond) become the heroes of the show. 'A lot more happened in 1969 than anyone remembers,' the Doctor announces, as they travel back to the White House in April 1969 and meet President Richard Nixon. One could not fail to marvel at how much the show had changed since the year that man first walked on the moon: Patrick Troughton, Smith's main inspiration, was the Doctor; and the show was a series of black and white, 25 minute episodes with suspect special effects. In fact, it wasn't until the end of the 1969 season that it was revealed that the Doctor was a Time Lord. Then Troughton left the show to make way for Jon Pertwee and the beginning of *Doctor Who* in colour. Back then William Hartnell was finding it difficult to get work, Tom Baker was treading the boards with Olivier, and Colin Baker was just starting out.

The beginning of Matt Smith's second season on Easter Saturday 2011 was also tinged with sadness, as it was the very week that Elizabeth Sladen died. Before the episode began, the screen went black and, fittingly, a tribute to late actress was displayed. Smith had played alongside Sladen in two episodes of *The Sarah Jane Adventures* and, along with other members of the *Doctor Who* family, he had paid his respects throughout the week.

Viewing figures for Smith's second season were strong. With the first episodes shot on location in the US and Amy Pond doing a Kiera Knightly from *Pirates of the Caribbean*, it was suggested that the show was trying to impress our American cousins.

With the two part story *The Rebel Flesh/The Almost People* (episodes 5 and 6) the programme unintentionally had echos of a real-life tragedy: the Japanese tsunami. The Doctor and his companions rode a solar wind and found a secret establishment that was bleeding toxic waste (not unlike a nuclear reactor) after being hit by the interstellar tsunami. Of course fans knew that the storyline wasn't a direct parallel, but the comparison was a spooky one nonetheless.

At the beginning of 2011, Matt Smith appeared in the drama *Christopher and his Kind*, playing the lead role of homosexual author Christopher Isherwood. Toby Jones co-starred as Gerald Hamilton in the programme, which focused on Isherwood's formative years in 1930's Berlin. Like David

Tennant and Tom Baker before him, Smith had found time to take on other roles while playing the Doctor, something that would have been impossible in William Hartnell's day.

With the possible exception of Hartnell, the role of Doctor Who has not had an adverse effect on any of the actors who have taken the part. Nevertheless they will probably always be known as the Doctor, despite making other great characters – from Worzel Gummidge to Hamlet – their own.

'Now step I forth to whip hypocrisy.'

Love's Labour's Lost
William Shakespeare

CONCLUSION

'But lips where smiles went out and in –
There was no guessing his kith and kin!'

The Pied Piper of Hamelin
Robert Browning

A SHOW THAT endures over 50 years must have something magical – and sustainable – about it. *Doctor Who* doesn't have a cult following, it has a broad and diverse following. It is today, as it has always been, family entertainment and if the younger ones get scared the older ones will reassure. For generations of British TV audiences, *Doctor Who* was an integral part of growing up. A mysterious man – a Pied Piper – who you know very little about but follow religiously nonetheless.

The Pied Piper analogy is a strong one. Look at the Doctor's many companions: they follow him, care for him, dance with him – love him. But he is an isolationist. The boy who never grew up, the man who can only watch people grow old and die, can never really love. The Pied Piper, just as William Hartnell described himself while playing the Doctor, just as Patrick Troughton depicted the Time Lord, with pipe and all, just as Jon Pertwee described him, just as Colin Baker dressed, and the very role Sylvester McCoy performed on stage before taking on *Doctor Who* and bringing back that air of mystery. And what about Tom Baker's pied scarf? Television viewers dance to the merry tune, but is it a merry tune, or something more sinister? As Queen Victoria stated to Christopher Eccleston's Doctor, there is something evil about him – the Time Lord – and, perhaps, there is something evil about the Pied Piper too. Something echoed in *The Sarah Jane Adventures* when she confronted clowns and the Pied Piper himself. It's as though, in an acting sense, the Pied Piper wears the two faces of variety theatre, the happy and the sad, and can change quickly between the two; surely that sums up the Doctor and his tetchy mood swings.

In 'Black Orchid', a two-part Peter Davison story, the Doctor wears a harlequin suit and mask – very Pied Piper-esque – and evil adopts the same costume too. Yes, there is something sinister about the Doctor, something that makes the actor playing him a little superior. Maybe this was the 'twist' Sydney Newman was looking for when developing the character all those years ago. We seem – like in all good stories – to get more from less. The fact that we don't know certain aspects of a character's make-up allows our imaginations to run riot; and, when the critic is at odds with himself, the artist is in accord with himself (to misquote Oscar Wilde).

So the Pied Piper continues to dance his merry dance, with hordes of TV companions and generations of real-life children behind him, happy to dance and play, and continue the legend that is *Doctor Who* into his fifth decade, more popular and sophisticated now than he has ever been before. And yes, we follow the Piper into his cave – the Tardis –

because he promises a life of happiness and excitement, but is it always?

What happens when the tune stops? When the Piper puts down his pipe exhausted and the rock rolls back and those that danced have all disappeared? What lies beyond that rock? Is there a happy land where only children play? The child inside us all? Is that why adults continue to watch *Doctor Who*, to regain their youth, the youth locked away in the mountainside of maturity? Or is it the secret yearning of the human race to dream of wandering the stars in search of... what exactly? The question to the answer 'forty-two' perhaps? Or maybe the reassurance that life goes on after death?

Doctor Who will one day stop forever. The Doctor – like every mortal creature – will have to die, like the original actors who have played him: William Hartnell, Patrick Troughton, Jon Pertwee and Peter Cushing so far; actors with incredible careers surrounding that iconic part. The part they played for little over four years at the most; but a part that has endured and remained in public memory for decades after they ceased to be.

If one watches *Brighton Rock* now, they will note that William Hartnell was Doctor Who. If one watches *The Omen* they will note that Patrick Troughton was Doctor Who. If one watches *Worzel Gummidge*, it will again be noted that the brilliant Worzel was also Doctor Who. The actor – despite great roles – will always be pulled back to that brief period where the universe was his oyster and they could knock on any family door in the nation at teatime on a Saturday afternoon and be invited in. And there is the Pied Piper effect on adults. We tell children to never talk to strangers, to never take sweets from strangers, but if Tom Baker's Doctor offered you a jelly baby, would you take it? Conversely, if Christopher Eccleston's

Doctor threw open the Tardis door and asked, 'Coming with me?' would you run inside and let that stone slip back?

Of course you would. The uniqueness of the show makes it special, and makes the lead actors immortal for ever more; and that begs the question after all this time – is it the immortality of the character that gives immortality to the actors? Yes, perhaps it does. But the price of that immortality will always be that all their other work pales into insignificance in comparison. I sincerely hope that this book has addressed that injustice, because the careers of the Doctor Whos are vitally important to the historical make-up of British TV, cinema and radio.

Furthermore, *Doctor Who* is full of British eccentricity – even though it was conceived by a Canadian – and, while turning a stream of eclectic actors into TV legends, the Time Lord for the present continues his pioneering journey through time and space. And that's exactly where we want him: fighting the most evil creatures in the universe and making children's minds more fertile.

Amid the horrors of everyday life, children still need the Doctor, for he is their guardian angel, the theme music his piper's music, and once the music stops and the Tardis door opens... a happy land awaits. But the adults also dance into that land to do battle with the evils of the universe. The Doctor, unlike Robert Browning's brilliant poem, is for both young and old alike.

'And folks who put me in a passion,
May find me pipe to another fashion.'

The Pied Piper of Hamelin
Robert Browning

PART TWO

FILM, TV AND THEATRE HIGHLIGHTS

CHAPTER ONE
ACTORS' CREDITS

WHAT FOLLOWS IS a detailed guide to the work of the actors who have played Doctor Who. Although extensive, I do not claim this to be complete. I have checked official sources, including film archives, official websites of the actors involved and cross-referenced all that information with additional information (theatre programmes, handbills, DVD/video cast lists) in private collections. I believe the end result is a very good reflection of what each actor achieved in his career. It clearly shows how much of a career the actors had outside of *Doctor Who* and also the importance of those roles in British theatre, television and cinema history.

I haven't included every voice-over or narration as that would take things to ridiculous levels, but a small selection of the most important are highlighted, apart from advertisements, which are not documented at all. Also, when an actor has appeared in a series, I have tried to identify the names of individual episodes; those programmes where they are not listed I have not found individual episode titles for, so have left them out.

Some inconsistency was found regarding release dates for films, as the copyright date (year of filming is not necessarily the year of release) was quoted in many archives. That year was largely, but not necessarily, the year prior to release, so I had to make a judgement as to what year to document as a 'release date'. The UK title is used for individual films and/or its foreign title if a foreign film. Additionally, a more general US title is given, if it makes it clear that the film is a sequel.

I have tried to include as many radio shows as possible, especially for Jon Pertwee who did much work there, but the main thrust of this long chapter is film and TV.

Finally, I didn't include dates and locations for theatre appearances because a lot of early information – from the 1960s and before – doesn't exist, especially for touring companies and appearances in repertory theatre. So what you have here is a useful user guide that highlights, at a glance, the strong body of work each actor has outside of *Doctor Who*, thus completely fulfilling the remit of this book.

WILLIAM HARTNELL

FILMS

The Unwritten Law (1929).

School for Scandal (1930), Man of Mayfair (1931), Diamond Cut Diamond (1932), Say it with Music (1932), That Night in London (1932), Follow the Lady (1933), I'm an Explosive (1933), The Lure (1933), Seeing is Believing (1934), The Perfect Flaw (1934), Swinging the Lead (1935), While Parents Sleep (1935), Old Faithful (1935), The Guv'nor (1935), The

Shadow of Mike Emerald (1935), La Vie Parisienne (1935) [aka Parisian Life, 1936], Crimson Circle (1936), Nothing but Publicity (1936), Midnight at Madame Tussaud's (1936), Farewell Again (1937), They Drive by Night (1938), Too Dangerous to Live (1939), Murder Will Out (1939).

They Came by Night (1940)*, Freedom Radio (1941)*, Flying Fortress (1942), They Flew Alone (1942), Suspect Person (1942), Sabotage at Sea (1942), The Peterville Diamond (1942), The Goose Steps Out (1942), The Bells Go Down (1943), The Dark Tower (1943), Headline (1943), San Demetrio London (1943), The Way Ahead (1944), The Agitator (1945), Strawberry Roan (1945), Murder in Reverse (1945), Appointment with Crime (1946), Temptation Harbour (1947), Odd Man Out (1947), Brighton Rock (1947), Escape (1948), Now Barabbas was a Robber (1949), The Lost People (1949).

Double Confession (1950), The Dark Man (1951), The Magic Box (1951), The Ringer (1952), The Holly and the Ivy (1952), The Pickwick Papers (1952), Will Any Gentleman? (1953), Footsteps in the Fog (1955), Josephine and Men (1955), Doublecross (1956), Private's Progress (1956), Tons of Trouble (1956), Yangtse Incident: the Story of HMS Amethyst (1957), Hell Drivers (1957), The Hypnotist (1957), Dates with Disaster (1957), On the Run (1958), Carry On Sergeant (1958), Shake Hands with the Devil (1959), The Mouse that Roared (1959), The Night We Dropped a Clanger (1959), Strictly Confidential (1959), The Desperate Man (1959).

And the Same to You (1960), Jackpot (1960), Piccadilly Third Stop (1960), Tomorrow at Ten (1962), This Sporting Life

(1963), Heavens Above! (1963), To Have and to Hold (1963), The World Ten Times Over (1963), Tomorrow at Ten (1964).

*uncredited and unconfirmed.

PLAYS

The Merchant of Venice (1926), She Stoops to Conquer (1926), Julius Caesar (1926), As You Like It (1926), Hamlet (1926), The Tempest (1926), School for Scandal (1926), The Merchant of Venice (1926), Macbeth (1926), Good Morning, Bill (1927), Monsieur Beaucaire (1928), Hamlet (1928), School for Scandal (1928), The Merchant of Venice (1928), The Man Responsible (1928?), The Lad (1928?), Good Morning, Bill (1928), Miss Elizabeth's Prisoner (1928), A Bill of Divorcement (1928/9), 77 Park Lane (1929).

The Ugly Duchess (1930), The Man Who Changed His Name (1931), The Young Idea (1931), The Man I Killed (1932), Too Good to be True (1932), Just Married (1933), While Parents Sleep (1934), Behold We Live (1934), Good Morning, Bill (1934), The Brontës (1934), Eliza Comes to Stay (1934), Counsellor at Law (1934), Apron Strings (1934), Pursuit of Happiness (1934), Nothing but the Truth (1934), Indoor Fireworks (1934), Lord Richard in the Pantry (1935), Mr Faintheart (1935), The Maitlands (1935), It Pays to Advertise (1935), The Ghost Train (1935), Charley's Aunt (1935), White Cargo (1935), A Little Bit of Fluff (1935), The Ghost Train (1936), Someone at the Door (1937), Paganini (1937), Take it Easy (1937), Power & Glory (1938), Happy Returns (1938), The Second Man (1938/9?), Faithfully Yours (1939).

Nap Hand (1940), What Ann Brought Home (1940?), Brighton Rock (1943).

What Ann Brought Home (1950), Seagulls Over Sorrento (1950 and 1954), Treble Trouble [aka Home and Away] (1955), Ring for Cathy (1956).

The Cupboard (1961), Puss in Boots (1967), Brothers and Sisters (1968).

TV

Douglas Fairbanks Jnr Presents, 'The Auction', Season 3, Episode 28, 25 May 1955; London Playhouse ,'The Inward Eye', Season 1, Episode 7, 10 November 1955; The Errol Flynn Theatre, 'The Red Geranium', Season 1, Episode 13, 1955; The Army Game, Season 1, Episode 1, 19 June 1957, Season 2, Episode 3, 3 January 1958; Probation Officer, Season 1, Episode 28; The Flying Doctor, 'The Changing Plain' Season 1, Episode 9, 1959; Dial 999, 'The Killing Job', Season 1, Episode 1, 6 July 1958, '50,000 Hands', Season 1, Episode 16, 1959.

Kraft Mystery Theatre, 'The Desperate Men', Season 1, Episode 11, 23 August 1961; Ghost Squad, 'High Wire', Season 1, Episode 4, 30 September 1961; The Plane Makers, Season 1, Episode 15, 20 May 1963; The Edgar Wallace Mystery Theatre, 'To Have and to Hold', Season 4, Episode 9, July 1963; Tomorrow at Ten, 1964; No Hiding Place, 'The Game', Season 10, Episode 2, 23 March 1967; Softly Softly, 'Cause of Death', Season 3, Episode 13, 4 January 1968;

Crime of Passion, 'Alain', Season 1, Episode 6, 27 April 1970; Doctor Who, 'The Three Doctors', Season 10, Story 6 (4 Episodes, 30 December 1922, 6 January 1973, 13 January 1973, 20 January 1973).

WILLIAM HARTNELL'S DOCTOR WHO

Season 1
Pilot episode (1 episode), An Unearthly Child (The Tribe of Gum) (4 episodes total), The Daleks (7 episodes), The Edge of Destruction (2 episodes), Marco Polo (7 episodes), The Keys of Marinus (6 episodes), The Aztecs (4 episodes), The Sensorites (6 episodes), The Reign of Terror (6 episodes).

Season 2
Planet of the Giants (3 episodes), The Dalek Invasion of Earth (6 episodes), The Rescue (2 episodes), The Romans (4 episodes), The Web Planet (6 episodes), The Crusade (4 episodes), The Space Museum (4 episodes), The Chase (6 episodes), The Time Meddler (4 episodes).

Season 3
Galaxy 4 (4 episodes), Mission to the Unknown (one-off episode that doesn't feature the Doctor), The Myth Makers (4 episodes), The Dalek Master Plan (12 episodes), The Massacre of St Bartholomew's Eve (4 episodes), The Ark (4 episodes), The Celestial Toymaker (4 episodes), The Gunfighters (4 episodes), The Savages (4 episodes), The War Machine (4 episodes).

Season 4
The Smugglers (4 episodes), The Tenth Planet (4 episodes).

PATRICK TROUGHTON

FILMS

Escape (1948), Hamlet (1948), Badger's Green (1949), Cardboard Cavalier (1949).

Chance of a Lifetime (1950), Treasure Island (1950), Waterfront (1950), The Woman With No Name (1950), The Franchise Affair (1951), White Corridors (1951), The Black Knight (1954), Richard III (1955), The Curse of Frankenstein (1957), The Moonraker (1958).

The Phantom of the Opera (1962), Jason and the Argonauts (1963), The Gorgon (1964), The Black Torment (1964), The Viking Queen (1967).

Scars of Dracula (1970), Frankenstein and the Monster From Hell (1974), The Omen (1976), Sinbad and the Eye of the Tiger (1977).

THEATRE

After the Second World War, Patrick Troughton returned to the theatre. He spent time at the Amersham Repertory Company, the Bristol Old Vic and the Pilgrim Players at the Mercury Theatre Nottingham. Little is known about his various appearances. He did play Adolf Hitler on stage in *Eva Braun* and he appeared a couple of times with William Hartnell, apparently once as an understudy.

TV

Hamlet (1947), King Lear (1948), RUR (1948).

Kidnapped (1952) (5 episodes)
'The Brig Covenant', 'Red Fox', 'The Flight in the Heather', 'The Quarrel', 'Back to Shaws'.

Robin Hood (1953) (6 episodes)
'Gathering the Band', 'The Abbot of St Mary's', 'Who is Robin?', 'The Silver Arrow', 'A King Comes to Greenwood', 'The Secret'.

Misalliance (1954).

Clementina (1954) (6 episodes)
'For the Sake of a Throne', 'A Man Needs His Friends', The Night of the 27th', 'The Road to Italy', 'For Love of a Queen', 'The End of a Journey'.

The Scarlet Pimpernel (1956) (10 episodes)
'The Elusive Chauvelin', 'Something Remembered', 'The Sword of Justice', 'Sir Andrew's Fate', 'The Ambassador's Lady', 'The Christmas Present', 'The Flower Woman', 'The Imaginary Invalid', 'Antoine & Antoinette', 'A Tale of Two Pigtails'.

The Count of Monte Cristo (1956) (3 episodes)
'Marseilles', 'The Portuguese Affair', 'The Island'.

Kidnapped (1956), Lilli Palmer Theatre 'The End of Justice' (1956).

Sword of Freedom (1957) (4 episodes)
'Vespucci', 'The Tower', 'The School', 'The Ambassador'.

Assignment Foreign Legion (1 episode) 'The Conquering Hero' (1957), Precious Bane (1957) (6 episodes), The New Adventures of Charlie Chan (1 episode) (1958), Queen's Champion (1958), Ivanhoe (1 episode) 'The Kidnapping' (1958), The Rebel Heiress (1958), William Tell (1 episode) 'The Golden Wheel' (1958), The Flying Doctor (1 episode) 'A Stranger in Distress' (1959), Dial 999 (2 episodes) '50,000 Hands', 'Thames Division' (1959).

The Cabin in the Clearing (1959) (4 episodes)
'Friends and Foes', 'Ordeal By Fire', 'The Desperate Plan', 'The Break Out'.

The Scarf (3 episodes) (1959), The Naked Lady (1 episode) (1959), The Moonstone (1 episode) (1959), Interpol Calling (1 episode) 'The Thirteen Innocents' (1959), H G Wells' Invisible Man (1 episode) (1959), The History of Mr Polly (2 episodes) (1959), Three Green Nobles (1 episode) 'The Painter' (1959).

BBC Sunday Night Theatre (6 episodes) (1950–59)
'The Family Reunion' (1950), 'Adventure Story' (1950), 'Lines of Communication' (1952), 'Midsummer Fire' (1955), 'The White Falcon' (1956), 'Maigret and the Lost Life' (1959).

Law of the Plainsman (1 episode) 'The Matriarch' (1960).

The Splendid Spur (6 episodes) (1960)
'The King's Messenger', 'The Road to the West', 'Bristol

Keep', 'The Godsend', 'Joan of the Tor', 'The End of the Gleys'.

The Four Just Men (2 episodes) 'The Night of the Precious Stones', 'The Moment of Truth' (1959 and 1960).

The Adventures of Robin Hood (8 episodes) (1959–60)
'The Friar's Pilgrimage' (1956), 'The Dream' (1957), 'The Blackbird' (1957), 'The Shell Game' (1957), The Bandit of Brittany (1957), 'Food For Thought' (1957), Elixir of Youth (1958) 'The Bagpiper' (1960).

Paul of Tarsus (2 episodes) 'The Feast of Pentecost', 'To the Gentiles' (1960), Danger Man (2 episodes) 'The Lonely Chair', 'Bury the Dead' (1961 and 1962), International Detective (2 episodes) 'The Marion Case', 'The Martos Case' (1960 and 1961), Maigret (1 episode) 'Raise Your Right Hand' (1961), Compact (1 episode) 'Efficiency Expert' (1962).
Sir Francis Drake (3 episodes) (1961–62)
'Doctor Dee' (1961), 'Drake on Trial' (1962), 'The Bridge' (1962).

Wuthering Heights (1962).

BBC Sunday Night Play (2 episodes) (1960–62)
'Twentieth Century Theatre: The Insect Play' (1960), 'Sword of Vengeance' (1962).

Man of the World (1 episode) 'Death of a Conference' (1962), The Sword in the Web (1 episode) 'The Alibi' (1962), The Old Curiosity Shop (11 episodes) (1962–63), Lorna Doone (1 episode) 'A Summons to London' (1963), No Cloak – No

Dagger (1963), Espionage (1 episode) 'He Rises on Sunday and We on Monday' (1963), The Sentimental Agent (1 episode) 'The Scroll of Islam' (1963), Crane (1 episode) 'Man Without a Past' (1964), The Midnight Men (1 episode) 'The Man From Miditz' (1964), Detective (1 episode) 'The Loring Mystery' (1964), The Third Man (1 episode) 'A Question in Ice' (1964).

Smuggler's Bay (5 episodes) (1964)
'On the Beach', 'A Reward of Fifty Pounds', 'The Auction', 'In the Vault', 'A Death and a Discovery'.

Thorndyke (1 episode) 'The Old Lag' (1964), HMS Paradise (1 episode) 'Thar's Gold in Them Thar Holes' (1964), Artist's Notebooks (1 episode) 'William Hogarth (1697–1764)' (1964), The Indian Tales of Rudyard Kipling (1 episode) 'The Brokenhurst Divorce Case' (1964), Sherlock Holmes (1 episode) 'The Devil's Foot' (1964), The Wednesday Play (1 episode) 'And Did Those Feet?' (1965), A Tale of Two Cities (10 episodes) (1965).

No Hiding Place (4 episodes) (1959–65)
'The Stalag Story' (1959), 'Two Blind Mice' (1960), 'Process of Elimination' (1961), 'The Street' (1965).

David Copperfield (1 episode) 'The Long Journey' (1966), Armchair Theatre (1 episode) 'The Battersea Miracle' (1966).

ITV Play of the Week (3 episodes) (1962–63)
'Freedom in September' (1962), 'The Misunderstanding' (1965), 'The First Thunder' (1966).

The Saint (2 episodes) 'The Romantic Matron', 'Interlude in Venice' (1966), Adam Adamant Lives! (1 episode) 'D For Destruction' (1966).

Paul Temple (1 episode) 'Swan Song for Colonel Harp' (1970).

The Six Wives of Henry VIII (5 episodes) (1970)
'Catherine of Aragon', 'Anne Boleyn', 'Jane Seymour', 'Anne of Cleves', 'Catherine Howard'.

ITV Playhouse (1 episode) 'Don't Touch Him, He Might Resent It' (1970).

Dr Finlay's Casebook (7 episodes) (1962–70)
'Snap Diagnosis' (1962), 'A Test of Intelligence' (1964), 'The Doctor Cried' (1964), 'The Control Group' (1965), 'A Little Learning' (1965), 'Crusade' (1966), 'Dust' (1970).

Little Women (4 episodes) (1970), Doomwatch (1 episode) 'In the Dark' (1971), On the House (1 episode) 'The Secret Life of Charlie Cattermole' (1971), Thirty-Minute Theatre (2 episodes) 'Give the Clown His Supper', 'Jilly' (1965 and 1971), Out of the Unknown (1 episode) 'The Chopper' (1971), The Persuaders! (1 episode) 'The Old, the New, and the Deadly' (1971), Softly Softly (2 episodes) 'Best Out of Three', 'Better Than Doing Porridge' (1966 and 1971), The Goodies (1 episode) 'The Baddies' (1972).

A Family at War (9 episodes) (1970–72)
'Line in Battle' (1970), 'The Gate of the Year' (1970), 'The Breach in the Dyke' (1970), 'The War Office Regrets' (1970),

'Salute the Happy Morn' (1971), 'The Thing You Never Told Me' (1971), 'Take It On Trust' (1971), 'This Year, Next Year' (1971), '... Yielding Place to New' (1972).

Jason King (1 episode) 'That Isn't Me, It's Somebody Else' (1972), The Befrienders (1 episode) 'Fallen Star' (1972), The Protectors (1 episode) 'Brother Hood' (1972), Colditz (1 episode) 'The Traitor' (1972), Whoops Baghdad! (1 episode) 'Ali and the Thieves' (1973), Ego Hugo (1973), Hawkeye, the Pathfinder (5 episodes) (1973), Stars on Sunday (1 episode) 'Glories of Christmas' (1973), Special Branch (1 episode) 'Alien' (1974), Village Hall (1 episode) 'The Magic Sponge' (1974), Sutherland's Law (1 episode) 'Who Cares?' (1974), Jeannie: Lady Randolph Churchill (2 episodes) 'Lady Randolph', 'Recovery' (1974), Thriller (1 episode) 'The Devil's Web' (1975), Churchill's People (1 episode) 'Silver Giant, Wooden Dwarf' (1975).

Z Cars (4 episodes) (1964–75)
'Inside Job' (1964), 'Pressure of Work' (1973), 'Squatters' (1975), 'Eviction' (1975).

The Sweeney (1 episode) 'Hit and Run' (1975), Crown Court (2 episodes) 'Pot of Basil', 'Will the Real Robert Randell Please Stand Up' (1974 and 1975), Our Mutual Friend (1 episode) (1976), Survivors (1 episode) 'Parasite' (1976), Angels (1 episode) 'Decision' (1976), Lorna Doone (5 episodes) (1976), Warship (1 episode) 'Robertson Crusoe' (1977), Yanks Go Home (1 episode) 'The Name of the Game' (1977), Van der Valk (1 episode) 'Accidental' (1977), BBC2 Play of the Week (1 episode) 'The Sinking of HMS Victoria' (1977), Treasure Island (4 episodes) (1977), A Hitch in Time (1978), Space 1999 (1 episode) 'The Dorcans' (1978), The Feathered Serpent (12 episodes) (1976–78).

The Devil's Crown (4 episodes) (1978)
'Bolt From the Blue', 'The Flowers Are Silent', 'Tainted King', 'To the Devil They Go'.

Edward and Mrs Simpson (3 episodes) (1978)
'The Decision', 'Proposals', 'The Abdication'.

The Famous Five (1 episode) 'Five Run Away Together' (1979), The Onedin Line (1 episode) 'The Suitor' (1979), Suez 1956 (1979), All Creatures Great and Small (1 episode) 'Hair of the Dog' (1980), Only When I Laugh (1 episode) 'Where There is a Will' (1980).
Bognor (6 episodes) (1981)
'Unbecoming Habits: Part 1 – Collingdale's Dead', 'Unbecoming Habits: Part 2 – Balty Tom', 'Unbecoming Habits: Part 3 – The Cross Country Monk', 'Unbecoming Habits: Part 4 – Lord Dismiss Us', 'Unbecoming Habits: Part 5 – Keeping Up With the Jones', 'Unbecoming Habits: Part 6 – Making a Bog of It'.

John Diamond (1981), BBC2 Playhouse (1 episode) 'The Pigman's Protege' (1982).

Nanny (5 episodes) (1981–82)
'A Pinch of Dragon's Blood' (1981), 'Other Peoples' Babies' (1981), 'Ringtime' (1982), 'Ashes to Ashes' (1982), 'A Twist of Fate' (1982).

Shine on Harvey Moon (1 episode) 'The Course of True Love' (1982), Foxy Lady (2 episodes) (1982), The Cleopatras (1 episode) '100 BC' (1983), King's Royal (1982–83), Jury (1983), Dramarama (1 episode) 'The Young Person's Guide to Getting Their Ball Back' (1983).

Play For Today (4 episodes) (1976–83)
'Love Letters on Blue Paper' (1976), 'No Defence' (1980), 'PQ17' (1981), 'Reluctant Chickens' (1983).

Amy (1984), Minder (1 episode) 'Windows' (1984), Swallows and Amazons Forever! The Big Six (1984).

The Box of Delights (3 episodes) (1984)
'When the Wolves Were Running', 'Where Shall the Knighted Showman Go?', 'Leave Us Not Little, Nor Yet Dark'.

The Two Ronnies 1984 Christmas Special, Long Term Memory (1985).

The Two of Us (5 episodes) (1986)
'Proposals', 'Family Pressures', 'The Limit', 'Cracks in the Pavement', 'The End of the Beginning'.

Yesterday's Dreams (4 episodes) (1987), Inspector Morse 'The Dead of Jericho' (1987), Supergran (1 episode) 'Supergran and the Heir Apparent', Knights of God (13 episodes) (1987).

Note: Troughton played a sizable role in an 11-part adaptation of Evelyn Waugh's *Sword of Honour* on radio in 1974.

PATRICK TROUGHTON'S DOCTOR WHO

Season 4 (cont.)
The Power of the Daleks (6 episodes), The Highlanders (4 episodes), The Underwater Menace (4 episodes), The Moonbase (4 episodes), The Macra Terror (4 episodes),

The Faceless Ones (5 episodes), The Evil of the Daleks (7 episodes).

Season 5
The Tomb of the Cybermen (4 episodes), The Abominable Snowmen (6 episodes), The Ice Warriors (6 episodes), The Enemy of the World (6 episodes), The Web of Fear (6 episodes), Fury From the Deep (6 episodes), The Wheel in Space (6 episodes).

Season 6
The Dominators (5 episodes), The Mind Robber (5 episodes), The Invasion (8 episodes), The Krotons (4 episodes), The Seeds of Death (6 episodes), The Space Pirates (6 episodes), The War Games (10 episodes).

JON PERTWEE

FILMS

Dinner at the Ritz (1937), A Yank at Oxford (1938), A Young Man's Fancy (1939), The Four Just Men (1939).

Trouble in the Air (1948), A Piece of Cake (1948), William Comes to Town (1948), Murder at the Windmill (1949), Helter Skelter (1949), Dear Mr Prohack (1949), Miss Pilgrim's Progress (1949).

The Body Said No (1950), Mister Drake's Duck (1951), Will Any Gentleman...? (1953), The Gay Dog (1954), A Yank in

Ermine (1955), It's a Wonderful World (1956), Evans Abode (1956), The Ugly Duckling (1959).

Just Joe (1960), Not a Hope in Hell (1960), Nearly a Nasty Accident (1961), Ladies Who Do (1963), Carry On Cleo (1964), I've Gotta Horse (1965), Runaway Railway (1965), You Must Be Joking! (1965), Carry On Cowboy (1966), Carry On Screaming (1966), A Funny Thing Happened on the Way to the Forum (1966), Up in the Air (1969).
The House That Dripped Blood (1971), One of Our Dinosaurs is Missing (1975), Wombling Free (1977), Adventures of a Private Eye (1977), No.1 of the Secret Service (1977), The Water Babies (1978).

Deus ex Machina (1984), Do You Know the Milkyway? (1985).

Carry On Columbus (1992).

THEATRE

Twelfth Night (1935), Lady Precious Stream (1935), Love From A Stranger (1938), Candida (1938), Judgement Day, To Kill A Cat, Goodbye Mr Chips, Night Must Fall (1942), George and Margaret (1942), HMS Waterlogged (1944), Waterlogged Spa (1946), The Breadwinner, A Funny Thing Happened on the Way to the Forum (1963), There's A Girl in My Soup (1966), Oh Clarence, Irene, Super Ted (1985), Worzel Gummidge (1989), Dick Whittington (1989), Aladdin (1990–91) (1991–92), Scrooge – The Musical (1992–93) (1993–94), Who Is Jon Pertwee (1995).

TV

Toad of Toad Hall (1946).

Ivanhoe (1 episode) 'The Swindler' (1958).

The TV Lark (1963)
Note: this series came between Season Four and Season Five of the radio show *The Navy Lark* and consisted of the same crew (unlike the movie, which only included Leslie Phillips from the original cast). Only titles for the first seven of the ten episodes have been traced: 'Opening Night', 'Advertising Drive', 'The Party Political Broadcast', 'Back to Portsmouth', 'Serial Programming, 'The African Incident', 'Yours or MINE!!!'

A Slight Case of... (1 episode) 'The Enemy Within' (1965), Mother Goose (1965), The Avengers (1 episode) 'From Venus With Love' (1967), Beggar My Neighbour (1 episode) (Season 1) (1967), Jackanory (10 episodes) 'The Green Witch', 'The Talking Cat', 'The Enchanted Children', 'The Clock That Wasn't There', 'Who is Tom Tildrum?' (1966) 'Little Grey Rabbit's Washing Day', 'Little Grey Rabbit and the Weasel', 'Little Grey Rabbit Goes to the Sea', 'Little Grey Rabbit Makes Lace', 'Little Grey Rabbit's Birthday' (1967).

Whodunnit (1974–78), Four Against the Desert (1975), The Goodies (1 episode) 'Wacky Wales' (1975).

Worzel Gummidge (1979–81)
Series 1: Worzel's Washing Day, A Home Fit For Scarecrows, Aunt Sally, The Crowman, A Little Learning, Worzel Pays A Visit, The Scarecrow Hop.

Series 2: Worzel and Saucy Nancy, Worzel's Nephew, A Fishy Tale, The Trial of Worzel Gummidge, Very Good Worzel, Worzel in the Limelight, Fire Drill, The Scarecrow Wedding. Series 3: Moving On, Dolly Clothes-Peg, A Fair Old Pullover, Worzel the Brave, Worzel's Wager, Choir Practice, A Cup o' Tea and a Slice o' Cake.

Series 4: Muvver's Day, The Return of Dolly Clothes-Peg, The Jumble Sale, Worzel in Revolt, Will the Real Aunt Sally...?, The Golden Hind, Worzel's Birthday.

Super Ted (10 episodes) 'Super Ted and the Pearl Fishers', '... and the Inca Treasure' (1982), '... and the Train Robbers', '... at the Funfair', '... and the Giant Kites', '... and the Gold Mine', '... and the Stolen Rocket', '... and the Elephant's Graveyard', '... at Creepy Castle' (1983), '... Meets Father Christmas' (1984).

Worzel Gummidge Down Under (1987–89)
Season 1: As the Scarecrow Flies, The Sleeping Beauty, Full Employment, Worzel's Handicap, King of the Scarecrows, Two Heads Are Better Than One, Worzel to the Rescue, Salve Scarecrow, The Traveller Unmasked, A Friend in Need.

Season 2: Stage Struck, A Red Sky in T'Morning, Them Thar Hills, The Beauty Contest, Balbous Cauliflower, Weevily Swede, Elementary My Dear Worty, Dreams of Avarish, The Runaway Train, Aunt Sally RA, Wattle Hearthbrush, The Bestest Scarecrow.

The Further Adventures of Super Ted (1989), Virtual Murder (1 episode) 'A Torch For Silverado' (1992).

RADIO

Note: It is simply impossible to list with any accuracy the amount of radio appearances Jon Pertwee had during his career, from the odd guest appearance to the uncredited extras he provided. What follows is a listing of his major work.

Lillibulero (Ireland only), Marmaduke Brown, Young Widow Jones, Stella Dallas, Mediterranean Merry-Go-Round (1946), Up the Pole (1947–52), Waterlogged Spa (1948–50), Puffney Post Office (1950), Pertwee Goes Round the Bend, Pertwee's Progress.

The Navy Lark (1959–77)
Note: *The Navy Lark* spanned 18 years and 15 seasons, plus specials. Certain episodes have now been lost from the archive and anyone who can offer any help in tracing individual episodes should contact the BBC or The Navy Lark Appreciation Society. A basic guide to *The Navy Lark* follows: Season 1: 16 episodes (1959), Season 2: 27 episodes (1959–60), Season 3: 20 episodes (1960–61), Season 4: 26 episodes (1961–62) plus Christmas Special, Season 5: 6 episodes (1963), Season 6: 19 episodes (1963–64), Season 7: 13 episodes (1965) plus Christmas Special, Season 8: 13 episodes (1966), Season 9: 20 episodes (1967), Season 10: 18 episodes (1968–69), Season 11: 16 episodes (1969–70), Season 12: 11 episodes (1971), Season 13: 13 episodes (1972), Season 14: 13 episodes (1973), Season 15: 11 episodes (1975–76). A special final episode was broadcast in 1977.

Doctor Who Paradise of Death (1993), The Ghosts of N Space (1996).

JON PERTWEE'S DOCTOR WHO

Season 7
Spearhead From Space (4 episodes), Doctor Who and the Silurians (7 episodes), Ambassadors of Death (7 episodes), Inferno (7 episodes).

Season 8
Terror of the Autons (4 episodes), The Mind of Evil (6 episodes), The Claws of Axos (4 episodes), Colony in Space (6 episodes), The Daemons (5 episodes).

Season 9
Day of the Daleks (4 episodes), The Curse of Peladon (4 episodes), The Sea Devils (6 episodes), The Mutants (6 episodes), The Time Monster (6 episodes).

Season 10
The Three Doctors (4 episodes), Carnival of Monsters (4 episodes), Frontier in Space (6 episodes), The Planet of the Daleks (6 episodes), The Green Death (6 episodes).

Season 11
The Time Warrior (4 episodes), Invasion of the Dinosaurs (6 episodes), Death to the Daleks (4 episodes), Monster of Peladon (6 episodes), Planet of the Spiders (6 episodes).

Special: The Five Doctors (1983).

Note: Jon Pertwee played the Doctor in two BBC audio stories before his death. He was scheduled to take part in more.

TOM BAKER

Note: Although Tom Baker is the voice of *Little Britain*, I haven't listed everything he has provided his in-demand voice for.

FILMS

The Winter's Tale (1968).

Nicholas and Alexandra (1971), The Canterbury Tales (1972), Cari Genitori (aka Dear Parents) (1973), The Vault of Horror (1973), The Golden Voyage of Sinbad (1974), The Mutation (1974), The Author of Beltraffio (1974).

The Curse of King Tut's Tomb (1980), The Zany Adventures of Robin Hood (1984).

Dungeons & Dragons (2000), The Magic Roundabout (voice only) (2005).

THEATRE

The Winter's Tale (1966), Apple a Day (1967), Stand Still and Retreat Onwards (1967), Shop in the High Street (1967), Dial M for Murder (1967), The Reluctant Debutante (1967), Late Night Lowther (1967), A Bout in the Backyard (1968), Ardon of Faversham (1968), The Strongbox (1968), Hay Fever (1968), The Travails of Sancho Panza (1969).
The Merchant of Venice (1970),The Idiot (1970), A Woman

Killed With Kindness (1971), The Rules of the Game (1971), Troilus and Cressida (1972), The White Devil (1972), Don Juan (1872), Macbeth (1973), The Trials of Oscar Wilde (1974).

Treasure Island (1981), Feasting With Panthers (1981), Educating Rita (1982–83), Hedda Gabler (1982–83), She Stoops to Conquer (1984), The Mask of Moriarty (1985), An Inspector Calls (1987), The Musical Comedy Murders of the 1940s (1988).

Little Britain Live (voice only) (2006).

TV

Dixon of Dock Green (2 episodes) 'Number 13', 'The Attack' (1968), Z Cars: 'Hudson's Way' (Parts 1 & 2) (1968), George and the Dragon (1 episode) 'The 10:15 Train' (1968), Market in Honey Lane (1 episode) (1968), Thirty-Minute Theatre 'The Victims: Frontier' (1969).

Softly Softly 'Like Any Other Friday...' (1970), Jackanory 'The Iron Man' (1972), The Millionairess (1972), Arthur of the Britons (1 episode) 'Go Warily' (1973), Frankenstein: The True Story, Piccadilly Circus (1 episode) 'The Author of Beltraffio' (1977),The Book Tower (22 episodes) (1979).

The Hound of the Baskervilles (4 episodes) (1982), Jemima Shore Investigates: Dr Ziegler's Casebook (1983). The Passionate Pilgrim (1984), Remington Steele (1984), The Life and Loves of a She-Devil (1986), The Kenny Everett Television Show (1 episode) (1986), Roland Rat: The Series (1 episode) (1986), Blackadder II (1986).

The Silver Chair Chronicles of Narnia (Parts 1 & 2) (1990), Hyperland (1990), The Law Lord (1991), Selling Hitler (1991).

Cluedo (Season 3, 6 episodes) (1992):
'A-Haunting We Will Go', 'Scared to Death', 'Blackmail and the Fourth Estate', 'And Then There Were Nuns', 'Deadly Dowry'.

Doctor Who: Dimensions in Time (1993), The Diary of Jack the Ripper: Beyond Reasonable Doubt? (narrator) (1993), Medics (3 & 4 episodes) (1992–95), Have I Got News For You (guest) (1998).

Max Bear (voice only) (2000), The Canterbury Tales (1 episode) 'The Journey Back' (voice only) (2000),This is Your Life (2000), Alter Ego (2001), Top Ten TV Sci-Fi (2001), Fun at the Funeral Parlour (1 episode) 'The Jaws of Doom' (2001), Top Ten Comic Book Heroes (2002).

Randall & Hopkirk (Deceased) (2 Seasons, 10 episodes):
'Mental Disorder', 'The Best Years of Your Death', 'Paranoia', 'A Man Called Substance' (2000), 'Whatever Possessed You?', 'Revenge of the Bog People', 'O Happy Isle', 'Painkillers', 'Marshall and Snellgrove', 'The Glorious Butranekh' (2001).

Swiss Toni: Cars Don't Make You Fat (2003), Strange (1 episode, Season 7) 'Asmoth' (2003), Fort Boyard (2003), Monarch of the Glen (Series 6 & 7, 12 episodes), Britain's Fifty Great Comedy Sketches (2005), Little Britain (23 episodes) (narrator) (2003–06), The Wind in the Willows (2006), Miss Marple: Towards Zero (2007), The Beep (45 episodes) (narrator) (2003–06),The Dame Edna Treatment (Episode 4, Season 1) (2007), Little Britain in America (6 episodes) (narrator) (2008), The Girls Aloud Party (voice only) (2008), Have I Got News For You (chair) (2008).

TOM BAKER'S DOCTOR WHO

Season 12
Robot (4 episodes), The Ark in Space (4 episodes), The Sontaran Experiment (2 episodes), Genesis of the Daleks (6 episodes), Revenge of the Cybermen (4 episodes).

Season 13
Terror of the Zygons (4 episodes), Planet of Evil (4 episodes), Pyramids of Mars (4 episodes), The Android Invasion (4 episodes), The Brain of Morbius (4 episodes), The Seeds of Death (6 episodes).

Season 14
The Masque of Mandragora (4 episodes), The Hand of Fear (4 episodes), The Deadly Assassin (4 episodes), The Face of Evil (4 episodes) The Robots of Death (4 episodes), The Talons of Weng-Chiang (6 episodes).

Season 15
Horror of Fang Rock (4 episodes), The Invisible Enemy (4 episodes), Image of the Fendahl (4 episodes), The Sun Makers (4 episodes), Underworld (4 episodes) The Invasion of Time (6 episodes).

Season 16
The Ribos Operation (4 episodes), The Pirate Planet (4 episodes), The Stones of Blood (4 episodes), The Androids of

Tara (4 episodes), The Power of Kroll (4 episodes), The Armageddon Factor (6 episodes).

Season 17
Destiny of the Daleks (4 episodes), City of Death (4 episodes), The Creature From the Pit (4 episodes), Nightmare of Eden (4 episodes), The Horns of Nimon (4 episodes), Shada (6 episodes).

Note: the shoot for *Shada* was never completed due to industrial dispute at the BBC, therefore the story was never shown on television, as the studio sequences were not finished. However, BBC Video did release it in their *Doctor Who* series of videos, complete with a small script book and links provided by Tom Baker himself.

Season 18
The Leisure Hive (4 episodes), Meglos (4 episodes), Full Circle (4 episodes), State of Decay (4 episodes), Warrior's Gate (4 episodes), The Keeper of Traken (4 episodes), Logopolis (4 episodes).

Note: Tom Baker had also taken part in the BBC audio *Doctor Who* series, reprising his role.

PETER DAVISON

FILMS

Black Beauty (1994), Parting Shots (1999).

THEATRE

Love's Labour's Lost (1972–73), Taming of the Shrew (1973), A Midsummer Night's Dream (1974), The Two Gentlemen of Verona (1974), Hamlet (1974).

Barefoot in the Park (1981), Cinderella (1981), Aladdin (1984), Barefoot in the Park (1984), Cinderella (1984), The Owl and the Pussycat (1986).

Arsenic and Old Lace (1991), The Decorator (1982), The Last Yankee (1995), An Absolute Turkey (1994), Mother Goose (1984), Dick Whittington (1995–96), Dial M For Murder (1996), Chicago (1999).

Under the Doctor (2001), Spamalot (2007–08), Legally Blonde The Musical (2010).

TV

Warship (1 episode) 'One of Those Days' (1974), The Tomorrow People (3 episodes) 'A Man for Emily' Parts 1, 2 & 3 (1975), Love For Lydia (7 episodes) (Season 1, Episodes 2, 3, 4, 6, 7, 8, 9) (1997), The Hitchhiker's Guide to the Galaxy (1 episode) (Season 1, Episode 5) 'Dish of the Day' (1981).

Holding the Fort (20 episodes) (1980–82)
'In Safe Hands', 'Jumping the Gun', 'Come to the Aid of the Party', 'Twelve Good Men and Pooh', 'After the Ball', 'Against the Grain', 'Over the Barrel' (1980), 'New Blood', 'Famous First Words', 'Over and Out', 'Under a Cloud',

'Lock, Stock and Barrel', 'A Sense of Duty' (1981), 'Feeling the Pinch', 'All Boys Together', 'A Place in the Sun', 'Under Pressure', 'One Careful Owner', 'Otherwise Engaged', 'News From the Front' (1982).

All Creatures Great and Small (65 episodes) (1978–90)
'Dog Days', 'It Takes All Kinds', 'Calf Love', 'Out of Practice', 'Nothing Like Experience', 'Golden Lads and Girls', 'Advice and Consent', 'The Last Furlong', 'Sleeping Partners', 'Bulldog Breed', 'Practice Makes Perfect', 'Breath of Life', 'Cats and Dogs', 'Attendant Problems', 'Fair Means and Fowl', 'The Beauty of the Beast', 'Judgement Day', 'Faint Hearts', 'Tricks of the Trade', 'Pride of Possession', 'The Name of the Game', 'Puppy Love', 'Ways and Means', 'Pups, Pigs and Pickle', 'A Dog's Life', 'Merry Gentlemen' (1978), 'Plenty to Grouse About' (1979), 'Charity Begins At Home', 'Every Dog His Day…', 'Hair of the Dog', 'If Wishes Were Horses', 'Pig in the Middle', 'Be Prepared', 'A Dying Breed', 'Brink of Disaster', 'Home and Away', 'Alarms and Excursions', 'Matters of Life and Death', 'Will to Live', 'Big Steps and Little 'Uns' (1980), 1983 special, 1985 special, 'One of Nature's Little Miracles', 'Barks and Bites', 'The Bull With the Bowler Hat', 'The Pig Man Cometh', 'Hail Caesar!', 'Only One Woof', 'Ace, Queen, King, Jack', '… The Healing Touch', 'For Richer, for Poorer', 'Against the Odds', 'Place of Honour', 'Choose a Bright Morning', 'The Playing Field'(1988), The Call of the Wild (1989), 'The Prodigal Returns', 'If Music Be the Food of Love', 'Knowing How to Do It', 'A Friend for Life', 'Spring Fever', 'A Cat in Hull's Chance', 'Hampered', 'Promises to Keep', 'Brotherly Love' (1990).

Sink or Swim (19 episodes) (1980–82)

'In the Beginning', 'Steve's Girlfriend', 'Croydon' (1980), 'The Turkey', 'The Car', 'The Boat', 'The Interviewer', 'Tourists', 'The Commune', 'The Folk Club', 'The Marrying', 'Ecology', 'University or What?' (1981), 'In the Pursuit of Learning', 'Nothing But Trouble', 'A Sporting Chance', 'A Slight Hankering', 'Making Amends', 'A New Departure' (1982).

Fox Tales (1985), Anna of the Five Towns (4 episodes) (Season 1, Episodes 1, 2, 3 & 4) (1985), Miss Marple: A Pocketful of Rye (1985), Magnum PI (2 episodes) 'Déjà Vu' Parts 1 & 2.

A Very Peculiar Practice (14 episodes) (1986–88)
'A Very Long Way From Anywhere', 'We Love You, That's Why We're Here', 'Wives of Great Men', 'Black Bob's Hamburger Suit', 'Contact Tracer', 'The Hit List', 'Catastrophe Theory' (1986), 'The New Frontier', 'Art and Illusion', 'May the Force Be With You' 'Bad Vibrations', 'Values of the Family', 'The Big Squeeze', 'Death of a University' (1988).

Tales of the Unexpected (1 episode) 'Wink Three Times' (1988), Kinsey (1988).
Campion (16 episodes) (1989–90)
'Look to the Lady' Parts 1 & 2, 'Police at the Funeral' Parts 1 & 2, 'The Castle of the Late Pig' Parts 1 & 2, 'Death of a Ghost' Parts 1 & 2 (1989), 'Dancers in Mourning' Parts 1 & 2, 'Flowers for the Judge' Parts 1 & 2, 'Mystery Miles' Parts 1 & 2 (1990).

Fiddler's Three (14 episodes) (1991)
'The Scapegoat', 'Norma Dove', 'The Dark Horse', 'The Whiz Kid', 'The Velvet Glove', 'Detective Story', 'Time Out', 'The Secret File', 'The Man Most Likely to', 'We Didn't Want to

Lose You' Parts 1 & 2, 'The Fiddle', 'Undue Influence', 'Cut and Dried'.

Harnessing Peacocks (1992), Screen One: A Very Polish Practice (1992), The Airzone Solution (1993), A Man You Don't Meet Ever Day (1994), Mole's Christmas (1994), The Zero Imperative (1994), Molly (1995), The Adventures of Mole (1995), The Devil of Winterbourne (1995), Ain't Misbehavin' (12 episodes) (two season of six episodes – 1994–95), Jeremy Hardy Gives Good Sex (1995), Ghosts of Winterbourne (1996), Cuts (1996), Dear Nobody (1997), Scene (1 episode), 'A Man of Letters' (1997), Jonathan Creek (1 episode) 'Danse Macabre' (1998), 'The Stalker's Apprentice' (1998), Verdict (1 episode), 'Be My Valentine' (1998), Wuthering Heights (1998), Hope & Glory (Season 1, Episode 1) (1999), 'The Nearly Complete and Utter History of Everything' (1999), The Mrs Bradley Mysteries (3 episodes) 'The Worsted Viper', 'The Rising of the Moon', 'Death at the Opera' (2000), At Home With the Braithwaites (26 episodes) (2000–03), Too Good to Be True (2003),The Complete Guide to Parenting (2006).
Fear, Stress and Anger (6 episodes) (2007)
'The Job List', 'Sex and Friends', 'Stress and Drugs', 'Julie's Interview', 'Health and Gran', 'Menopause'.

Agatha Christie's Miss Marple 'At Bertram's Hotel' (2007).

The Last Detective (17 episodes) (2003–07)
Pilot Episode, Moonlight, Tricia, Lofty (2003), Christine, The Long Bank Holiday, Benefit to Mankind, Dangerous and the Lonely Hearts (2004), Friends Reunited, Towpaths of Glory, Three Steps to Hendon, Willesden Confidential (2005), Once Upon a Time on the Westway, Dangerous Liaisons, A Funny

Thing Happened on the Way to Willesden, The Man From Montevideo, The Dead Peasants Society (2007).

Doctor Who: Time Crash (2007), Distant Shores (12 episodes) (2005–08), Unforgiven (2009), Al Murray's Multiple Personality Disorder (1 episode) (Season 1, Episode 4), Midsomer Murders (1 episode) 'Secrets and Spies' (2009), Micro Men (2009), Miranda (1 episode) 'Teachers' (2009), The Queen (1 episode) (2009). Sherlock (voice only) (2010).

PETER DAVISON'S DOCTOR WHO

Season 19
Castrovalva (4 episodes), Four to Doomsday (4 episodes), Kinda (4 episodes), The Visitation (4 episodes), Black Orchid (2 episodes), Earthshock (4 episodes), Time-Flight (4 episodes).

Season 20
Arc of Infinity (4 episodes), Snakedance (4 episodes), Mawdryn Undead (4 episodes), Terminus (4 episodes), Enlightenment (4 episodes), The King's Demons (2 episodes).

20th Anniversary Special, The Five Doctors

Season 21
Warriors of the Deep (4 episodes), The Awakening (2 episodes), Frontios (4 episodes), Resurrection of the Daleks (2 episodes), Planet of Fire (4 episodes), The Caves of Androzani (4 episodes).

COLIN BAKER

FILMS

Zandorra (1989), Clockwork (1989).

THEATRE

Plaintiff in a Pretty Hat (1969), The Other House (1969), Shakespeare Cabbages & Kings: 1959 and All That, The Wizard of Oz, Green Julia, Everyman, Long Christmas Dinner, New Lamps For Old (1969–70).

Reunion in Vienna (1971), Caesar & Cleopatra (1971), The Price of Justice (1971), Conduct Unbecoming (1972), Vivat! Vivat Regina! (1972), Christie in Love (1972), A Game Called Arthur (1972), A Christmas Carol (1972), A Lion in Winter (1973), Guys and Dolls (1973), Journey's End (1973), Hamlet (1973), French Without Tears (1973), Move Over Mrs Markham (1973), September Tide (1975), Let's Do It Your Way (1977), Underground (1977), The Flip Side (1978), Trap For A Lonely Man (1978), Macbeth (1978), Odd Man In (1979).

Dick Whittington (1980), Doctor in the House (1979), Traitors (1980), Private Lives (1981), The Norman Conquest (1981), Stagestruck (1981), Goldilocks (1982), Suddenly At Home (1983), The Mousetrap (1983–84), Cinderella (1984), Aladdin (1985), Cinderella (1986), Corpse (1987), Robinson Crusoe (1987), Death Trap (1988), Run For Your Wife

(1989), Doctor Who The Ultimate Adventure (1989), Private Lives (1989), Peter Pan (1989).

Born in the Gardens (1990), Spider's Web (1990), Jack and the Bean Stalk (1990), Privates on Parade (1991), Time and Time Again (1991), Frankie and Johnny in the Claire De Lune (1992), Death and the Maiden (1992), Dick Whittington (1992), Nightfright (1993), Peter Pan (1993), Not Now Darling (1994), Aladdin (1994), Peter Pan (1995), Great Expectations – The Musical (1985–86), Fear of Frying (1995), Dick Whittington (1996), Peter Pan (1997), Babes in the Wood (1997), Kind Hearts and Coronets (1998), Jack and the Bean Stalk (1998), Peter Pan (1999), Dick Whittington (1999).

Love Letters (2000), Out of Order (2000), Why Me? (2000), Snow White and the Seven Dwarfs (2000), Aladdin (2001), Flare Path (2002), Corpse (2002), Dick Whittington (2002), Corpse (2003), HMS Pinafore (2003), The Haunted Hotel (2004), Love Letters (2004), Dick Whittington (2004), Love Letters (2005), Dracula (2005), Snow White and the Seven Dwarfs (2005), Love Letters (2006), Strangers on a Train (2006), Bedroom Farce (2007), She Stoops to Conquer (2007), Dick Whittington (2007), She Stoops to Conquer (2008), Noises Off (2008), Jack and the Bean Stalk (2008–09).

TV

My Wife's Sister (1954).

Roads to Freedom (13 episodes – Baker appears in 3, 5 & 6) (1970), The Adventures of Don Quick (Episode 2, Season 1)

(1970), No That's Me Over Here! (Episodes 10 & 11, Season 3) (1970), The Mind of Mr J G Reeder 'The Shadow Man' (Baker appears in 1 of 16 episodes) (1971), Public Eye 'The Man Who Didn't Eat Sweets' (Episode 9, Season 5) (1971), Cousin Bette (5 episodes) 'Family Angel', 'Bitter Harvest', 'Delilah and Her Handmaid', 'The House of Pleasure', 'Poor Relations' (1971), The Moonstone (Episode 1 only of 5) (1972), The Man Outside (13 episodes) (1972), War and Peace (4 episodes of 17), 'Name Day', 'Madness', 'Sounds of War', 'A Letter and Two Proposals' (1972), The Edwardians 'Daisy' (1 episode of 8) (1973), Harriet's Back in Town (2 episodes) (1973), Orson Welles Great Mysteries 'A Terrible Strange Bed' (1973), Within These Walls 'Prisoner By Marriage' (1974), The Camforth Practice 'Undue Influence' (1974), Fall of Eagles (2 episodes) 'End Game', 'The Secret War' (1974).

The Brothers: (46 episodes) (1974–76)
'Partings', 'Hit and Miss', 'Public Concern', 'A Big Mistake', 'The Fall Guy', 'The Self-Made Cross', 'Tiger By the Tail', 'Breakdown', 'Special Licence', 'Flight of Fancy', 'A Very Short Honeymoon', 'Big Deal', 'Package Deal', 'End of a Dream', 'The Judas Sheep', 'Jennifer's Baby', 'War Path', 'Red Sky at Night', 'A Clean Break', 'Red Sky in the Morning', 'Orange and Lemons', 'When Will You Pay Me?', 'Tender', 'The Mole', 'The Chosen Victim', 'Blood and Water', 'The Devil You Know', 'Try, Try, Again', 'The Bonus', 'Birthday', 'To Honour and Obey', 'Home and Away', 'Invitations', 'The Female of the Species', 'Manoeuvres', 'Arrivals and Departures', 'The Distaff Side', 'Cross Currents', 'Ripples', 'Celebration…', 'Windmills', 'The Golden Road', 'Out of the Blue', 'The Knock on the Door', 'The Ordeal', 'The Christmas Party'.

Blakes 7 (1 episode) 'The City at the Edge of the World' (1980), For Maddie with Love (1980), Dangerous Davies: The Last Detective (1981), Juliet Bravo 'The Intruder' (1982), The Citadel (Episode 4 of 10) (1983), Swallows and Amazons Forever! Coot Club (1984), Swallows and Amazons Forever! The Big Six (1984), Roland Rat: The Series (Episode 3, Season 1) (1986).

Summoned By Strangers (1992), More Than a Messiah (1992), The Stranger: In Memory Alone (1993), The Airzone Solution (1993), The Zero Imperative (1994), Breach of the Peace (1994), The Stranger: The Terror Game (1994), Eye of the Beholder (1995), The Harpist (1997), The Famous Five 'Five Go To Billycock Hill (Parts 1 & 2) (1997), Jonathan Creek 'The Wrestler's Tomb' (1997), The Knock (Episodes 3, 4, 5 & 6, Season 3), A Dance to the Music of Time (1 episode of 4) 'Post War' (1997), The Bill 'Going Down' (1997), Casualty (2 episodes) 'Accidents Happen' (1989), 'An Eye For An Eye' (1998), Souls Ark (1999), Sunburn (Episode 2, Season 1) (1999), The Adventures of Young Indiana Jones: Daredevils of the Desert (1999), The Waiting Time (1999), Dangerfield 'Haunted' (1999).

The Asylum (2000), Travel Wise (2000), Hollyoaks 'The Judge' (1 episode) (2000), Time Gentlemen Please 'Day of Trivheads' (2000), The Impressionable Jon Culshaw (Episode 2, Season 1) (2000), Little Britain (2005), D'Artagnan et les trios Mousquetaires (2005), The Afternoon Play 'Your Mother Should Know' (2006), Kingdom (Episode 2, Season 3) (2009), Doctors (3 episodes) 'Matters of Principle' (2001), 'Honourable Gentlemen' (2006), 'The Romantics' (2006), Tiger Troubles (2010), Hustle (1 episode) (2010), Doctors 'Every Heart That Beats' (2011)'

COLIN BAKER'S DOCTOR WHO

Season 21 cont.
The Twin Dilemma.

SEASON 22
Attack of the Cybermen (2 episodes), Vengeance on Varos (2 episodes), The Mark of the Rani (2 episodes), The Two Doctors (3 episodes), Timelash (2 episodes), Revelation of the Daleks (2 episodes).

SEASON 23
The Mysterious Planet (4 episodes), Mindwarp (4 episodes), Terror of the Vervoids (4 episodes), The Ultimate Foe (2 episodes).

Note: the above season comes under the heading The Trial of a Time Lord.

Additional Note: Colin Baker also took part in the BBC audio *Doctor Who* and has completed other audios dramas such as Sapphire and Steel.

SYLVESTER MCCOY

FILMS

Dracula (1979). The Hobbit (2011).

Leapin' Leprechauns (1995), Spellbreaker: Secret of the Leprechauns (aka Leapin' Leprechauns 2) (1996).

Eldorado (2010), Back2Hell (2010).

THEATRE

The Ken Campbell Roadshow 'Modern Myths' (circa 1975), Twelfth Night (1976), She Stoops to Conquer (1976).

The Secret Policeman's Ball (1981), Pirates of Penzance (1982), Dracula (1985), The Pied Piper (1987), Aladdin (1989).

Cinderella (1993), The Government Inspector (1993–94), The Invisible Man (1993–94), Zorro: the Musical (1995), Life is a Dream (1998).

The Hypochondriac (2000), The Lion, the Witch and the Wardrobe (2001–02), King Lear (2001), The Dead Move Fast (2001), Live From Golgotha (2002), Hello Dali (2002), Noises Off (2003), Dick Whittington (2003/04), Arsenic & Old Lace (2005), Dick Whittington (2005/6), A Midsummer Night's Dream (2006), Me and My Gal (2006), The Pocket Orchestra (2006), The Lion, the Witch and the Wardrobe (2007), King Lear (2007), The Mikado (2008), The Lovely Russell Concert (2008), Little Shop of Horrors (2009), Cinderella (2010).

Other theatrical productions: Buster's Last Stand, Gone With Hardy, Robin Hood.

TV

Vision On (1965).

Robert's Robots (1 episode) 'Dial C for Chaos' (1973), Lucky Feller (1 episode) 'Lucky Feller: pilot' (1975), For the Love of Albert (TV mini-series) (1977), Tiswas (1974–82), Jigsaw (1979), All the Fun of the Fair (1979).

BBC2 Playhouse (1 episode) 'Electric in the City' (1980).

Big Jim and the Figaro Club (1979–81)
'Pilot: Big Jim and the Figaro Club' (1979), 'Dung From a Rocking Horse' (1981), 'Laughing Like a Drain' (1981), 'Hearts of Oak' (1981), 'The Pursuit of Courtly Love' (1981), 'Tiny Revolutions' (1981).

Eureka (1982).

The Last Place on Earth (6 episodes) (1985)
'Leading Men', 'Rejoice', 'Foregone Conclusion', 'The Glories of the Race', 'Gentlemen and Players', 'Minor Diversion'.

No 73 (1 episode) 'Moving Space' (1985), Dramarama (1 episode) 'Frog' (1985), Three Kinds of Heat (1987), What's Your Story? (1988), The Noel Edmonds Saturday Roadshow (1 episode) (1989), Thrill Kill Video Club (1991), The Airzone Solution (1993), Jackanory (1979–93), The Zero Imperative (1994), Frank Stubbs Promotes (1 episode) 'Mrs Chairman' (1994), Rab C Nesbitt (1 episode) 'Father' (1996), Beyond Fear (1997), The History of Tom Jones, a Foundling (4 episodes) (1997), Destiny of the Doctor (1998).

The Mumbo Jumbo (2000), Do You Have a Licence to Save This Planet (2001), See It, Saw It (1 episode) 'Courage and Adventure' (2001), Hollyoaks (1 episode) (2002), The Shieling of the One Night (2002), Still Game (1 episode) 'Oot' (2004), Mayo (1 episode) (2006), The Bill (2 episodes) '010', '457' (2002 and 2006), Great Performances (1 episode) 'King Lear' (2008), Doctors (1 episode) 'The Lollipop Man' (2008), Casualty (2 episodes) 'Life and Soul', 'The Evil That Men Do' (2001 and 2008), Al Murray's Multiple Personality Disorder (Season 1, Episode 6) (2009), The Academy (2009), The Academy Part 2: First Impressions (2009).

Other television: Starstrider, Space Cadets, Today is Saturday, Wake Up Smiling, The Foot Doctor, Light in Dark Places, Hell's Kitchen, The 100 Great Kids TV Shows.

SYLVESTER MCCOY'S DOCTOR WHO

Season 24
Time and the Rani (4 episodes), Paradise Towers (4 episodes), Delta and the Bannerman (3 episodes), Dragonfire (3 episodes).

Season 25
Remembrance of the Daleks (4 episodes), The Happiness Patrol (3 episodes), Silver Nemesis (3 episodes), The Greatest Show in the Galaxy (4 episodes).

Season 26
Battlefield (4 episodes), Ghost Light (3 episodes), The Curse of Fenric (4 episodes), Survival (3 episodes).

PAUL MCGANN

FILMS

Withnail and I (1987), Empire of the Sun (1988), Snowball (1988), Tree of Hands (1989), The Rainbow (1989), Streets of Yesterday (1989), Dealers (1989).

A Paper Mask (1990), The Monk (1990), Afraid of the Dark (1991), Alien 3 (1992), The Three Musketeers (1993), Catherine the Great (1996), The Hanging Gale (1996), Fairytale: A True Story (1997), Downtime (1997), The Dance of Shiva (1998), Our Mutual Friend (1988).

My Kingdom (2001), Queen of the Damned (2002), Listening (2003), Y Mabinogi (voice only) (2003), Fables of Forgotten Things (2005), Naked in London (2005), Gypo (2005), Poppies (2006), Voice From Afar (2006), Always Crashing in the Same Car (2007), Lesbian Vampire Killers (2009), The Odds (2010).

THEATRE

John, Paul, George, Ringo and Bert (1981), Much Ado About Nothing (1981), Cain (1981), Piaf (1981), Godspell (1981), Oi! For England (1982), Yakety Yak (1982–83), The Genius (1984), Loot (1984), The Seagull (1986), A Lie of the Mind (1987).

Sabina (1998).
Mourning Becomes Electra (2003), Little Black Book (2003),

The Gigli Concert (2005), Helen (2009), Sonnet 115 (2010), Butley (2011).

TV

Play for Today (1 episode) 'Whispering Wally' (1982), Give Us a Break (1983), Sharpe's Rifles (1983), The Importance of Being Earnest (1986).

The Monocled Mutineer (4 episodes) (1986)
'The Making of a Hero', 'A Dead Man on Leave', 'When the Hurly-Burly's Done', 'Before the Shambles'.

Screenplay (1 episode) 'Cariani and the Courtesans' (1987), Jackanory (1 episode) 'The Whipping Boy' (1989).

Drowning in the Shallow End (1990), Nice Town (3 episodes) 'Idyll', 'Unto Us a Child is Born', 'Immaculate Conception' (1992), The Merchant of Venice (1996), The One That Got Away (1996), Breathless Hush (1999), Forgotten (1999), Nature Boy (2000), Fish (2000), Hotel! (2001).

Hornblower (4 episodes) (2001–03)
Mutiny (2001), Retribution (2001), Loyalty (2003), Duty (2003).

My Kingdom (2001), Sweet Revenge (2001), Blood Strangers (2002), The Biographer (2002), Agatha Christie's Poirot (1 episode) 'Sad Cypress' (2003), Lie With Me (2004), Twisted Tales (1 episode) 'Txt Msg Rcvd' (2005), Kidnapped (2005), Agatha Christie's 'Sleeping Murder' (2006), Sea of Souls (1 episode) 'Rebound' (2006), If I Had You (2006), Tripping Over (6 episodes) (2006), True Dare Kiss (6 episodes) (2007),

Voice From Afar (2007), The True Story: Escape From Alcatraz (2008), Fables of Forgotten Things (2008), Collision (5 episodes) (2009), Jonathan Creek (1 episode) 'The Judas Tree' (2010), Luther (2010).

PAUL MCGANN AS NARRATOR

(Due to the seriousness of some of McGann's documentary narrations, it was deemed important to list some of his most memorable pieces of work in this line of business)

Dispatches: Hope for the Last Chance Kids, Cutting Edge: Leaving Home at 8, The Making of *Alien 3* (1992), Bible Mysteries (3 episodes) 'Joseph and his Coat of Many Colours', 'Peter and the First Church', 'David and Saul' (1996),The Making of *Alien* (2003), Behind the Crime (2004), Wacko About Jacko (2005), Cathedral (2005), Daphne Ashbrook in the UK (2005), Kill Me if You Can (2005), The Sperminator (2005), Foetus Snatcher (2005), Adopt Me, I'm A Teenager (2005), The Ripper Hoaxer: Wearside Jack (2006), Mr Miss Pageant (2007), World of Compulsive Hoarders (2007), Zero Hour (3 episodes) 'One of America's Own', 'The Sinking of the Estonia', 'Capturing Saddam' (2006, 2007 and 2007), The Foreign Legion: Tougher Than the Rest (2007), The Ties That Bind Us (2008), Getting A Head (2008).

PAUL MCGANN'S DOCTOR WHO

Doctor Who – The Movie
Note: It must be noted that, although Paul McGann only

appeared in one feature-length TV film, he did provide continuity to the series by regenerating on screen from Sylvester McCoy. McGann signed a contract for a series, but unfortunately this didn't happen. However, his version of the interior of the Tardis was used when the show was relaunched in the new millennium.

It must also be noted that Paul McGann has been the most prolific audio and drama Doctor Who, all of which are available on BBC audio CDs.

CHRISTOPHER ECCLESTON

FILMS

Let Him Have It (1991), Anchoress (1993), Shallow Grave (1994), Jude (1996), Death and the Compass (1996), Elizabeth (1998), A Price About Rubies (1998), Heart (1999), eXistenZ (1999), With or Without You (1999).

The Tyre (2000), Gone in 60 Seconds (2000), The Others (2001), This Little Piggy (2001), Strumpet (2001), The Invisible Circus (2001), 24 Hour Party (2002) I Am Dina (2002), Revengers Tragedy (2002), 28 Days Later (2002), The Seeker: The Dark is Rising (2007), New Orleans, Mon Amour (2008), GI Joe: The Rise of the Cobra (2009), Amelia (2009), GI Joe 2: The Revenge of the Cobra (2011).

THEATRE

Lock Up Your Daughters (Salford Tech), A Streetcar Named

Desire (1998), Woyzeck, The Wonder, Dona Rosita – The Spinster, Bent (1990), Abingdon Square (1990), Aide Memoire (1990), Encounters, Waiting at the Water's Edge (1993).

Miss Julie (2000), Hamlet (2002), Romeo and Juliet (2004), Electricity (2004), A Doll's House (2009).

TV

Blood Rights (1990), Casualty (1 episode) 'A Reasonable Man' (1990), Inspector Morse (1 episode) 'Second Time Around' (1991), Boon (1 episode) 'Cover Up' (1991), Rachel's Dream (1992), Agatha Christie's Poirot (1 episode) 'One, Two, Buckle My Shoe' (1992), Friday On My Mind (1992), Business With Friends (1992), Roots (1992), Cracker (10 episodes) 'The Mad Woman in the Attic' Part 1 & 2, 'To Say I Love You' Parts 1, 2 & 3, 'One Day A Lemming Will Fly' Parts 1, 2 & 3, 'To Be A Somebody' Parts 1, 2 & 3 (1993), Our Friends in the North (9 episodes) '1964', '1966', '1967', '1970', '1974', '1979', '1984', '1987', '1995' (1996).

Wilderness Men (2000), Killing Time: The Millennium Poem (2000), Clocking Off (2 episodes) 'Yvonne's Story', 'Steve's Story' (2000), Othello (2001), Linda Green (1 episode) 'Twins' (2001), The League of Gentlemen (1 episode) 'How the Elephant Got His Trunk' (2002), Lost in La Mancha (2002), Flesh and Blood (2002), Sunday (2002), The King and Us (2002), The Second Coming Parts 1 & 2 (2003), Only Human (1 episode) 'Bosom Buddies' (2006), Heroes (5 episodes) 'Chapter Twelve: Godsend', 'Chapter Thirteen: The Fix', 'Chapter Fourteen: Distraction', 'Chapter Sixteen: Unexpected',

'Chapter Seventeen: Company Man' (2007), Perfect Parents (2006), The Sarah Silverman Program (1 episode) 'I Thought My Dad Was Dead, But It Turns Out He's Not; (2008), The Happiness Salesman (2009), The Beautiful Fantastic (2010), Lennon Naked (2010), The Shadow Line (five episodes) (2011).

RADIO

Chancer (1 episode) 'Jo' (1991), Room of Leaves (1998), Pig Paradise (1998).

Some Fantastic Places (2001), Bayeux Tapestry (2001), The Importance of Being Morrissey (2002), The Iliad (2002), Cromwell: Warts and All (2003), Life Half Spent (2004), Crossing the Dark Sea (2005), Sacred Nation (2005), Born to Be Different (2005), A Day in the Death of Joe Egg (2005), E=mc2 (2005), Dubai Dreams (2005), Wanted: Mum and Dad (2005), Children in Need (2005), This Septic Isle (2005), The 1970s: That Was the Decade That Was (2006).

CHRISTOPHER ECCLESTON'S DOCTOR WHO

Relaunched TV series.
Series I
Rose (1 episode), The End of the World (1 episode), The Unquiet Dead (1 episode), Aliens of London/World War Three (2 episodes), Dalek (1 episode), The Long Game (1 episode), Father's Day (1 episode), The Empty Child/The Doctor Dances (2 episodes), Boom Town (1 episode), Bad Wolf/The Parting of the Ways (2 episodes).

DAVID TENNANT

FILMS

Jude (1996), Bite (1997), LA Without A Map (1998), The Last September (1999), Being Considered (2000), One Eyed Jacques (2001), Nine ½ Minutes (2002), Bright Young Things (2003), Old Street (2004), Harry Potter and the Goblet of Fire (2005), Free Jimmy (2006), Glorious 39 (2009), St Trinians: The Legend of Fritton's Gold (2009), How to Train Your Dragon (voice only) (2010), The Decoy Bride (2011), Fright Night (2011).

THEATRE

The Resistible Rise of Arturo Ui (1991), Shinda The Magic Ape (1991–92), Jump The Life to Come (1992), Hayfever (1992), Tartuffe (1992), Merlin (1992–93), Antigone (1993), The Princess and the Goblin (1993), The Slab Boys Trilogy (1994), What the Butler Saw (1995), An Experienced Woman Gives Advice (1995), The Glass Menagerie (1996), Long Day's Journey into Night (1996), Who's Afraid of Virginia Woolf? (1996), As You Like It (1996), The General From America (1996), The Herbal Bed (1996), Hurly Burly (1997), The Real Inspector Hound/Black Comedy (1998), Vassa – Scenes From Family Life (1999), Edward III (1999), King Lear (1999), The Comedy of Errors (2000), The Rivals (2000), Romeo & Juliet (2000), A Midsummer Night's Dream (2001), Comedians (2001), Push Up (2002), Lobby Hero (2002), The Pillowman (2003), Look Back in Anger (2005–06), Hamlet

(2008–09), Love's Labour's Lost (2008), Much Ado About Nothing (2011).

TV

Dramarama 'The Secret of Croftmore' (1988), Rab C Nesbitt 'Touch' (Season 3, Episode 2) (1993), Taking Over the Asylum (6 episodes) (1994), The Tales of Para Handy (9 episodes/2 seasons) (1994–95), The Bill 'Deadline' (1995), A Mug's Game (1996), Holding the Baby (Season 1, Episode 2) (1997), Duck Patrol (7 episodes) (1998), Love in the 21st Century 'Reproduction' (episode 1) (1999), The Mrs Bradley Mysteries 'Death at the Opera' (Season 1, Episode 1) (2000), Randall & Hopkirk (deceased) (episode 1, Season 1) (2000), People Like Us 'The Actor' (Season 2, Episode 4) (2001), Sweetnightgoodheart (2001), 'Foyle's War' in Crime in Wartime Britain (Episode 3) (2002), Posh Nosh (Episodes 3 & 8) (2003), Trust (Season 1, Episode 6) (2003), Spine Chillers 'Bradford in My Dreams' (2003), The Deputy (2004), He Knew He Was Right (4 episodes) (2004), Blackpool (6 episodes) (2004), Traffic Warden (2004), Casanova (3 episodes) (2005), The Quatermass Experiment (2005), Secret Smile (2 episodes) (2005), The Romantics (3 episodes) (2006), The Chatterley Affair (2006), Recovery (2007), Dead Ringers (Season 7, Episode 6) (2007), Learners (2007), Extras 'Christmas Special' (2007), Einstein and Eddington (2008), The Sarah Jane Adventures (2 episodes) (2009), Hamlet (2009), Rex is Not Your Lawyer (2010), Single Father (4 episodes) (2010), Twenty Twelve (6 episodes) (2011), United (2011).

DAVID TENNANT'S DOCTOR WHO

Specials: Doctor Who: Children in Need, The Christmas Invasion

Series 2

New Earth (1 episode), Tooth and Claw (1 episode), School Reunion (1 episode), The Girl in the Fireplace (1 episode), Rise of the Cybermen/The Age of Steel (2 episodes), The Idiot Lantern (1 episode), The Impossible Planet/The Satan Pit (2 episodes), Love and Monsters (1 episode), Fear Her (1 episode), Army of Ghosts/Doomsday (2 episodes).

Special: The Runaway Bride

Series 3

Smith and Jones (1 episode), The Shakespeare Code (1 episode), Gridlock (1 episode), Daleks in Manhattan/Evolution of the Daleks (2 episodes), The Lazarus Experiment (1 episode), 42 (1 episode), Human Nature/The Family of Blood (2 episodes), Blink (1 episode), Utopia/The Sound of Drums/Last of the Time Lords (3 episodes).

Special: The Voyage of the Damned

Series 4

Partners in Crime (1 episode), The Fires of Pompeii (1 episode), Planet of the Ood (1 episode), The Sontaran Stratagem/The Poison Sky (2 episodes), The Doctor's Daughter (1 episode), The Unicorn and the Wasp (1 episode), Silence in the Library/Forest of the Dead (2 episodes), Midnight (1 episode), Turn Left (1 episode), The Stolen Earth/Journey's End (2 episodes).

Series 4 (specials)

Christmas 2008 The Next Doctor (1 episode), Easter 2009 Planet of the Dead (1 episode), Autumn Special 2009 The Waters of Mars (1 episode), Winter Specials 2009–10 The End of Time (2 episodes).

Animated Specials

The Infinite Quest (13 episodes), Dreamland (6 episodes).

MATT SMITH

THEATRE

Murder in the Cathedral (2003), The Master and Margarita (2004), Fresh Kills (2004), On the Shore of the Wild World (2005), The History Boys (2005–06), Burn/Chatroom/Citizenship (2006), Swimming With Sharks (2007–08), That Face (2008).

TV

The Ruby in the Smoke (2006), The Shadow in the North (2007), In Bruges (2007), The Street (2007), The Secret Diary of a Call Girl (2007), Party Animal (2007), Moses Jones (2009), Together (2009), Womb (2010), The Sarah Jane Adventures (2 episodes) (2010), Christopher and His Kind (2011).

MATT SMITH'S DOCTOR WHO

Series 5

The Eleventh Hour, The Beast Below, Victory of the Daleks, The Time of the Angels/Flesh and Stone, The Vampires of Venice, Amy's Choice, The Hungry Earth/Cold Blood, Vincent and the Doctor, The Lodger, The Pandorica Opens/The Big Bang.

Special: A Christmas Carol

Series 6

The Impossible Astronaut/Day of the Moon (2 episodes), The Curse of the Black Spot (1 episode), The Doctor's Wife (1 episode), The Rebel Flesh/The Almost People (2 episodes), A Good Man Goes to War (1 episode), Let's Kill Hiter (1 episode), Night Terrors (1 episode), The Girl Who Waited (1 episode), The God Complex (1 episode), episode twelve, episode thirteen.

CHAPTER TWO
MISSING DOCTOR WHO EPISODES

WHAT FOLLOWS IS a list of *Doctor Who* episodes missing from the BBC archive. The BBC has spent much time and trouble recovering old stories from the William Hartnell and Patrick Troughton eras, but many episodes are still missing, feared lost forever. If any film collector has anything they feel may be valuable to the BBC, albeit clips, whole episodes or complete stories, they would dearly like to hear from you.

WILLIAM HARTNELL MISSING EPISODES

Marco Polo eps 1–7; The Reign of Terror eps 4 & 5; The Crusade eps 2 & 4; Galaxy 4 eps 1–4; Mission to the Unknown (this story is only one episode long and does not feature the Doctor); The Myth Makers 1–4; The Dalek Master Plan eps 1, 3, 4, 6, 7, 8, 9, 11, 12; The Massacre of St Bartholomew's Eve eps 1–4; The Celestial Toymaker 1–3; The Savages eps 1–4; The Smugglers eps 1–4; The Tenth Planet ep 4.

PATRICK TROUGHTON MISSING EPISODES

The Power of the Daleks eps 1–6; The Highlanders eps 1–4; The Underwater Menace eps 1, 2, 4; The Moonbase eps 1, 3; The Macra Terror eps 1–4; The Faceless Ones eps 2, 4, 5, 6; The Evil of the Daleks eps 1, 3, 4, 5, 6, 7; The Abominable Snowman eps 1, 3, 4, 5, 6; The Ice Warriors eps 2 & 3; The Enemy of the World eps 1, 2, 4, 5, 6; The Web of Fear eps 2, 3, 4, 5, 6; Fury From the Deep eps 1–6; The Wheel in Space eps 1, 2, 4, 5; The Invasion eps 1 & 4; The Space Pirates 1, 3, 4, 5, 6.

Note regarding Jon Pertwee stories: although there is a record of every single episode featuring Jon Pertwee's Doctor, the quality of some of the prints are not up to scratch, and again the BBC would dearly like to hear from anybody who owns individual episodes in order to upgrade the quality of prints they have in archive.

Worthy of mention here is the multitude of other shows missing from the BBC archive, from Patrick Troughton's *Robin Hood* to the TV *Navy Lark*. There are also many missing early performances from legendary double acts such as Morecambe and Wise and the BBC would dearly like to hear from anyone who may hold copies of those too.

CHAPTER THREE
HIGHLIGHTS OF A CULT TV SHOW

WHAT FOLLOWS IS an essay about the very best *Doctor Who* stories in the opinion of one writer. Although few will agree with the shortlist of 25 best stories, because everybody has their own personal favourite, the essay is important because it brings true highlights together from the whole history of the show and goes a long way to explain why the show is such a major success generation after generation; aside from the actors that have taken on the main role.

It is an accepted fact that many people who will buy this book are *Doctor Who* fans and therefore it is right to celebrate the programme – as well as the actors – for some of its/their finest moments.

WHY DOCTOR WHO ENDURES

INTRODUCTION

Doctor Who has been one of the most popular and discussed children's programmes of all time. Why? This essay explains through one person's top 25 favourite stories, which are:

STORY		DOCTOR
1.	The Deadly Assassin	Tom Baker
2.	Blink	David Tennant
3.	Genesis of the Daleks	Tom Baker
4.	State of Decay	Tom Baker
5.	The Abominable Snowman	Patrick Troughton
6.	The Daemons	Jon Pertwee
7.	The Planet of the Ood	David Tennant
8.	An Unearthly Child	William Hartnell
9.	The Visitation	Peter Davison
10.	The Girl in the Fireplace	David Tennant
11.	The Pyramids of Mars	Tom Baker
12.	The Robots of Death	Tom Baker
13.	The Caves of Androzani	Peter Davison
14.	Human Nature/The Family of Blood	David Tennant
15.	The Time Meddler	William Hartnell
16.	The Keeper of Traken	Tom Baker
17.	Father's Day	Christopher Eccleston
18.	The Rescue	William Hartnell
19.	The Two Doctors	Colin Baker
20.	Midnight	David Tennant
21.	Logopolis	Tom Baker
22.	Dalek	Christopher Eccleston

STARMAN

In order to understand the enigma of *Doctor Who*, one must watch the very first episode. Largely taken for granted nowadays, episode one of *Doctor Who* – 'An Unearthly Child', is eerie, inspirational and very unsettling for its time.

Imagine the small black and white TV in the corner of the room. A dark winter's evening about to begin, the news of the assassination of President John F Kennedy still in everybody's minds. Then the TV screen goes black and a strange electronic music starts. No one had ever heard the like before – and, many would say, no one has heard the like since. Like a quality space-age Bowie record, the music for this programme was unearthly and haunting, instantly preparing the watcher for a show like no other. A policeman walks through a fog, a clock tolls 3am, a scrap-yard door creaks open and an everyday police telephone box gives off a faint hum as the theme tune fades. The anticipation was palpable, and the rollercoaster started its 50-year-plus ride, thrilling minds both young and old.

The magic of *Doctor Who* is there in those first couple of minutes: from the start of the theme tune to the living-hum of the Tardis. There is suddenly an expectation of something unusual, which is both captivating and slightly scary, especially for the younger viewers.

The first episode of *Doctor Who* was about two school-teachers (Ian and Barbara) worried about one of their pupils who is brilliant in some things and terrible in others. They decide to follow her home, and end up at the junk yard from the beginning of the episode. They see her enter the yard and follow, but on entering the yard they lose her. She has disappeared. They are about to go and fetch a policeman when an old man enters. They hide but he notices them when Ian knocks over some old junk.

The first meeting with the Doctor enhances the viewers' curiosity and overall mystery of the episode. It's clear the old man knows more about Susan than he is letting on, but he is not saying anything. When they are about to give up, Susan opens the police-box door and the two schoolteachers push their way into the Tardis; they are amazed by the giant control room beyond. The doors close and the Doctor refuses to let them go. There is a scuffle and the Tardis is started on course to a new world and its first TV adventure.

But who is this strange old man known only as the Doctor? Doctor Who? And who is the girl – the pupil from the school?

As far as the Doctor was concerned, no one would find out about his home world for seven years and, with regard to his 'granddaughter', it would be 50 years before the original draft of the script was found to explain all to expectant fans. And around all this, a legend grew.

But how did that legend endure?

One of the fundamental reasons is the Daleks. Since their first appearance in 1963, they have made viewing figures soar and critics shake their heads in wonder.

For many years the Daleks had a problem climbing stairs, but not any more. Since Sylvester McCoy's Doctor, the Daleks have managed to climb the human staircase. This became more established after the relaunch of the show in the new millennium and the story 'Dalek'.

'Dalek' was significant. No longer could a Dalek be blinded with mud on its eye-piece. Not only could they climb stairs but they could effectively fly too! Not only that, they didn't trundle along like an old dustbin, they moved with menace like the most sophisticated armoured tank, which is what effectively they are and what we would grow to appreciate with the new series.

Although the visual effects of *Doctor Who* are so much better nowadays, the Daleks – and indeed the programme itself – endured because of great storylines. For the Daleks, there is no clearer example than the Tom Baker story 'Genesis of the Daleks'.

For years 'Genesis of the Daleks' was the archetypical *Doctor Who* story. It had everything. Not only did it feature the Doctor's arch enemy, it was the debut of their evil creator Davros too, so brilliantly played by Michael Wisher.

Between Terry Nation and Robert Holmes, they not only created a story that showed the birth of the Daleks, but they also formed a direct parallel between the Nazis and the Kaleds (the race that created the mutations that became the Daleks through their inhuman experiments). The story was so well conceived that none of this was overplayed. But where the story succeeded the most was in its allegory. The Doctor doesn't kill the Daleks off at birth; he lets them live because so many races would become allies because of the Daleks. Simply, he knew that out of their evil would come something good. And that was probably the final verdict of Adolf Hitler and the Nazi party: what they did sickened the whole of mankind so much, it probably made the 'super powers' stop and think that one second more before contemplating a Third World War – out of the Nazis' evil came something good.

There are several classic scenes within 'Genesis of the

Daleks', the first being where the Doctor wires up the incubator room where the mutations are being born. He has two wires that if he touches them together would destroy the Daleks forever. But he hesitates. He asks himself: if I kill them would I not be just as bad as them (exterminating a whole race)? Through the second half of the 20th century, many people asked themselves: if I had a time machine, would I go back in time and kill Adolf Hitler? So many people morally said that they would; but 'Genesis of the Daleks' gave the reason for saying no. And it was the right reason. People learned from the Nazis' atrocities. So bad and terrible they were that people realised that they couldn't – as a species – stoop so low again.

Another important scene and, to me, the greatest scene in the show's history, is one in which the Doctor has a private conversation with Davros. He needs to see if he really is mad. He asks him: if he created a virus so terrible it could wipe out entire races, would he use it? Davros ponders but not the Yes or No answer. He has instantly decided that the answer is Yes, of course he would do it, but he ponders – wallows – in the excitement that, if he could hold in his hand a tiny vial of agent, and that the slightest pressure of his fingers, just enough to break the glass, would destroy the universe, then yes, he would do it, because that power would set him up among the Gods.

Adolf Hitler incarnate.

'Genesis of the Daleks' is probably the most important *Doctor Who* story ever. It asks important questions and tackles the implications of those answers, thus dealing with highly moral issues. If Sydney Newman had seen 'Genesis of the Daleks' rather than the first Dalek story back in 1963, he would not have had any issue with the Daleks at all. The moral implications were there, the parallel with the Nazis was a plain as day, and the allegory was purely *brilliant* writing.

There is only one *Doctor Who* story that has had as much moral impact as 'Genesis of the Daleks' and that is 'Planet of the Ood'. Again, one could make the comparison with the Nazis' extermination of the Jews, or the American settlers' extermination of the Native American, but, for me, it is more of a direct analogy with slavery through the ages. It is about people, emotions and cruelty. Again, the story tackles big questions and presents them primarily to a young audience. *Doctor Who* can do this; Newman wanted children to learn about history through the programme's stories. To see Belsen would be too much, but an alien race being slaughtered, or at least persecuted, was a watered-down, more palatable, interpretation of the truth; but the moral implications are still there, the issues can still be discussed. Stories like 'Genesis of the Daleks' and 'Planet of the Ood' do not come along every season. In fact, they don't come along every decade, they are one of the surprises the show throws out from time to time and people marvel at.

Sometimes an audience can get so much more from less. One of the very best stories for this was 'Midnight'. The story works on the premise that there is something hostile outside the ship and, although we can't see it, we know it's there.

'Midnight' is a very clever tale as it builds tension with an eerie wonder. We see the hinterland, we know there's something out there but we can't see what it is, we can't feel it, we can't communicate with it, but it kills us all the same, so we are hopelessly lost. We are terrified, we are out of our depth, and so much behind the 'superior' being. Indeed is it 'superior'? What is it? Could we befriend it? Probably not, but it's the not knowing, and that's the way it ends.

The thing disappears. We suddenly realise that we'll never know any more about the entity that conspired against the vessel. We have to carry on as normal, with no answers, no explanations, nothing, apart from the fact that there are forces in the universe we know nothing about, that are far greater than us, and that we will never be allowed to learn from. 'Midnight' is a humbling story, it tells us not to take things for granted and, perhaps as importantly, not to be scared of the unknown. 'There are more things in Heaven and Earth than dreamed of in your philosophy', Shakespeare tells us, and 'Midnight' showcases this quote perfectly.

Not since William Hartnell and Patrick Troughton's day has there been such foreboding from a story. In the surviving episode of 'The Abominable Snowman', we have ancient powers locked deep in a monastery, the flickering flames and shadows in black and white, we hear ancient chanting in the deserted monastery from 'The Time Meddler' and an evil creature that lurks in the caves and visits the space ship in 'The Rescue'. All these things speak of an otherness, and evoke a deep foreboding, that uneasy place that we as human beings dare not let our senses go, not willingly; but we enjoy those feelings of fear, we wallow in them. We need to explore those feelings, because they are an essential part of being human, and if *Doctor Who* allows us to enjoy that feeling in the secure environment of our living room – behind the obligatory sofa or cushion – then so be it. That is the reason why we watch, it is this very feeling that makes us love the programme.

On the subject of more from less, there is a story in which the Doctor hardly appears but is hailed as one of the greatest *Doctor Who* stories ever, and that is 'Blink'. The story of the Weeping Angels and how Sally Sparrow and her friends try to thwart them with the Doctor is legendary. It's a great lesson in

Doctor Who scriptwriting: pace, scare factor, good character development is what it's all about. Sometimes the Doctor isn't needed, but unusually he is, to release the tension, to explain things and reassure in a 'timey-wimey' sort of way. He is the crackpot professor, the stranger that rides into town to sort things out (a Clint Eastwood-like character). Simply, he is the Doctor who makes people better. But in what way better? Surely, some die because of his dabbling?

Sometimes *Doctor Who* wallows in darkness, a gothic horror that deals with tried and proven legends, and this enhances the mystique of the show. Stories such as 'State of Decay' are under-rated in the *Doctor Who* canon. 'State of Decay' deals with exploitation, corruption, traditional values and legends – both Earth legends and those of the Doctor's home planet Gallifrey. The very idea that a castle could be a spaceship and simultaneously a giant stake is ingenious to say the least. 'State of Decay' is often overlooked today because it falls within a trilogy of stories about 'E Space', a universe in a different dimension; but for me it sticks out as one of the great gothic masterpieces in the history of the show. Another story that falls within this category is 'The Daemons', from the Jon Pertwee era. An ancient barrow is opened and a creature not unlike the Devil is released to cause havoc.

Jon Pertwee rated 'The Daemons' as a personal favourite, and with its beautiful location, sinister demons and devils – as well as the Master and UNIT – it ticks many boxes, proving that you don't need the biggest budget to tell a great story, you just need a great script and a dose of eeriness.

There are two stories that go even deeper within the gothic realm and place the Doctor way out of his comfort zone. Only very occasionally do we see him covered in mud, his clothes ripped, his knees scraped. Rarely do we see the

Doctor actually bleed but, in 'The Caves of Androzani' and 'The Deadly Assassin', we get plenty of this, and an exciting story follows.

With 'The Caves of Androzani' the Doctor actually gives his life to save that of his companion. Effectively, he loses, but, because he is a Time Lord, he escapes to fight another day, the proverbial cat with nine – twelve? – lives. He regenerates.

'The Caves of Androzani' is also suspenseful because of the deranged masked man that hides down under the Citadel; he is, like the wicked master in 'The Talons of Weng-Chiang', a *Phantom of the Opera*-like creature. But what 'Androzani' has over 'Weng-Chiang' is gothic romance. Peri (the Doctor's companion) becomes the Phantom's (Sharaz Jek) love interest in 'The Caves of Androzani', and the Doctor doesn't just have to save her from the madman but he must also save both Peri and himself from a killer disease. In the end, it all becomes too much for him and he passes away to his next regeneration.

In 'The Deadly Assassin', the Doctor is again at full stretch. Powerful mind games send the Doctor into a schizophrenic limbo world where he is shot at, partially drowned, blown up, run over by a speeding train and just generally terrified. For me, 'The Deadly Assassin' is the best *Doctor Who* story ever for sheer imagination and gothic appeal; it is the Doctor alone on his home planet, pitted against the Master in his new more sinister incarnation, with the Time Lords seemingly against him too. At one stage, the Master is thought to be dead, but he has only drugged himself and he comes back to kill and destroy all that he surveys. The whole High Council of the Time Lords put the Doctor on trial and torture him, believing him to be the murderer of the President himself – the Assassin; but the whole thing is a set-up by the Master. Ingenious, brutal and incredibly imaginative, 'The Deadly Assassins' showcases some of the best scares *Doctor Who* has to offer, not dissimilar to the gothic horror of rats, disfigured madman and bleeding dolls in a foggy Victorian London, as seen in 'The Talons of Weng-Chiang'.

Both 'The Deadly Assassin' and 'The Talons of Weng-Chiang' come from an era in the Tom Baker years known as the Hinchcliffe Years, where Philip Hinchcliffe was the producer and brought a more sinister, gothic edge to the stories, not unlike Steven Moffat in the new-look *Doctor Who* of Matt Smith (indeed, he has vampires, Weeping Angels and a host of other great foes to draw from in the very first season). Other stories from these Hinchcliffe Years worthy of note include 'The Pyramids of Mars' and 'The Robots of Death', run-of-the-mill *Doctor Who* fodder, but great Saturday-night entertainment.

'The Pyramids of Mars' was an interesting blend of several ideas: Egyptian Gods as aliens, photos of pyramid-like structures found on the surface of Mars and the mysteries of Tutankhamen.

With all these ideas running around, it was no surprise that 'The Pyramids of Mars' would feature as an all-time classic and another story in which the Doctor doesn't easily get away with it. The evil ruler Sutekh in the story is both evil and unsettling, and a real sense of suspense is drawn from the imaginative script.

'The Robots of Death' worked Isaac Asimov's laws of robotics from *I, Robot*, not dissimilar to how 'The Daemons' played with Arthur C Clarke's devil creatures from *Childhood's End*. Sometimes classic SF does influence current SF, inasmuch as it encourages good practice.

'The Robots of Death' is not a brilliant allegory or, for that matter, a radical script. It's a good script with interesting robots and a supporting cast you actually care for – well, some of them anyway.

Louise Jameson is terrific as Leela and really comes into her own in this story, which has the obligatory mad man wanting to take over. A murder is committed and the Doctor and Leela turn up just in time to be the prime suspects. It's a tried and tested pathway, but every time there's a subtle difference and the Doctor's way of remedying the evil in the story is both amusing and ingenious.

Doctor Who does sometimes have its poignant moments but stories that pull at the heart strings are rare, especially those done exceptionally well. Stories such as 'Father's Day', 'Human Nature/Family of Blood' show off this theme tremendously well. In 'Father's Day', Rose Tyler (the Doctor's companion) wants to travel back in time and see her dead father. But instead of just observing him she saves his life in a road accident and releases creatures into the world that need to repair the break in time. One of the creatures eats the Doctor and it is left to Rose Tyler, his trusted companion, to right the wrong she has created. The way the story builds into a credible basis for Rose's parents to understand the truth is nothing short of quality scriptwriting, and the poignancy that is evoked with the end of the episode, make it both tender and moving.

In the double bill 'Human Nature/Family of Blood', the Doctor toys with the mortality of being human and the horror humans bestow upon each other (the backdrop is the Great War). One of the greatest scenes in the history of the show is Martha Jones putting a poppy on the Doctor's lapel as the Great War veteran looks on. What brings home the underlying message are the words of a great poem ('For the Fallen'), which start with 'They will not grow old…' and indeed the time travellers haven't aged a day since they last saw the veteran as a boy about to go to war. The Doctor and Martha haven't grown old, they've simply jumped forward seconds in time, but the veteran has taken 90 Earth years to get to that moment. He sees them, and is humbled by their respect, in a wonderfully poignant scene.

The waste of human lives through war is also brought home, but also one thing more: the Doctor's longing for true companionship. His love of human females but despair that they just don't live long enough is painfully clear. In 'Human Nature', he becomes human, falls in love, and, in an amazing visual projection, has children and then sees his wife die. There is something very *Highlander* about this part of the story, something very sad but telling.

The one thing the new-millennium *Doctor Who* gives us is a sense of love captured and lost, a true sense of loneliness. The Doctor's home planet has been destroyed, there is only his adopted planet left – Earth; but there he is nothing more than a stranger in a strange land, a Robert Heinlein exile that harks back to Jon Pertwee's Doctor so brilliantly as he drives Bessie away from Jo Grant.

'Human Nature' recalls the very first *Doctor Who* story, or the original draft of the script ('An Unearthly Child'), where Suzanne (Susan Foreman) and the Doctor explain that a race of creatures is after them to kill them and steal the Tardis, so they must hide. The only reason the Doctor became human was to hide from some terrifying creatures who wanted him and his Tardis. In a way it was history repeating itself. In fact, could this be the race of creatures that wanted to kill the Doctor and Susan all those years ago? Nobody knows, but maybe time will tell. If

Susan became human, that would explain a lot about her motives and calling the Doctor grandfather.

Androids are a constant in *Doctor Who*. The placid, such as the unaffected in 'Robots of Death', to the totally scary, e.g. 'The Girl in the Fireplace' and 'The Visitation'. But one thing most have in common – indeed all of the above – is that *something* or *somebody* made them do wrong. They are only scary because the person who programmed them made them dangerous.

One could stretch the android theme and suggest that the original Cybermen – those scary mechanical men from 'The Tenth Planet' – are an extension of this. In a way, they are the product of a self-wounding race at odds with their own bodies and emotions. Although the Cybermen look fantastic in the new series of *Doctor Who*, they have lost their free will to become what they are, and that is wrong. We pitied the original Cybermen and admired their intelligence; the new breed are just plain sick grotesques of the human form encased in metal, a side-effect of a Nazi system already populated by Davros. It doesn't work for me, guys.

Humour has its place in *Doctor Who*, from the Doctor's return from a Jacobean wild party to thwart the clockwork men in 'The Girl in the Fireplace', to the theatrical – and slightly pitiful – antics of Richard Mace in 'The Visitation'. Humour has always been there to counterbalance the scary bits and that certainly happened in 'The Girl in the Fireplace' and even 'The Sound of Drums' (where the Master gasses all of the British Cabinet but first puts a gas mask on, and gives a choking man the thumbs-up when he tells him he's mad).

The humour shared between the Second Doctor and an alien chef in a restaurant ('The Two Doctors') while craving human flesh is of particular note, especially as it defuses a stabbing scene seconds later, but even that degenerates into a comic chase scene. Comedy is so important to *Doctor Who*. When overplayed it highlights its worst scenes, but, when it's done well, it's magical.

There has been a wealth of emotion and incident in *Doctor Who* over the years, but there is a recurring theme of death. From the natural – the Fourth Doctor falling a great height and smashing his body ('Logopolis') – to the macabre – the Master taking over a person's body at the end of 'The Keeper of Traken'. Death is everywhere in *Doctor Who*. In 'The Last of the Time Lord', we look back at the Doctor's dead race, we see into the madness of the Master, and see him will himself to death while the Doctor grieves over him. In fact, in all of the stories I have discussed in this essay, somebody dies or, more accurately, somebody is killed. It's as though somebody always has to pay for the Doctor's – and his companions' – thrills. But in legend, isn't it true, any time the Grim Reaper is called up he must take a soul away with him.

From the very beginning of *Doctor Who* to its current position, there is something very unsettling about the main character. He is the Pied Piper who leads his merry companions on a dance, but, when he leaves them behind, they have to pay – mentally – for what happened to them on their journey with him. And perhaps the actors who have played the Doctor have had to pay a price too, because they will always be known as the Doctor, while their other work will be largely regarded as second best.

Doctor Who endures because children keep being born, and children want adventure. If that adventure is a somewhat bumpy ride, then perhaps that's just a portent of what the future may bring and, of course, the one constant in life is death. While the Doctor lives on, it is all us earthlings that pass away, and that's another reason why the character fascinates us, he doesn't die, while everybody else does. He is immortal... the one thing most earthlings admire.

'You'll delay an execution to pull the wings off a fly.'

The Doctor to the Master

'The Deadly Assassin'

CHAPTER FOUR
KING
DOCTOR

'Splendid chap, all of them.'

Nicholas Courtney, Brigadier Alistair Gordon Lethbridge-Stewart'

'The Five Doctors'

SO WHO IS King Doctor? The very best of the best? Short answer: nobody.

The thing is so many people have a favourite Doctor Who; normally the one they first encountered. But let us look through the list of actors and what they brought to the part:

William Hartnell, the very first Doctor, brought an air of mystery and crotchetiness second to none. He made the part his own as Doctor Who, i.e. in the days before anyone knew where he came from. But his career was over after the show due to a mixture of ill health and media persecution.

Patrick Troughton was the second Doctor and the first to take over the regeneration mantle. His Doctor was the monster Doctor, with many classic stories that sadly no longer reside in the BBC archives. It was Patrick Troughton who influenced Peter Davison to only take three years in the part, and inadvertently influenced Matt Smith in his interpretation of the Doctor.

Jon Pertwee, classic comedy actor, played the role straight and even injected his own personality into the role. His seriousness and James Bond-like personality really brought a new edge to the character and Pertwee was a great ambassador to the show, working closely with the fans, especially those who needed him.

Tom Baker built upon this and really took the character out on to the streets where he was taken extremely seriously. His Doctor was angelic: he didn't eat, drink or smoke near children. He even signed photos as the Doctor, so much was his passion and loyalty to the show.

Tom Baker is widely regarded as 'King Doctor', even those who don't like him much, but his successor, Peter Davison, was a worthy, but widely different, Doctor, whose compassion and rapport with his companions was more prominent than any other Doctor Who.

Colin Baker's Doctor was passionate and over-the-top. His exasperation with extreme scenes endeared him to many, but his outlandish clothes, poor scripts (for the most part) and tacky monsters alienated him somewhat.

Sylvester McCoy was the radical update to Colin Baker's Doctor and, although he brought the mystery back to the role, along with better storylines, the decision had been made that the programme would be exterminated…

Paul McGann brought the show back with a new-look Tardis, a kiss from his assistant, and a pace that could have challenged any new-millennium Doctor. McGann was the catalyst that took *Doctor Who* on to a new level, although no one would realise it at the time.

Christopher Eccleston, a great actor, brought the show back and reinvented it along with companion Billie Piper, but it was

David Tennant who won the hearts of the nation and became the most popular Doctor since Tom Baker. But was Tennant the best actor, a man who could be considered King Doctor?

No. The legacy was too long. Hartnell had started it and Pertwee had advanced it – both through transition to colour and a more serious/adult outlook – and widened the canvas with his enthusiasm for gadgets.

Matt Smith followed David Tennant and some people felt sorry for him because of Tennant's popularity in the role. But Smith has weathered the storm, playing the Doctor his own way, reminding us that the character is bigger than the actor who plays him.

In retrospect, Patrick Troughton will probably go down as the most important Doctor. He took on the legacy, he added humour, he was the Pied Piper with his recorder and clown-like leadership. Troughton was a friend of Pertwee during the war, he advised Davison to only play the Doctor for three years, and was the main inspiration for the classical-looking Matt Smith. Couple that with an incredibly impressive career in theatre and TV, Patrick Troughton must reign as one of the very best Doctor Whos; but King Doctor? That is for you to decide, maybe I'll stick with Tom.

'If heroes don't exist it is necessary to invent them.'
Cardinal Borusa to the Doctor

'The Deadly Assassin'

FURTHER READING

THE FOLLOWING BOOKS are essentially the core of any *Doctor Who* book collection. They are suggested further reading for anyone interested in the genesis of the show, some of which were also used in research for this book.

Doctor Who and the Daleks (Frederick Muller, 1964)
Doctor Who and the Daleks (Armada Paperbacks, 1965)
Doctor Who and the Zarbi (Frederick Muller, 1965)
Doctor Who and the Crusaders (Frederick Muller, 1965)
Doctor Who and the Crusaders (Green Dragon p/back, 1967)
The Dalek Pocket Book and Space Travellers Guide, Terry Nation (Panther Books, 1965)
The Making of Doctor Who (Pan Books limited-edition hardback 1972 – the rarest Doctor Who book ever published). Laminated boards, limited release to libraries only
The Making of Doctor Who, Malcolm Hulke and Terrance Dicks (Piccolo Books, 1972)
Doctor Who 10th Anniversary Radio Times Special (1973)
The Doctor Who Monster Book (originally issued with poster) (Target Books, 1975)

The Making of Doctor Who, Malcolm Hulke and Terrance Dicks (Target Books, 1976)

Doctor Who and the Daleks Omnibus (St Michael, 1976)

The Second Doctor Who Monster Book (Target Books, 1977)

Terry Nation's Dalek Special (Target, 1979)

A Day With a Television Producer (Day in the Life), Graham Rickard (Hodder Wayland, 1980)

Doctor Who – Making of a Television Series, Alan Road (Andre Deutsch, 1982)

Doctor Who 20th Anniversary Radio Times Special (originally issued with poster) (1983)

Doctor Who – A Celebration, Two Decades Through Time and Space, Peter Haining (W H Allen, 1983) (also available as a limited-edition leather-bound edition)

Doctor Who – The Key to Time, A Year-By-Year Record, 21st Anniversary Special, Peter Haining (W H Allen, 1984) (also available as a limited-edition leather-bound edition)

Moon Boots and Dinner Suits, Jon Pertwee (Elm Tree Books, 1984)

The Tardis Inside Out, John Nathan-Turner (Piccadilly Press, 1985)

The Companions of Doctor Who, K9 and Company, Terence Dudley (Target, 1987)

The Gallifrey Chronicles, John Peel (Virgin Publishing, 1991)

The Nine Lives of Doctor Who, Peter Haining (Headline, 1991)

Doctor Who – The Sixties, David J Howe, Mark Stammers and Stephen James Walker (Virgin, 1992)

Doctor Who – The Seventies, David J Howe, Mark Stammers and Stephen James Walker (Virgin, 1994)

Classic Doctor Who – The Hinchcliffe Years, Seasons 12–14, Adrian Riglesford (Boxtree, 1995)

Doctor Who – The Eighties, David J Howe, Mark Stammers and Stephen James Walker (Virgin, 1996)

Who's There? The Life and Career of William Hartnell, By His Granddaughter Jessica Carney (Virgin, 1996)

Who on Earth is Tom Baker? An Autobiography, Tom Baker (HarperCollins, 1997)

Jon Pertwee: The Biography, Bernard Bale (Andre Deutsch, 2000)

Doctor Who: The Scripts, Tom Baker 1974/5 (BBC, 2001)

DOCTOR WHO ANNUALS

1965 (Hartnell), Invasion From Space (Hartnell – Special Edition, 1966),1966 (Hartnell), 1967 (Troughton), 1968 (Troughton), 1969 (Troughton), 1970 (Pertwee), 1971 – no annual, 1972 – Countdown Annual (featuring Doctor Who strips and Behind the Camera feature regarding the filming of The Daemons), 1973 (Pertwee), 1974 (Pertwee), 1975 (Pertwee), 1976 (T Baker), The Amazing World of Doctor Who (Special with wall chart to go with series of Typhoo Tea cards), 1977 (T Baker), 1978 (T Baker), 1979 (T Baker), 1980 (T Baker), 1981 (T Baker), 1982 (T Baker/ Davison), 1983 (Davison), 1984 (Davison), 1985 (C Baker). 1986–1989 Doctor Who Holiday Annual series of four, 2007 (Eccleston), 2008 (Tennant), 2009 (Tennant), 2010 (Tennant), 2011 (Smith – with colour poster).

K9 Annual 1983 (World International, 1982).

The Dalek Book 1964 (Souvenir Press), The Dalek World 1965 (Souvenir Press), The Dalek Outer Space Book 1966 (Souvenir Press).

Terry Nation's Dalek Annual 1976 (World Distributors), Terry Nation's Dalek Annual 1977 (World Distributors), Terry Nation's Dalek Annual 1978 (World Distributors), Terry Nation's Dalek Annual 1979 (World Distributors).